LIGHTING DESIGN BASICS

MARK KARLEN

JAMES R. BENYA

WILEY

JOHN WILEY & SONS, INC.

Published by John Wiley & Sons, Inc., Hoboken, New Jersey

Published simultaneously in Canada

For general information on our other products and services or for technical support, please contact our Customer Care Department within the United States at (800) 762-2974, outside the United States at (317) 572-3993 or fax (317) 572-4002.

Wiley also publishes its books in a variety of electronic formats. Some content that appears in print may not be available in electronic books. For more information about Wiley products, visit our web site at www.wiley.com.

Library of Congress Cataloging-in-Publication Data:

Karlen, Mark.
    Lighting design basics / by Mark Karlen and James Benya.
         p. cm.
Includes index.
    ISBN 0-471-38162-4 (Paper)
    1. Lighting. 2. Lighting, Architectural and decorative I. Benya, James
        TH7703.K27 2003
        621.32—dc21

                                                          2002153109

Printed in the United States of America

10 9 8 7 6 5 4 3 2 1

THE SURREY INSTITUTE OF ART & DESIGN
UNIVERSITY COLLEGE

Farnham Campus, Falkner Road, Farnham, Surrey GU9 7DS
Return on or before the last date stamped below fines will be charged on overdue books

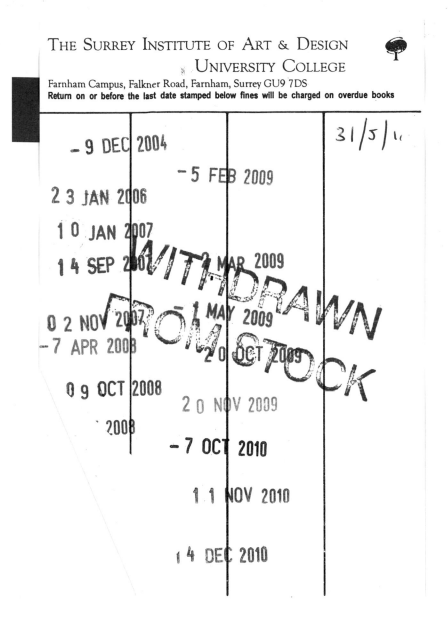

CONTENTS

PREFACE

This book had its origins several years ago when we were both repeat presenters as part of a series of professional education events across the country over a period of a couple of years. After a few casual meetings over lunch or dinner we discovered we had many interests and points of view in common. Much of that commonality was based on the fact that each of us were deeply involved in our professional lives; Jim as a lighting designer and electrical engineer; and Mark as an architect, interior designer, and educator.

Each of us has spent many years lecturing and teaching architects and designers, and knew the need for design professionals to understand the concepts and basic principles of lighting design. In our experience, too many of those professionals have not had the opportunity to develop that understanding. We believe there is a need for a different kind of lighting design textbook; one that focuses on design, rather than terminology and technology; one that will lead architects and interior designers to work with lighting design in an appropriately professional manner.

Working together has had its logistical difficulties. Jim is based in Portland, Oregon, with an extremely busy nationwide professional practice, as well as a calendar full of lecture engagements at universities and professional conferences. Mark is based at Pratt Institute in Brooklyn, New York, with a full schedule of teaching and administrative duties as Chair of the Interior Design Department, as well as many other professional involvements, including delivering several weekend "STEP" workshops each year for ASID, preparing young designers for taking the NCIDQ exam.

Despite the occasional problems of our bicoastal home bases, and with the marvelously professional and undaunting efforts of John Wiley and Sons' editorial staff, particularly Amanda Miller, Publisher for Architecture and Design, and Jennifer Ackerman, Technical Project Editor, what follows is the concerted effort of the past couple of years. This book is dedicated to our understanding and loving families, and to all of our students—former, present, and future.

James R. Benya and Mark Karlen

LIGHTING DESIGN BASICS

Chapter 8

LIGHTING CONCEPTS: THE LAYERS APPROACH

As in architecture and interior design, the extent to which aesthetics in lighting matters varies from project to project. There is hardly any aesthetic concern, for example, in designing an ordinary office using inexpensive lay-in troffers. However, the type and location of every luminaire in a cathedral is critical in the appearance of the space itself, not just the lighting. Even though many real-world projects require simple, primarily economical lighting designs, it is still beneficial to tackle each with a common approach that permits an appropriate result.

ABOUT LIGHTING SYSTEMS AND LAYOUTS

In great deal of contemporary architecture, electric lighting was treated as a building system, much like plumbing, structure, and heating, ventilation, and air conditioning (HVAC). The general practice was to eliminate ornament and non-essentials. At the same time, energy was plentiful and inexpensive. The result was to design general lighting at relatively high lighting levels. This was best done with a single lighting system laid out in a regular pattern or grid. A great deal of the public's distaste for fluorescent lighting is due to this practice, which was seldom aesthetically pleasing and usually produced glaring light.

The word *system* has a number of specific connotations and uses in modern lighting. We still refer to the building's *lighting system*, but we also refer to the *track lighting system* or the *indirect lighting system*. The use of the word *system* in all of these instances is more vernacular than meaningful.

But in a few cases, the word *system* actually refers to a group of parts and components that work together. This becomes critical when, for reasons of performance, safety, or code, the "lighting system" or the "control system" must be used in a particular manner. It is probably best that the term *system* be used in this way.

Because traditional electric lighting is a system or grid of lights, engineers "laid out" the lighting grid more as an engineering exercise than a design process. Today, the expression *layout* persists, but because we are, arguably, better designers, the expression has a different meaning. Now, *layout* is just another term for a *lighting plan*.

LIGHTING LAYERS

The principle of layering provides a framework for understanding and achieving composition and aesthetics in lighting design. Layers of lighting, like layers of clothing, combine to make a composition. Layering permits judicious choices that ensure that obvious design requirements such as period, theme, and style can be met without compromising good lighting design. For example, when lighting a dining room, the chandelier is only one layer. To dramatically light the table or centerpiece, another layer, called *accent lighting*, might be added. The chandelier is chosen for its style, but the accent lighting should be inconspicuous or hidden.

LAYERED DESIGN

Each layer has unique responsibilities to light certain tasks, but because lighting is seldom so carefully controlled, the layers often work together to light portions of the space.

The Ambient Layer

Providing overall lighting in a room is the role of *ambient lighting*. Ambient lighting does not illuminate specific tasks but rather provides the light that allows moving around in the space and other basic visual recognition. The amount of ambient light is important; if the ambient light level in the space is significantly lower than the task levels, the contrast between task and ambient light will be high and the space will appear more dramatic. On the other hand, if the ambient light levels are nearly as high as the task levels, the room will be brighter, cheerier, and more relaxing. Because of its impact on the mood or ambience of the room, choice of ambient lighting is surprisingly critical.

For instance, the ambient lighting in a museum or boutique store is often low to create significant contrast with the feature displays and heighten the sense of drama. One way to do this is with downlights that illuminate the floor but not the walls and ceiling. People can safely walk around, but the room appears dark.

To achieve a relaxed ambience, on the other hand, it is important to increase the brightness of room surfaces, especially ceilings and upper walls. Uplighting is an excellent way to achieve this effect. Generally, the more even the uplighting, the more relaxed the room.

The Task Layer

Among visual tasks in a space, many work tasks, such as reading, occur on a table or desk. It is common to provide task lights at locations where these tasks occur. Task luminaires include table lamps, floor lamps, desk lamps, drafting lamps, undercabinet lights, and shelf lights. Overhead luminaires, such as pendants, troffers, and downlights, can also be located to illuminate a task.

Interestingly, the can downlight, a common light fixture in all types of modern construction, was invented to illuminate tasks in churches. Traditional chandelier lighting, while providing ambient light, does not illuminate hymnals and prayer books well. While the downlight has been put to many other uses, it remains an important task light.

Because much more task light than ambient light is needed in most rooms, providing the higher task lighting levels only where needed is usually energy efficient. In offices, factories, and other workspaces, the *task-and-ambient* or *task/ambient* approach to lighting is a common design of separate lighting layers whose primary purpose is to minimize lighting energy use.

The Focal Layer

Focal lighting is one of two types of aesthetic lighting that is usually used only in projects that demand it for style and appearance. Focal lighting's primary purpose is to illuminate features and displays such as artwork, architectural features, retail displays, and signs.

Most of the time, the focal layer utilizes lighting designed to be adjusted. Track lighting is perhaps the most popular form of focal lighting, and it is used extensively in museums, galleries, and stores to permit rapid changes in the lighting to suit changing display needs. Other types of focal lighting include recessed adjustable accent lights, wallwashers, monopoint accent lights, and theatrical equipment. The focal layer is usually meant to be innocuous; the idea is to draw attention to the display, not the lights.

Chapter 1 INTRODUCTION
How to Use This Book

This book is an instructional tool designed to develop the necessary knowledge and skills for solving lighting design problems for typical rooms and spaces. Of equal importance is the development of the necessary knowledge and skills for collaborating with lighting design professionals in solving problems for complex rooms and spaces. The book is directed to both students and professionals in architecture and interior design as well as those in related fields such as facilities management, construction management, store planning, and electrical engineering.

The primary focus is on design, not on technology or terminology. *Design* is here defined as the development of a lighting design concept and the selection and placement of luminaires to achieve the desired result. Lighting technology (and related terminology) will be covered in enough depth to serve the design orientation of the book's methodologies. For more information related to these technical factors, the Bibliography identifies the best sources.

This is a how-to instructional textbook, the goal of which is to provide its users with the tools of lighting design required to function effectively in the many design and construction fields of which lighting is an essential part.

ORGANIZATION

Beyond this introductory chapter, Lighting Design Basics is organized in four parts, plus Appendixes and a Bibliography. Here is a description of these parts.

Part I: Basics About Lighting. Chapters 2 through 6 provide background for the technical (and related terminology) aspects of lighting design—enough to serve this book's purpose but without unnecessary emphasis on technical issues. More specifically, the technical factors addressed are light sources (and their color implications), luminaires, switching and controls, daylighting, and calculations (including rule-of-thumb techniques).

Part II: Design Process. Chapters 7 through 9 provide a basic approach or methodology for developing successful lighting design concepts and solutions, including the graphic representation tools and techniques used to convey the solutions. In this context, success is defined as meeting functional visual requirements, achieving satisfying aesthetic results, and using lighting design technology (including code compliance) intelligently.

Part III: Applications and Case Studies. Chapters 10 through 15 focus on the typical lighting design problems encountered in the five major building use

1

types: (1) residential, (2) office/corporate, (3) hospitality/foodservice, (4) institutional/health care, and (5) retail store. Case studies are provided for many of the typical rooms and spaces found in these building use types. This is the heart of the book, where design problems, their solutions, and the rationales for the solutions are presented in detail.

Part IV: Professional Skills. Chapters 16 through 18 provide additional and necessary information about functioning as a designer or design-related professional in matters concerning lighting design. They are intended to serve as a transition from learning to professional practice.

Appendixes

Appendix A is a brief overview of lighting design for the exterior of buildings and exterior spaces. This specialized aspect of lighting design is complex and requires an extensive study of its own. This Appendix provides a starting point and direction for those interested in pursuing the subject more fully.

Appendix B is a summary of energy codes and how they affect design. Included are Internet references for obtaining the most recent energy code information within the United States.

GETTING THE MOST OUT OF THIS BOOK

This book is meant to be worked with, not just read. Doing the exercises after reading and understanding the related case studies is the heart of the learning process presented here.

The case study examples and the exercises represent typical lighting design applications. Beyond these examples, lighting design becomes increasingly complex and challenging, even for the most knowledgeable and experienced professionals. The purpose here is not to prepare the reader for those complex problems but rather to provide understanding of lighting design concepts, techniques, and realistic goals so collaboration with a lighting design professional can achieve the best possible results. One must learn to communicate design intentions in a way that a lighting designer can use. Those communication skills require a conceptual understanding of lighting design, the acquisition of which should be one of the major learning goals in working with this book.

Many technical aspects of lighting design go considerably beyond the scope of this book. Issues such as the fine points of color rendition, code compliance, project budget, and lighting live performance spaces can be extremely complex. Working knowledge of these factors is not expected of broad-based design and built environment professionals. However, general familiarity is required to collaborate productively with lighting designers. To acquire deeper knowledge in these technical matters, consult the Bibliography.

In a classroom setting, the value of this book is enhanced by an exchange of ideas among students working on the same exercises as well as the instructor's critiques and open classroom critiques and discussion. Beyond the classroom, one should take advantage of every opportunity to discuss exercise solutions with design professionals, particularly those with extensive practical experience. Such discussion can be invaluable.

Two readily available learning tools should be used concurrently with this book. First is the deliberate observation and critique of existing lighting design applications. Be aware of the lighting in public and semipublic spaces, making note of lamp and luminaire types—and, more important, what works well and what doesn't. A great deal can be learned from the successes and failures of others. Second, many architecture and interior design professional publications present enough programmatic, plan, and spatial information about interesting spaces that one can use them as additional exercises for enhancing one's skills.

It all begins with working on paper or the computer and trying a variety of lighting design solutions to typical design problems.

While this book prescribes a particular approach to solving lighting design problems, it should be understood that several potentially successful methodologies exist. In the professional community of lighting designers and the other design professionals who work with them, the problem-solving process enjoys many workable variations. It is expected that individual professionals, after repeated experience with actual problems, will gradually develop a personalized methodology.

Chapter **2** LIGHT SOURCES

Light occurs in nature, and sunlight, moonlight, and starlight are the most important sources of light to life. But because of their need for additional light, humans have learned to create light as well. Understanding the fundamental difference between natural and man-made light is the beginning of understanding light sources.

Natural light sources occur within nature and are beyond the control of people. These include sunlight, moonlight, starlight, various plant and animal sources, radioluminescence, and, of course, fire.

Man-made light sources can be controlled by people, more or less when and in the amount wanted. These include wood flame, oil flame, gas flame, electric lamps, photochemical reactions, and various reactions, such as explosives.

Due to their obvious advantages in terms of availability, safety, cleanliness, and remote energy generation, electric lamps have displaced almost all other man-made sources for lighting of the built environment. However, because man-made sources consume natural resources, natural light sources should be used to the greatest extent possible. Exploiting natural light sources remains one of the biggest challenges to architects and designers.

QUALITIES OF LIGHT SOURCES

In practical terms, light sources can be discussed in terms of the qualities of the light they produce. These qualities are critical to the result and must be understood when choosing the source for a lighting plan.

How Light Is Generated

Most natural light comes from the sun, including moonlight. Its origin makes it completely clean, and it consumes no natural resources. But man-made sources generally require consumption of resources, such as fossil fuels, to convert stored energy into light energy. Electric lighting is superior to flame sources because the combustion of wood, gas, and oil produces pollution within the space being illuminated. Moreover, electricity can be generated from natural, nondepletable sources of energy, including the energy generated by wind, hydro, geothermal, and solar sources.

Edison Lamp

How an electric lamp operates determines virtually everything about the light created by it. The common incandescent lamp generates light through the principle of incandescence, in which a metal is heated until it glows. Most other lamps, however, generate light by means of a complex chemical system in which electric energy is turned into light energy where heat is a side effect. These processes are usually much more efficient than incandescence—at the cost of complexity and other limitations. For instance, a fluorescent lamp generates light by a discharge of energy into a gas, which in turn emits ultraviolet radiation, which is finally converted to visible light by minerals that "fluoresce." This process generates light about 400 percent more efficiently than incandescence and is the reason fluorescent lamps are promoted as environmentally friendly.

The Spectrum of Light

The spectrum of light is seen in a rainbow or from a prism, and it includes all of the visible colors. We tend to organize color into three primaries (red, green, and blue) and three secondaries (yellow, cyan, and magenta). When primaries of light are combined, the human eye sees white light

Historically, using a filter to remove colors from white light generated colored light. Blue light, for instance, is white light with green, and red removed. Filtered light is still common in theatrical and architectural lighting.

However, most nonincandescent light sources tend to create specific colors of light. Modern fluorescent lamps, for example, create prime colors of light (red, green, and blue) that appear to the human eye as white light. Other lamps, such as low-pressure sodium lamps, create monochromatic yellow light. While most lamps are intended to appear as white as possible, in some cases lamps are designed to create specific colors, such as green or blue.

However, the intent of most light sources is to produce white light, of whose appearance there are two measures:

1. *Color temperature*, which describes whether the light appears warm (reddish), neutral, or cool (bluish). The term *temperature* relates to the light emitted from a metal object heated to the point of incandescence. For instance, the color temperature of an incandescent lamp is about 2700K, appearing like a metal object heated to 2700° Kelvin (2427° Celsius or 4400° Fahrenheit).
2. *Color rendering index* (CRI), which describes the quality of the light on a scale of 0 (horrible) to 100 (perfect).

All white light sources can be evaluated by color temperature and CRI. Color temperature is the more obvious measure; two light sources of the same color temperature but different CRI appear much more alike than do two light sources of similar CRI but different color temperature.

Natural light is generally defined as having a CRI of 100 (perfect). Color temperature, however, varies a great deal due to weather, season, air pollution, and viewing angle. For instance, the combination of sun and blue skylight on a summer day at noon is about 5500K, but if the sun is shielded, the color of the blue skylight is over 10,000K. The rising and setting sunlight in clear weather can be as low as 1800K (very reddish). Cloudy day skylight is around 6500K.

When choosing electric light sources, it is generally best to select source color temperature and CRI according to the following table. Note that even if daylight enters the space, it is usually not a good idea to try to match daylight with electric light, as daylight varies considerably.

Color Classification of Light Sources

Color Temperature (Kelvins or K)	Applications
2500	Bulk industrial and security High Pressure Sodium (HPS) lighting.
2700–3000	Low light levels in most spaces [10 foot candles (FC)]. General residential lighting. Hotels, fine dining and family restaurants, theme parks.
2950–3500	Display lighting in retail and galleries; feature lighting.
3500–4100	General lighting in offices, schools, stores, industry, medicine; display lighting; sports lighting.
4100–5000	Special-application lighting where color discrimination is very important; uncommon for general lighting.
5000–7500	Special-application lighting where color discrimination is critical; uncommon for general lighting.
Minimum Lamp CRI	**Applications**
50	Noncritical industrial, storage, and security lighting.
50–70	Industrial and general illumination where color is not important.
70–79	Most office, retail, school, medical, and other work and recreational spaces.
80–89	Retail, work, and residential spaces where color quality is important.
90–100	Retail and work spaces where color rendering is critical.

Point Source, Line Source, or Area Source

Light sources vary in shape. The three basic shape types are point sources, line sources, and area sources. Each radiates light differently, thus causing distinctive effects.

Ballast or Transformer

In order to operate correctly, many electric light sources require an auxiliary electric device, such as a transformer or ballast. This device is often physically large and unattractive and can create an audible hum or buzz when operating.

Lamp Size

The physical size of the lamp affects the size of the luminaire and, in turn, determines how some sources might be used. Small, low-wattage lamps permit small luminaires, such as undercabinet lights and reading lights; large, high-powered lamps, such as metal halide stadium lamps, require a large luminaire, both for heat and for the reflector needed to aim the light properly.

Voltage

The electric power needed to operate a lamp is measured first by voltage. In the United States, the standard voltage services are 120 volts, 240 volts, 277 volts, and 480 volts. The standard 120-volt service is available in all building types; 240-, 277-, and 480-volt services are available only in large industrial and commercial buildings. Service voltage varies from country to country.

Many types of low-voltage lamps, operating at 6, 12, or 24 volts, are used throughout the world. Transformers are used to alter the service voltage to match the lamp voltage.

Bulb Temperature

The bulb of a lamp can get quite hot. The bulb temperature of incandescent and halogen lamps and most high-intensity discharge (HID) lamps is sufficiently high to cause burns and, in the case of halogen lamps, extremely severe burns and fires. Fluorescent lamps, while warm, are generally not too hot to touch when operating, although contact is not advised.

Operating Temperature

Fluorescent lamps are sensitive to temperature caused by the ambient air. If the bulb of the lamp is too cool or too hot, the lamp will give off less light than when operated at its design temperature. Most other lamps give off the same amount of light at the temperatures encountered in normal applications.

Operating Position

Some lamps produce more light or have longer lamp life when operated in specific positions with respect to gravity. Metal halide lamps are especially sensitive; some versions will not operate unless in the specified position.

Starting, Warming Up, and Restarting

Some lamps, especially incandescent, start operating as soon as power is applied, but most other types, especially discharge lamps, like fluorescent and metal halide lamps, require the lamp to be started by a high-energy pulse. The lamp warms up gradually, first glowing faintly and then, after a modest period, giving off full light. If then extinguished, fluorescent lamps can be restarted right away, but most HID lamps, like metal halide lamps, must cool considerably before restarting, potentially causing several minutes of unwanted darkness. Obviously, these considerations can dramatically affect design when safety or security might be compromised by a long warm-up or restart time.

Dimming Characteristics

Dimming is the process by which lamps are operated at less than full light, often as an energy-saving or mood-creating method. With incandescent lamps, dimming is simple and inexpensive, but with other types, dimming can be considerably more complex, and, in some cases, not advisable.

Energy Efficiency

The energy efficiency of a light source is called its *efficacy* and is measured in lumens per watt. Like miles per gallon, the higher the number, the better. Low-efficacy lamps, like incandescent lamps, are less than 20 lumens per watt. Among good colored light sources, metal halide and fluorescent lamps can achieve up to about 100 lumens per watt; distorted color sources, like low-pressure sodium lamps, presently achieve almost 180 lumens per watt.

Incandescent Lamps

INCANDESCENT AND HALOGEN LAMPS

Incandescent lamps generate light when electric current heats the lamp's filament. The hotter the filament, the whiter the light. The problem is that as the lamp filament gets hotter, the more rapid the evaporation of metal from the filament. A very dim lamp giving off yellow-orange light (2200K) may last a long time; a lamp giving off pure white (5000K) light will probably last for a few seconds only. The evaporated filament material blackens the bulb wall.

Standard incandescent lamps today use tungsten filaments that generate a warm-colored white light and last about 750 to 1000 hours. Two special types of incandescent lamps—krypton-incandescent lamps and xenon-incandescent lamps—make lamps last a bit longer. The temperature of the incandescent lamp bulb is generally too hot to touch but luminaires are designed to prevent inadvertent contact, so in general, the lamp's heat is not a problem. The color temperature of incandescent lamps is about 2700K, generating a warm-toned light.

Tungsten-halogen lamps (also called *TH* or simply *halogen* lamps) give off whiter light and last longer than standard incandescent lamps. Lamp life for halogen lamps ranges from 2000 hours up to 10,000 hours. Some types of halogen lamps use a quartz glass bulb and get extremely hot, requiring special protection for safety. The color temperature of halogen lamps is about 3000K, making their light appear slightly whiter and cooler than incandescent.

Low-voltage incandescent and tungsten-halogen lamps are smaller than regular lamps, a trait that has numerous advantages for accenting and display. Low-voltage lighting is particularly popular for specialty lights and for display lighting in retail, museums, homes, and other applications. For instance, most popular do-it-yourself landscape lighting is low-voltage. Transformers are needed to change the primary power, usually 120 volts, to the low voltage. The most common systems are 12 volts; these are used to power the popular MR16 and PAR36 display lamps. Some transformers are part of the luminaire, while in other applications a remote transformer can power a lighting system consisting of many lamps.

Halogen Lamps

Points to Remember About Incandescent and Halogen Lamps

Incandescent and halogen lamps operate in virtually any position. They start and warm up almost instantly and can be extinguished and restarted at will. Incandescent and halogen lamps can be dimmed easily and inexpensively. Dimming generally extends lamp life significantly.

Incandescent lamps are among the least energy-efficient sources available. Standard incandescent lamps generate between 5 and 20 lumens per watt; halogen lamps generate between 15 and 25 lumens per watt. The most efficient incandescent light sources are the latest infrared-reflecting halogen lamps, which generate between 20 and 35 lumens per watt.

Designers tend to prefer incandescent and halogen lamps for their color and versatility. When dimming, incandescent lamps are the only type that shifts color toward red as intensity decreases. While other source types have some size and shape versatility, no source other than incandescent can range from $\frac{1}{2}$-watt peanut lamps to 10,000-watt stage lamps. However, their inefficiency and short life are critical drawbacks that must be resolved in the design.

Most Common Applications

Standard incandescent lamps, such as A and R lamps, are still commonly used in residences, hotels and motels, and some retail environments where a residential-like quality is desired. In these applications, the designer is trading the low energy efficiency and short life of the incandescent lamp for its warm color and low costs.

Halogen PAR lamps are commonly used in residential downlighting and outdoor lighting, hotels and motels, and especially in retail display. IR/HIR lamps, the most common display light source in service, are used in recessed lighting, track lighting, and other lampholders in stores of all types.

MR16 and PAR (Parabolic Aluminized Reflector Lamp) low-voltage lamps are commonly used in museums and galleries, residences, landscape lighting, and other applications where a modest amount of light and excellent beam control are called for. Other types of low-voltage lighting are used in residential and hospitality lighting for details and special effects like cove lights and illumination inside and under cabinets.

FLUORESCENT LAMPS

The fluorescent lamp is the workhorse light source for commercial and institutional buildings. Fluorescent lamps use the principle of *fluorescence*, in which minerals exposed to ultraviolet light are caused to glow. Electric energy excites the gas inside the lamp, which generates ultraviolet light. The ultraviolet light in turn excites the phosphors, which are a mixture of minerals painted onto the inside of the bulb. Phosphors are designed to radiate particular colors of white light, thus enabling the choice of both the color temperature and CRI of a lamp. The color of the lamp is described by the name or designation. Traditional lamp colors include *cool white, warm white,* and *daylight.* However, modern lamps are identified by a color "name" that designates its color temperature and CRI. For example, a lamp having a color temperature of 3500K and a CRI between 80 and 90 is known as the color 835.

A fluorescent lamp requires a *ballast* in order to work properly. A ballast is an electrical component that starts the lamp and regulates the electric power flow to the lamp. Some ballasts can operate up to four lamps. There are two types, *magnetic* and *electronic*, of which the latter is generally more energy-efficient and quieter, and it reduces lamp flicker considerably.

Fluorescent lamps can be dimmed through the use of an electronic dimming ballast. Most electronic dimming ballasts require specific dimmers. Dimming range is typically 10 to 100 percent of light or better, with the best ballasts allowing a dimming range of 0.5 to 100 percent. Fluorescent lamps change color slightly when dimmed; their light tends to appear more purple at lower output levels.

Fluorescent lamps are sensitive to temperature. Bulb temperature is critical for proper light output, and lamps operated in very cold or very warm situations generally do not give off as much light as when operated at room temperature. Also, lamps may not start if they are too cold. The minimum starting temperature of a lamp depends on the ballast; minimum starting temperature ratings are available for ballasts to help choose the right type. Most fluorescent lamps get warm, but a person can touch one in operation without being burned.

Standard Straight and U-bent Lamps

Most common fluorescent lamps are straight tubes. The longest standard fluorescent lamps are 8' long and the shortest are 4". The most common length is 4', and the most common diameters are ⅝" (T-5), 1" (T-8), and 1½" (T-12). U-bent lamps are straight lamps that are manufactured in a *U* shape but otherwise perform about the same as straight lamps.

Standard straight and U-bent lamps are preferred for general illumination because of their cost effectiveness and energy efficiency. In current designs, the T-8 is the most commonly used general-purpose lamp, and the T-5 and T-5 high-output lamps are becoming increasing popular for a number of specific lighting systems. The T-12 lamps are an older style that is less energy efficient.

Compact Fluorescent Lamps

There are two major types of compact fluorescent lamps: those with screw bases, designed to directly replace incandescent lamps in incandescent lamp sockets, and those with plug-in bases designed to fit into sockets in luminaires designed specifically for compact fluorescent lamps.

Because compact fluorescent lamps, like all fluorescent lamps, require a ballast, lamps with screw bases are larger and costlier than those for dedicated

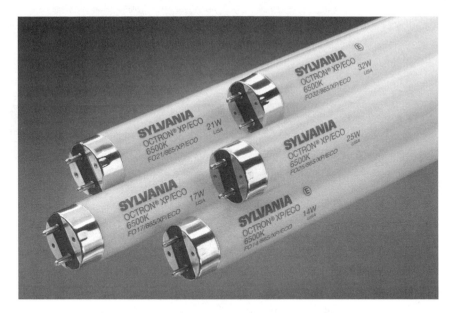

Flourescent Lamps

Compact Flourescent Lamps

compact fluorescent luminaires. As a result, it is generally best to employ dedicated compact fluorescent luminaires in new designs. Screw-based compact fluorescent lamps should be used to convert incandescent type luminaires only after the fact.

Points to Remember About Fluorescent Lamps

Fluorescent and compact fluorescent lamps provide good energy efficiency, good to excellent color, dimming, and many other features expected of modern light sources. Improvements in fluorescent lighting since 1980 now make it useful in homes, businesses, and for almost every other type of lighting application.

The challenge of the designer remains to determine the best light source to meet the user's expectations, and fluorescent lighting is still not a *direct* replacement for incandescent lighting. Fluorescent and compact fluorescent lamps can be used in many places, however, and it is important to develop expertise in using these energy-efficient sources.

HID LAMPS

High-intensity discharge (HID) lamps are designed to emit a great deal of light from a compact, long-life light source. They are most often used for street and parking lot lighting and for large indoor spaces like gymnasiums and industrial work floors. Most HID lamps approximate a *point source* of light, making them excellent sources for spot lighting equipment such as track lights, display lights, and even stadium lights. HID lamps are generally energy efficient, producing 50 to 100 lumens per watt.

As in fluorescent lamps, a ballast regulates the amount of power flowing into HID lamps. Magnetic ballasts are generally used for most HID lamps, although electronic ballasts are becoming increasingly popular. Ballasts can be bulky, heavy, and noisy, but some types can be mounted remotely from the luminaire.

HID lamps can get quite hot and generally should be protected from direct touch. In addition, some metal halide lamps must be totally enclosed due to a small possibility of lamp explosion. HID lamps start and operate over a relatively wide temperature range, and they are well suited to both indoor and outdoor applications.

HID lamps require time to warm up; they get progressively brighter over several minutes until reaching full light output. The lamp's true light output and color is often not reached for two to five minutes. If power to an operating HID lamp is interrupted, the lamp must cool before the ignition circuit can restart it. The cool-off period is called the *restrike time*. Some HID lamps must cool more than 10 minutes after being extinguished before they can restrike and warm back up.

Types of HID Lamps

Metal Halide Lamps

Metal halide lamps produce white light of a good color quality and are available in many sizes, from compact lamps that can be used in track lighting and table lamps to huge lamps for lighting stadiums. Standard metal halide lamps tend to have a color temperature of 3700 to 4100K and appear cool and slight-

Metal Halide Lamps

ly greenish. Their CRI is 65 to 70. Standard metal halide lamps typically are used where color is not critical, such as sports arenas, parking lots, landscape lighting, and building floodlighting.

The latest metal halide lamps are called *ceramic metal halide* lamps. They exhibit superior color rendering (80 to 85) and a choice of warm (3000K) or cool (4100K) lamps. They can be used for interior lighting, such as downlighting, display lighting, and wallwashing, as well as for exterior lighting.

Sodium Lamps

The two types of sodium lamps are *high-pressure sodium (HPS) lamps* and *low-pressure sodium (LPS) lamps*. Sodium lamps tend to be yellowish in color. HPS lamps exhibit a golden-pinkish light that tends to create spaces with a distinctly brown or dirty quality. Low-pressure sodium emits monochromatic yellow light, creating stark scenes devoid of color altogether. Although HPS lamps offer very high lumens per watt, their color deficiencies limit use to lighting roads, parking lots, heavy industrial workspaces, warehousing, security lighting, and other applications where light color is not important. LPS lamps are even higher in lumens per watt, but their color is so poor that their use is limited to security lighting.

Mercury Vapor Lamps

Mercury vapor lamps are an older type of lamp that remains in common use as streetlights and security lights. However, compared to other HID lamps, mercury vapor lamps have relatively poor color and low energy efficiency. They are almost never used in new construction.

OTHER LIGHT SOURCES

Induction Lamps

Induction lamps are a type of fluorescent lamp that uses radio waves rather than an electric arc to cause the gas in the lamp to give off ultraviolet energy. Induction lamps have most of the characteristics of fluorescent lamps, including 70 to 80 lumens per watt, choice of color, and high CRI. However, because induction lamps have no electrodes, the lamps are rated to 60,000 to 100,000 hours. An induction lamp used every day for 12 hours will last more than 20 years. Typical applications include streetlighting and lighting in hard-to-maintain locations.

High Pressure Sodium Lamps

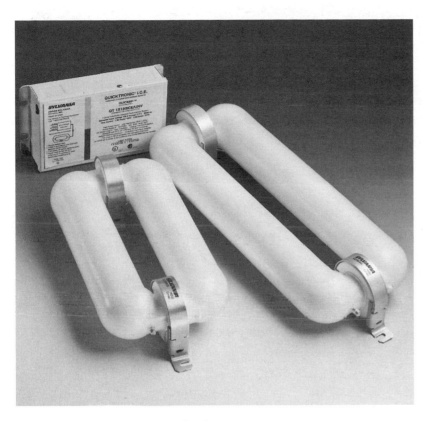

Induction Lamps

Light Emitting Diodes (LEDs)

Light-Emitting Diodes

Light-emitting diodes (LEDs) are presently limited in color and efficiency, making them still too costly to serve as general-purpose light sources. This is expected to change as technological growth in this source progresses.

However, LED lamps can be used in specialty applications, including signs and display lighting. Systems employing red, green, and blue LED lamps can be used to create changing color washes. At present, the most common architectural application of LED lamps is in exit signs. Automotive and sign lighting applications, including traffic signals, are multiplying rapidly.

Neon and Cold Cathode Lamps

Neon and cold cathode lamps are closely related to fluorescent lamps in operating principles. While their primary applications are signs and specialty lighting, both neon and cold cathode lamps can be used for architectural lighting applications. Both types last 20,000 to 40,000 hours, are reasonably energy efficient, and can be dimmed and even flashed on and off without affecting lamp life.

When thinking of neon and cold cathode lamps, imagine tubular lighting that can be formed into just about any shape and be made to create just about any color of light. Cold cathode lighting is like neon, but generally the lamps are larger in diameter and the light source is used for architectural rather than sign lighting. Cold cathode lamps are also distinguished by having a plug-in base, where neon tubing usually terminates in base wire connectors.

In architecture, neon lighting is most often used for special effects, such as cove lighting, building outlining, and color accents, especially in casinos and retail lighting. Cold cathode lamps produce more light than neon; they are typically used for cove lighting and outlining in conventional building types, such as hotels, convention centers, and office buildings.

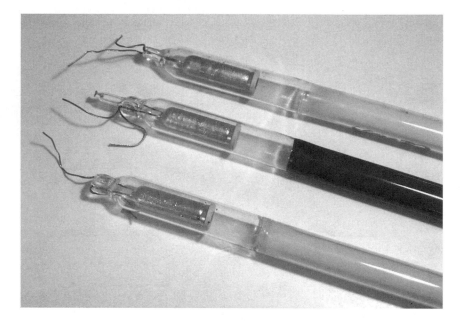

Neon and Cold Cathode Lamps

sizes are 2' x 4', with 2' x 2' and 1' x 4' also readily available. Most troffers are designed to lay in to acoustic tile ceilings. Recessed troffer depth varies from 3½" to over 7", so make certain to coordinate troffers with other elements above the ceiling.

Troffers can be equipped with most fluorescent technologies, including dimming, magnetic or electronic ballasts, and T-12 or T-8 lamps. They can be equipped with emergency battery packs to power some or all of the lamps during a power outage or emergency condition.

Commercial Fluorescent Fixtures

Commercial fluorescent fixtures comprise several types of fluorescent direct luminaires. The most common type is the wraparound, wherein a lens or diffuser top surrounds the lamps, hiding them from direct view while radiating light downward and to the sides. Commercial luminaires are among the lowest-cost lighting fixtures. They are typically used for general and utility lighting in modest projects.

The majority of commercial fixtures are rated for dry locations. They use T-12 or T-8 lamps. Some have damp labels, and most can be equipped with a battery pack for emergency power.

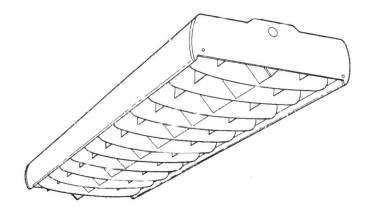

Commercial Flourescent Fixture

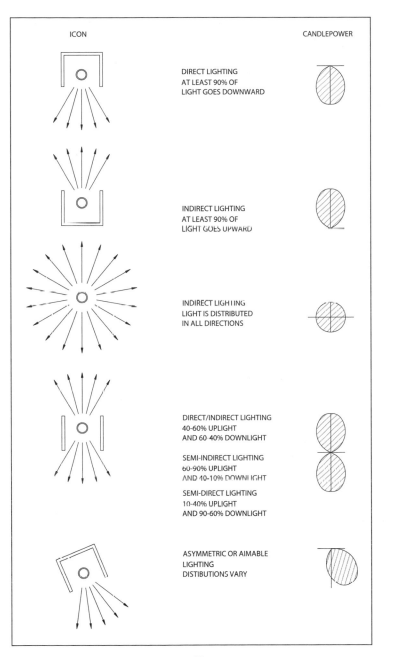

ICON		CANDLEPOWER
	DIRECT LIGHTING AT LEAST 90% OF LIGHT GOES DOWNWARD	
	INDIRECT LIGHTING AT LEAST 90% OF LIGHT GOES UPWARD	
	INDIRECT LIGHTING LIGHT IS DISTRIBUTED IN ALL DIRECTIONS	
	DIRECT/INDIRECT LIGHTING 40-60% UPLIGHT AND 60-40% DOWNLIGHT	
	SEMI-INDIRECT LIGHTING 60-90% UPLIGHT AND 40-10% DOWNLIGHT	
	SEMI-DIRECT LIGHTING 10-40% UPLIGHT AND 90-60% DOWNLIGHT	
	ASYMMETRIC OR AIMABLE LIGHTING DISTIBUTIONS VARY	

Troffers

Industrial Luminaires

Industrial luminaires generally have a utilitarian or functional appearance. Fluorescent industrials are strip lights and open fixtures with simple reflectors designed to be surface-mounted or hung by chains or rods. HID industrials include high-bay downlights and low-bay downlights. Industrial fixtures are generally used in factories, warehouses, and, increasingly, in schools and retail stores where a less finished appearance is desired. Although most industrials are direct lighting, many are semi-direct—that is, having a small percentage of uplight to improve visual comfort.

Most industrial fixtures are listed for dry locations. Some are finished in glass or porcelain to resist corrosion caused by airborne gases or particles. Others utilize aluminum or plastic construction. Certain fixtures are specifically designed for demanding environmental applications ranging from wet and salt-water marine luminaires to explosion-proof products for use in petrochemical plants, grain storage facilities, and other hazardous locations.

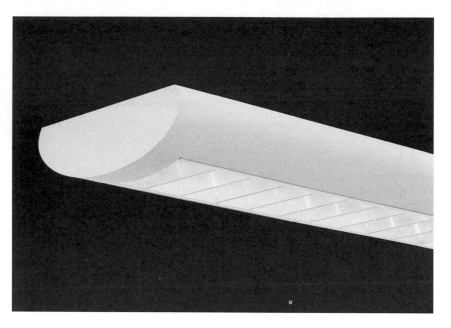

Linear Lighting System

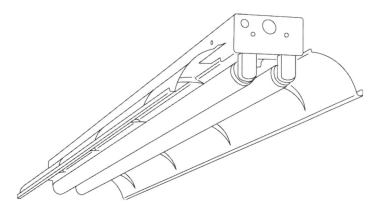

Industrial Fluorescent Fixture

Linear Lighting Systems

Linear lighting systems are fluorescent luminaires having indirect, semi-indirect, and direct-indirect lighting distribution; they are designed to illuminate offices and other more finished spaces. Because the luminaires can be obtained in varying lengths and assembled into patterns, they are called *linear systems*.

Indirect lighting systems produce uplight only. Generally, they are mounted at least 15" to 18" below the ceiling; longer suspension lengths improve unifor-

mity of light on the ceiling. To maintain adequate clearance, it is usually necessary for ceilings to be at least 9' high. Semi-indirect systems having a small percentage of downlight should be used in the same manner.

Direct-indirect lighting systems are intended to produce both indirect lighting, for its comfort and balance, and direct light, for task lighting. Suspension length and ceiling height are not as fixed as for indirect lighting. The ratio of uplight to downlight varies; generally, the higher the ceiling, the greater the downlight percentage should be.

Almost all luminaires of this type are for dry and relatively clean indoor locations. They usually use T-8, T-12, or T-5 lamps and often are equipped with battery packs for emergency lighting. Some versions permit track or low-voltage accent lighting on the bottom of the luminaire together with fluorescent uplight.

Architectural Lighting Fixtures

Architectural lighting fixtures are fixtures that are not decorative but rather functional and inconspicuous. They are used to illuminate architectural shapes and forms.

Wallwashers

Wallwashers are available in several types:

- *Eyelid* wallwashers are, essentially, downlights with an eyelid-shaped shield on the room side.
- *Recessed lens* wallwashers resemble downlights but use an angled lens to throw light to one side.
- *Surface and semirecessed lens* and *open* wallwashers throw light onto an adjacent wall and generally work best; they can also be mounted to track.
- *Downlight* wallwashers are downlights designed to illuminate rather than scallop an adjacent wall, but not well enough for display purposes.

Wall Grazing Fixtures

Wall grazing fixtures, sometimes called *wall slots*, are used to illuminate walls in lobbies, corridors, and core areas. They are especially well suited to textured and polished surfaces.

Accent Fixtures

Accent fixtures allow light to focus on art and building surfaces.

- *Recessed accent lights* appear as downlights but internally permit rotation and elevation of the light beam.
- *Eyeballs* and *pulldown accents* resemble downlights, but their appearance belies the ability to be adjusted.
- *Track lighting systems* are designed to accent art and retail displays; for ease and flexibility of use, lampholders can be relocated to any point on the track.

Cove Lights

Cove lights permit uplighting from coves or other architectural elements more efficiently than do strip lights, and without socket shadows.

Task Lights

Task lights are specially designed to illuminate a desk area while minimizing veiling reflections.

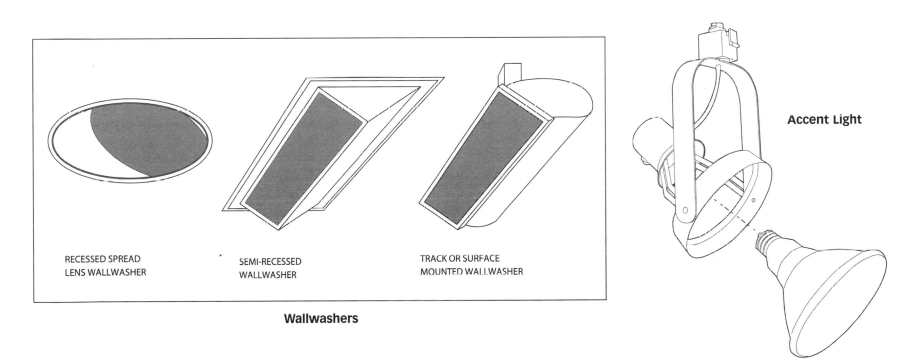

Accent Light

RECESSED SPREAD LENS WALLWASHER

SEMI-RECESSED WALLWASHER

TRACK OR SURFACE MOUNTED WALLWASHER

Wallwashers

Decorative Lighting

Lighting is the jewelry of architecture and, in many building types, plays a significant role in building style, period, or motif.

- *Chandeliers* are ornate luminaires generally consisting of many small incandescent lamps that simulate the effect of candle flames. Chandeliers are hung from the ceiling and are used for general illumination in dining rooms, foyers, and other formal spaces.
- *Pendants* are also ceiling-hung decorative fixtures. In general, the term *pendant* is used for hanging luminaires less formal than chandeliers that are used in offices, restaurants, and many other places. Most pendant luminaires use incandescent lamps, although modern variations are also available with HID and fluorescent sources.
- *Close-to-ceiling luminaires* are similar to pendants but mount closely to the ceiling to allow use in most rooms with conventional ceiling heights.
- *Sconces* are ornate or decorative wall-mounted luminaires. Often, sconces match an adjacent chandelier; at other times, they are the sole decorative lighting element. Sconces exhibit a wide range of style, from crystal fixtures with flame-tip lamps to modern designs.

Torchièr

Floor Lamp

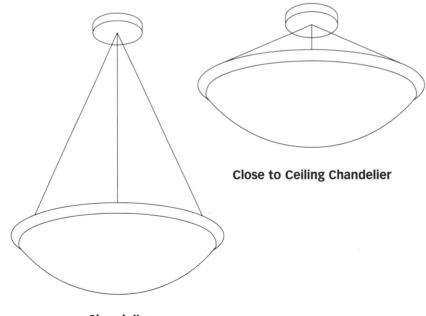

Close to Ceiling Chandelier

Chandelier

- *Torchièrs* are floor lamps designed specifically for uplighting. Most use incandescent or halogen sources, although compact fluorescent options should be considered for commercial and hospitality applications.

- *Lanterns* are outdoor luminaires mounted to ceilings, walls, posts, or poles.

Most decorative luminaires can be used in dry indoor spaces only. A few types, notably lanterns and some sconces, are wet-labeled, meaning they can be exposed to direct rain.

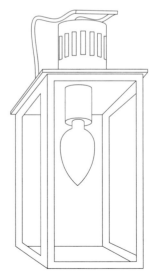

Lantern

STANDARDS OF THE INDUSTRY

Many design problems have reasonably obvious solutions determined by a combination of budget, energy code, and standards of the industry. Unless project requirements call for unique or specialized lighting, it is often best to design using common luminaire types. Here are some of them:

2' x 4' Lay-in Troffer with Pattern 12 Acrylic Lens

This is the least expensive lighting system for use in suspended ceilings for a wide variety of projects. In general, these luminaires should be specified with two or three T-8 lamps and an electronic ballast. They tend to have a low-budget appearance. They are not recommended for use in computer workspaces.

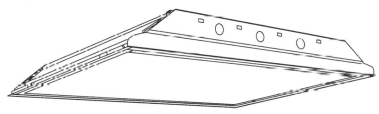

Lens Troffer

2' x 4' Lay-in Troffer with Large-Cell Parabolic Louver

This standard lighting system is appropriate for offices, stores, and many other building types with suspended ceilings. In general, the luminaires should be specified with two or three T-8 lamps and an electronic ballast; the number of rows of cells should equal the number of lamps. They tend to have an upgraded appearance and are at the low end of acceptable lighting quality for computer workspaces.

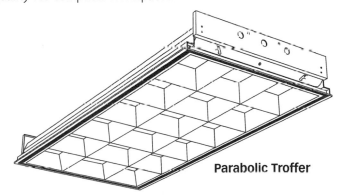

Parabolic Troffer

Wraparound Surface Fluorescent

This low-cost lighting system can be used in a variety of applications and ceiling systems. In general, the luminaires should be specified with two T-8 lamps, electronic ballast, and a prismatic acrylic lens. Wraparound luminaires are suited for low-ceiling applications; in general, they should not be used above 10'. These tend to have a utilitarian appearance and are unsuitable for computer workspaces.

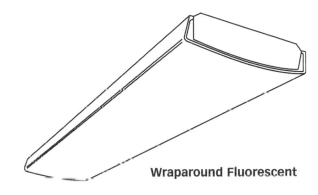

Wraparound Fluorescent

Fluorescent Strip

This very low-cost lighting system can be used in a variety of applications, ceiling systems, and architectural details, such as valances. In general, the luminaires should be specified with T-8 lamps and electronic ballast. Further, they should be specified in single-lamp, two-lamp, two-lamp end-to-end (tandem), and four-lamp tandem luminaires using 4' or 8' lamps.

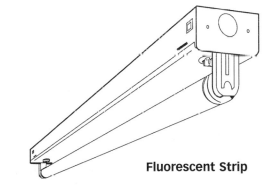

Fluorescent Strip

Fluorescent Industrial

This low-cost lighting system is used in a variety of applications, usually as general lighting in areas without suspended ceilings. The luminaires should be specified in two-lamp or four-lamp tandem luminaires using 4' or 8' T-8 lamps and electronic ballast. They are available as solid reflectors and reflectors with uplight slots.

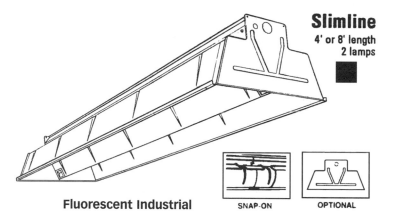

Slimline
4' or 8' length
2 lamps

Fluorescent Industrial

SNAP-ON   OPTIONAL

HID Industrial Downlight

This low- to moderate-cost lighting system type is used for industrial medium and high bay spaces (generally over 20' mounting height) as well as gyms, big box stores, and other spaces with an open, industrial character. The luminaires should be specified with metal halide pulse start lamps regardless of wattage.

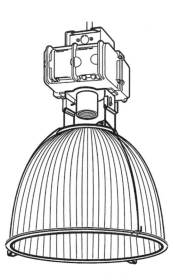

HID Industrial Downlight

Compact Fluorescent Industrial Downlight

This moderate-cost lighting system looks like a metal halide industrial downlight, but it employs multiple compact fluorescent lamps. It can be used at mounting heights up to 30'. While lower in efficacy than pulse-start HID, multiple compact fluorescent lamps offer superior color, rapid starting and restarting, and the ability to switch in groups to achieve lower lighting levels for daylighting or varying uses.

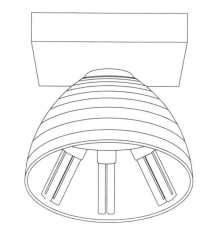

Multiple Compact Fluorescent Industrial

Suspended Fluorescent Indirect Lighting

Fluorescent lighting systems suspended from and uplighting the ceiling use T-5, T-5HO, or T-8 lamps, generally 4', and electronic ballasts. They may offer a small downlight component of less than 10%. This type of lighting must be suspended at least 18" below the ceiling, which necessitates a ceiling height of 9' or more. These systems are applicable as general lighting for offices, classrooms, and some medical spaces, and as ambient light in offices, retail stores, and other locations. They are considered good lighting for computer workspaces. Low-cost versions are made of sheet steel, while more expensive and styled versions are made from extruded aluminum. Various combinations of lamps are available; the most common selections are two or three T-8 or T-5 lamps or one T-5HO lamp across. The elements are installed in continuous rows approximately 10' to 12' apart and laid out in 4' increments.

Suspended Fluorescent Direct-Indirect Lighting

These suspended fluorescent lighting systems produce both downlight and uplight using T-5, T-5HO, or T-8 lamps generally 4' long and electronic ballasts. This type of lighting must be suspended at least 12" below the ceiling, necessitating a ceiling height of 9' or more. These systems are applicable as general lighting for offices, classrooms, libraries, and some medical spaces, and as ambient light in offices, retail stores, and other locations. They are considered good lighting for computer workspace. Moderate-cost versions are made of sheet steel or plastic, while more expensive and styled versions are made from extruded aluminum. The most advanced luminaires use wave guide lens technology. Various combinations of lamps are available; the most common selections are two or three T-8 or T-5 lamps or one T-5HO lamp across. The systems are installed in continuous rows approximately 10' to 12' apart and laid out in 4' increments.

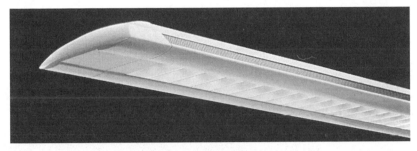

Suspended Direct-Indirect Lighting

Recessed Indirect Troffers

A relative and attractive newcomer, recessed indirect troffers are slightly more expensive than parabolics but offer a fresh, contemporary appearance for stores, offices, and other sites. They are not a good luminaire for open office areas and other large workrooms, however, so apply them with some caution for their glare potential. The 2' x 4' version uses two or three 4' lamps.

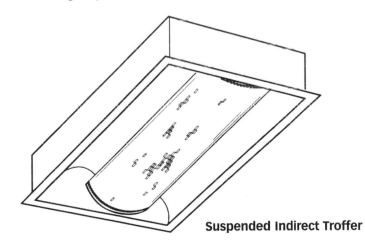

Suspended Indirect Troffer

Recessed and Surface Downlights

Also known as *cans* and *top hats*, downlights are an attractive and formal lighting system used for corridors, lobbies, meeting spaces, malls, and many other spaces where a modest amount of well-shielded light is desired. Apertures range from 4" to over 10", and the dozens of types include open reflector, open baffle, adjustable, lensed, and decorative ring styles. While the downlight was developed for incandescent lighting, energy-efficient variations include single and multiple compact fluorescent lamps and HID lamps.

Adjustable Downlights

A variation of the downlight using PAR lamps and low-voltage lamps, adjustable downlights are important for display lighting.

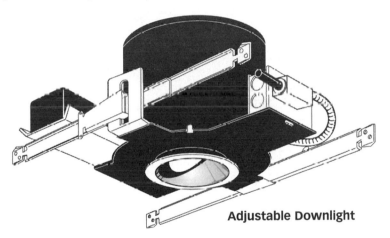

Adjustable Downlight

Track and Canopy Monopoints

These display lights, which come in many styles, are suitable for illuminating single objects. The appearance of the luminaire can play an important role. Similar to cans, monopoint variations employ compact fluorescent lamps, MR16 low-voltage lamps, PAR halogen lamps, and low-wattage metal halide lamps.

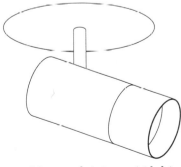

Monopoint Accent Light

Track, Canopy, and Semirecessed Wallwashers

These display lights are suitable for illuminating a wall of objects or displays. They are typically used with ceilings or soffits up to 12' and wash an area of wall about 3' to 4' wide. Lamp choices include high-wattage tungsten halogen lamps (100-500 watts), T-5 twin tube fluorescent lamps, and metal halide lamps. Wallwashing is one of the most energy-intensive techniques, so limit the number of washed surfaces to those that really need it.

Wall Sconces

Wall sconces are a decorative lighting source that can be equipped with incandescent or compact fluorescent lighting to provide an attractive and effective light. They can be used in hotels and motels, office corridors and lobbies, and a wide variety of other space types.

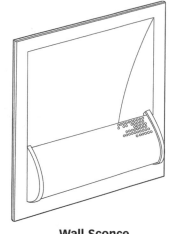

Wall Sconce

Pendants

Pendants are decorative lights that hang from the ceiling. They are often used in stores, hotels, and restaurants as much for their appearance as for light. While usually designed to use incandescent or halogen lamps, the increasing number of lamp choices includes hard-wired compact fluorescent lamps.

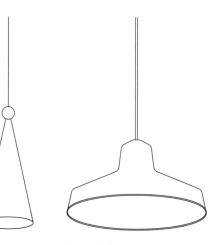

Pendant Lights

Ceiling Drums

Ceiling drums are round or square luminaires that mount to the ceiling surface. They typically are used as corridor lights, rest room lights, closet lights, and in many locations where a modest amount of light is needed. Drums tend to be inexpensive. A lens or diffuser surrounds and protects the lamp. Drums can be utilitarian or ornamental; rough service drums are available that can be used where vandal resistance is important.

Drum Luminaire

Portable Table and Floor Lamps

Table lamps are traditionally supplied as an incandescent lighting system, although versions are now being reinvented to employ hardwired compact fluorescent lamps. The secret of using a fluorescent lamp in a traditional luminaire is to divide the preferred incandescent watts by 3.5 to determine fluorescent watts.

Table Lamp

Task Lights

Since the invention of the classic architect lamp decades ago, the flexible task light has been a useful and attractive tool. Modern lamp options include low-voltage halogen and compact fluorescent versions.

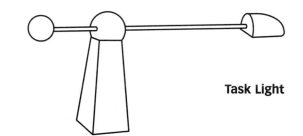

Task Light

Undercabinet Lights

These are task-oriented lights. Undercabinet lights should be mounted under the *front* edge of a shelf or cabinet and should be as continuous as possible. Undercabinet lights using fluorescent lamps are the most energy-efficient and least costly, but upscale types using halogen and xenon incandescent lamps are excellent choices in many situations.

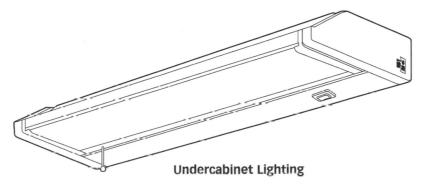

Undercabinet Lighting

Vanity Lights

The vanity light is a task light for bath vanity and mirror areas. It can mount horizontally above the mirror or vertically to the sides. Vanity lights can be highly ornamental, but many versions are utilitarian and designed for abuse. Fluorescent lamps should always be considered an alternative to incandescent and halogen vanity lights.

Vanity Lighting

Exit Signs

Exit signs can employ one of several energy-efficient light sources. Most modern exit signs now employ LED lamps to illuminate the face of the sign. However, where greater face brightness or a downlight is needed, look into cold cathode lamp exit signs. Other versions, including incandescent and compact fluorescent, are also available but lack the extreme energy efficiency and long life of both LED and cold cathode.

Exit Sign

Chapter 4

SWITCHING AND DIMMING

Since lighting was invented, switching has been essential. Even candles and gaslights were turned on and off and sometimes even dimmed. With electric lighting, switching and dimming is easy.

PRINCIPLES OF CONTROL

Controlling Operating Time

First, we control the operating time of lights for convenience and to save energy. By turning lights off, we both save the cost of electricity and preserve lamp life. Of course, we turn lights off when we wish to darken a room for sleep. This is generally called *switching*.

Controlling Power

Most light sources operate even if their power is varied. This results in a source that is less bright than normal, which we call *dimming*. Dimming is generally used to create an intimate mood, as in a dining room or restaurant. In addition, it is now frequently used to save energy. In many spaces, windows introduce enough light to permit interior lights to be dimmed; the combination of daylight and reduced electric light still provides adequate illumination.

Code Requirements

Building codes require lighting controls in two ways:

1. The National Electric Code requires switches by every door in residential occupancies, including private homes, apartments, and condominiums. This is primarily for safety and convenience.
2. Energy codes, like ASHRAE/IESNA 90.1 (American Society of Heating, Refrigerating, and Air Conditioning Engineers/Illuminating Engineering Society of North America) and various state codes, require switching in every nonresidential space but not necessarily beside every door. This is primarily to encourage people to turn lights off when they are not needed. In many cases, the switching must be automatic, as with a motion sensor.

Common Sense

In addition to specific code requirements, switches or other controls for lights are frequently chosen by the designer to enable the proper use of the lighting. Think about how a room is meant to be used. The best designs anticipate needs and resolve them prior to construction. Where should a light switch or dimmer be located? Should switching or dimming be provided in more than one location? Is dimming rather than switching more suited to the activities that will take place in the room? Once code requirements are met, the best approach is always common sense.

Preset Dimming

Preset dimmers permit the light level from each dimmer to be set and memorized. Then, when a button is pushed, the dimmer responds by fading to its preset level, creating a lighting scene. The most common preset dimming device is a four-dimmer, four-scene controller typically used to control light in large residential living rooms, hotel ballrooms, and restaurants where combinations of lighting are used for different times of day or for different functions. Each of the four scenes is memorized; when the proper button is pressed, the scene is recalled and the lights readjust accordingly.

Time Control

Many lighting systems are best controlled automatically by time. For instance, the lights in a store with fixed hours of operation can go on and off automatically through the use of a *time switch* (sometimes called a *time clock*). Simple clock mechanisms operate a switch by operating a contact closure at set times. People often use a residential version of a time switch to control lights as a security measure.

In larger buildings, computerized energy management systems may be programmed to run many time schedules for various lighting systems. These systems operate relays but have the advantage of computer control, centralization, and convenience. Major buildings employ this type of control so a single building engineer can effectively manage the facility.

Some time control systems can automatically change the set times according to the time of year, thus replacing photoelectric eyes. This type of control device is called an *astronomic time switch*.

A Four Scene Four Channel Preset Dimmer (Lutron). Four Buttons Are Scenes—Four LED Ladders with Up Down Buttons Are the Four Channels, or Separately Dimmed Circuits

Motion Sensor Wallbox

Motion Sensing

Motion sensors detect the presence of people and respond by automatically turning lights on. It is possible to replace an ordinary switch with a motion sensor switch, making lighting control hands-free and assuring that lights will go off when people are no longer present. Motion sensors mounted in the ceiling can be connected to relays, and several sensors can connect to the same relay. This assures that any motion in a relatively large space, such as a cafeteria or gym, will keep the lights on throughout the space. Also, in spaces such as rest rooms where walls or privacy dividers prevent motion sensing, multiple sensors assure that no one is left in the dark.

Daylighting Controls

Daylighting controls are photoelectric eyes that turn lights off or dim them when daylight is sufficient. In basic applications, photoelectric switches turn off parking lot lights and streetlights during the day. For interior spaces, photoelectric dimmers reduce the energy used by electric lights in spaces where windows or skylights provide most of the light actually needed in the space and increase light levels at night and on dark days.

Lumen Maintenance

Lumen maintenance controls are designed to take advantage of the overdesign of lighting systems so that as lamps age and luminaires become dirty, designed lighting levels are maintained. This means that for the period right after construction or maintenance, lighting systems can often be dimmed 20% to 30% and still provide the desired maintained light levels. Systems to perform this function use a special type of interior photoelectric cell and dimming of fluorescent or HID ballasts.

Adaptation Compensation

Adaptation compensation, which involves dimming lights at night, is intuitive. Especially in commercial buildings like grocery stores, lights can be dimmed considerably at night because shoppers' eyes are already accustomed to darkness. Adaptation compensation can be performed by a photoelectric eye or programmed into a computer according to the known sunset and sunrise times at the location.

CONTROL DEVICES

Here are the most common control devices and how to use them.

Switches

Switches turn lights on and off. Most switches are levers and mechanical devices that open and close electrical contacts in the power circuit directly feeding the lights.

The two most common switches types are *toggle* and *decora* (paddle). Some switches feature a finder light (the switch is illuminated in the dark) or a pilot light (the switch is illuminated when the lights are turned on). A switch should be located next to the door as you enter a room, preferably on the latch side, and mounted 42" above the floor in order to conform with ADA requirements. Switches must be located at each entry of a room. Multiple switch locations require switches called *three-way* and *four-way* that permit any switch location to turn the lights on and off.

Use one switch for each group of lights to be controlled together. For example, in office buildings, place luminaires near windows on separate switches from those further into the building. This permits energy savings by allowing the occupant to turn off lights near windows during the day.

Dimmers

Dimmers are control devices that vary the light level and power to lights. For incandescent lights, dimmers or dimmer switches are usually used in place of regular switches, either wall-mounted or on the luminaire itself. For fluorescent lights, the fluorescent ballast must be a dimming type connected to a compatible dimmer switch.

Dimmers almost always combine the dimming electronics with a switch, so they are really switch-dimmers. How the switch part works is just as important as the dimmer part. In a single-action dimmer, the lights must be dimmed completely before the switch action occurs. In a preset dimmer, the switch and the dimmer require separate actions. Preset dimmers are generally better because they allow three-way and four-way switching, and they permit setting a preferred light level and leaving it there even when lights are switched.

Among the several styles of dimmer, the most common are the rotary dimmer and the slide dimmer. In the rotary dimmer style, the preset dimmer often has a push-on, push-off dial. In the slide dimmer style, the preset dimmer may have a rocker switch, a push-on, push-off switch, or a touch switch with a separate dimmer slide.

Lighting designers, in addition to considering dimmer style differences, must also select dimmers according to their load, called the *dimmer rating*. Here are the most common dimmer ratings.

- Standard dimmers for incandescent lamps. The minimum rating is 600 watts; dimmers can be rated up to 2000 watts.
- *Dimmers for low-voltage incandescent lights.* These dimmers "dim" the transformer feeding the lights. Such dimmers are rated for magnetic transformers or electronic transformers. These dimmers can also dim regular incandescent lamps and mixed loads of incandescent lamps and low-voltage lighting. They are usually rated in volt-amps (VA), which are roughly the same as watts. Magnetic-rated dimmers are rated at least 600 VA; and electronic rated dimmers are rated at least 325 VA.
- *Dimmers for fluorescent lighting.* To dim fluorescent lighting, the lamps must have dimming ballasts. In addition, the dimmer must be designed to operate with the specific dimming ballast being used.
- *Dimmers for neon and cold cathode lights.*

Dimmer

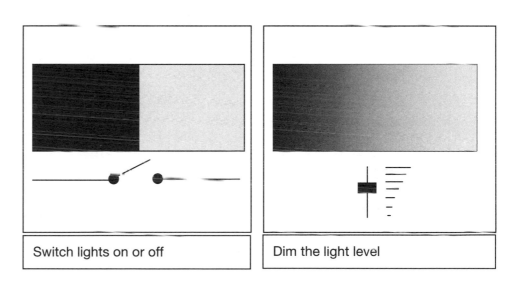

| Switch lights on or off | Dim the light level |

Dimmer Control Icon

Motion Sensors

Motion sensors are automatic switches that turn lights on when motion is detected and leave them on until some designated time after the last motion occurs. Motion sensors save energy and add convenience.

The most common motion sensors are wall-switch types, designed to replace ordinary manual switches. Several types are available, including one that is both a motion sensor and dimmer. Unfortunately, wall motion sensors are not always located in the best spot to detect motion; the better approach is to place a sensor close to the smallest regular motions that must be detected.

Motion sensors are also made to be mounted on the ceiling, on the upper walls, in corners, or on workstation shelves. These types of sensors usually operate a relay located above the ceiling. One type, designed for connection to a specific type of plug strip, can control task lights and office equipment like computer monitors and printers.

Time Clocks

A time clock is an electromechanical clock that opens and closes a circuit at specific times each day. Some models of time clock have stored energy to maintain timekeeping during power outages; others have astronomic time dials to automatically compensate for the changing sunrise and sunset times of the year. Modern versions of time clocks replace the timekeeping mechanism with a programmable electronic clock

Timers

A timer is a switch that turns lights off automatically after a certain period. Historically, timers used a wind-up mechanical dial. One of the most common applications is switching heat lamps in bathrooms. Modern timers use a push-button start and a programmable timeout period.

Photoswitches

For basic dusk-to-dawn lighting controls, it is possible to use a simple photoswitch in which a photocell throws a switch when the ambient light levels are sufficiently low. Photoswitches are most common in streetlights and parking lot lights, but they can also be used to switch indoor lights, especially in daylighted spaces like malls and lobbies.

CONTROL SYSTEMS

In large facilities, it is often a good idea to connect lighting control devices so they work as a system. Systems enable building operators to control lights better. In some very large and complex facilities, like stadiums and arenas, lighting controls are essential.

Relay Systems

A low-voltage control system can be used to remotely control lighting through relays. Relays are devices that control lighting power by mechanically opening or closing according to signals sent from low-voltage rocker switches, time clocks, or computer-based energy management systems. Relay systems are typically used in large commercial and institutional buildings like high-rise offices, convention centers, and airports.

In a relay control system, each group of lights that are switched together must be connected to the same relay. Many relays are located together in a panel, usually next to the circuit breaker panel. Relay systems are best for large facilities with big rooms that do not require dimming, such as schools, laboratories, factories, and convention centers.

Energy Management Systems

Energy management systems employ a computer to control many relay panels as well as mechanical motors, dampers, and so on. The primary difference between a relay system (above) and an energy management system is that the latter controls not just lighting but all energy use in the building.

Preset Dimming Systems

Preset dimming systems have a number of dimmers, usually in cabinets, that are designed to work together to create scenes of light. These complex systems are used in hotel function spaces, airports, convention centers, casinos, and other facilities where a number of rooms or spaces are controlled from a central computer-based preset controller. These systems are especially powerful and include the following features:

- The dimmer setting of each channel of lighting for each scene
- Groups of unique lighting scenes for each room

- The ability to manually choose scenes and, in many cases, change scene settings
- Partition switches, which enable the lighting control system to operate in conjunction with the various positions of movable partitions, as in hotel ballrooms
- Completely programmable automatic operation based on time of day, astronomic time, motion, daylight, or manual override

Daylighting Control Systems

Automatic daylighting control systems feature a photoelectric sensor that generates a signal to dim interior lights when adequate daylight enters the room through windows and skylights. Modern sensors are designed to connect directly to fluorescent dimming ballasts, enabling automatic dimming in almost any office, school, health care facility, or other building with small and medium-sized spaces near windows.

Chapter 5 DAYLIGHTING

Daylighting is the complete process of designing buildings to utilize natural light to its fullest. It includes all of the following activities.

- *Siting* the building—that is, orienting it for optimum solar exposure
- *Massing* the building—that is, presenting the optimum building surfaces toward the sun
- Choosing *fenestration* to permit the proper amount of light into the building, taking into account seasons, weather, and daily solar cycles
- *Shading* the façade and fenestration from unwanted solar radiation
- Adding appropriate operable *shading devices*, such as blinds and curtains, to permit occupant control over daylight admission
- Designing *electric lighting controls* that permit full realization of the energy savings benefit of daylighting

Because daylighting practice involves fundamental architectural considerations, it is difficult to undertake once the building has been designed, or, in the case of an interior design project or tenant improvement, almost impossible to carry out. For this reason, daylighting design is not dealt with in detail in this book. (See the bibliography for a number of excellent references, both modern and traditional.)

POINTS TO REMEMBER ABOUT DAYLIGHTING

Daylighting is an excellent light source for almost all interior spaces. It is best for offices, schools, and workspaces requiring a lot of light and for public spaces such as malls, airports, and institutions. Windows, skylights, and other forms of fenestration are used to bring daylight into the interiors of buildings. Daylight is highly desirable as a light source because people respond positively to it.

The amount of available daylight varies according to time of day, time of year, weather, pollution levels, and so on. The maximum amount of daylight is about 10,000 foot-candles on a sunny summer day. For energy efficiency in buildings, however, only about 5% of the daylight, or a peak of about 500 foot-candles, should be allowed into a building; more will generate so much heat that energy will be wasted in air conditioning.

The color of daylight varies as well. The color temperature of the setting sun is as low as 2000K, and the normal sun-and-sky color temperature at noon on a sunny day is 5500#6000K. The cold blue light from the winter north sky is over 10,000K. The color quality (CRI) is excellent. However, daylight has a relatively high ultraviolet (UV) light content, which has potential negative side effects such as sunburn and skin cancer. Extreme care must be exercised when using daylight in places such as museums where damage, called *photodegradation*, causes bleaching of pigments and other harm to irreplaceable art and antiquities. Ordinary interiors may also experience photodegradation in the form of fading fabrics.

From an energy efficiency perspective, daylight enjoys a significant advantage over electric light. At least 2.5 times as much air conditioning is needed to cool the heating effect of the most efficient electric light producing the same lighting level as daylight. Thus, if daylight is employed at light levels comparable to or even 50% higher than electric lighting and electric lights are extinguished, a building can be illuminated while saving *all* of the electric lighting energy and about half of the energy needed to cool the building load ordinarily created by electric lights.

INTEGRATING DAYLIGHTING AND ELECTRIC LIGHTING

To harvest the energy-saving benefits of daylighting, electric lights must be switched off or dimmed. This can be designed in several ways.

- Adequate manual switching or dimming to encourage the user to turn off or dim electric lights
- An automatic photoelectric device in each daylighted zone that either switches off lights during daylight periods or dims lights in proportion to the amount of daylight
- An automatic photoelectric system that dims or switches off lighting systems throughout a building in response to daylight
- An automatic time-of-day control system, preferably with astronomic time functions, that switches or dims lights according to a fixed solar schedule

Each approach has merit. It is generally agreed that switching lights is least expensive but dimming lights is most desired. Step dimming has been found disruptive in many situations.

Daylighted Airport Terminal with Most of the Electric Lighting Extinguished

The use of both electric light and daylight often raises the question of whether the electric light source should match the natural light. In most cases, choosing an electric light source that is appropriate independent of daylight is probably best. To match daylight, a light source of a very high color temperature is needed; this light would probably appear unusually cool as interior illumination at night.

When integrating electric and natural light, it is common to want to illuminate a skylight to imitate daylight at night, but this approach should be pursued carefully, if at all. Uplighting a skylight tends to send light through the glass and into the sky, wasting both the light and the energy consumed in creating it. What little light is reflected tends to create glare. However, illuminating the skylight well and splay can be effective. The goal is to create the illusion of skylighting without trying to match the illumination level.

TOP LIGHTING

One of the most common ways to introduce daylight is through skylights and other means of top lighting. Top lighting behaves as direct electric lighting does—by radiating light downward. Principles commonly used for designing electric lighting systems can also be used for top lighting, which is the easiest form of daylighting and is relatively unaffected by site orientation and adjacent buildings.

Here are several classic prototypes for top lighting.

- The *skylight*, or horizontal glazing, permits direct solar and sky radiation through a fenestrated aperture.
- The *single clerestory* produces both direct and indirect lighting by introducing light through a vertical clerestory window. Depending on the adjacent roof, some of the light may be reflected downward by the ceiling into the space. However, depending on site orientation, the relatively high percentage of direct light can be glaring.
- The *sawtooth single clerestory* produces both direct and indirect lighting but, by bouncing a high percentage off the adjacent slanted ceiling, increases the amount of downward light and can minimize the amount of direct light. If the sawtooth glazing faces north, it can be an excellent source of natural light for a large interior area.
- The *monitor or double clerestory* also permits abundant daylight, especially in buildings where solar orientation or weather do not permit the sawtooth or other more unusual designs. With proper choice of glazing and overhang, a monitor can produce exceptionally balanced and comfortable daylight.

Toplighting Concepts

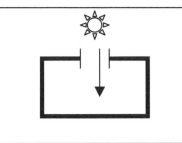

SKYLIGHT TOPLIGHTING
The use of skylights to introduce light from above. Best done with a diffusing or prismatic skylight to prevent direct sun rays from causing overly bright spots. Skylights should generally be no more than 5–6% of the roof area.

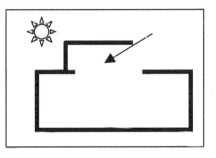

CLERESTORY TOPLIGHT
The use of high windows, above the ceiling line. Best done when the window faces north to prevent direct solar radiation. With north facing fenestration, ceiling aperture can be very large. Interior finishes of well are important, but appealing surfaces such as wood can used.

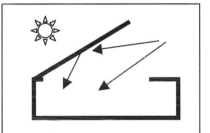

SAWTOOTH CLERESTORY TOPLIGHT
Angled ceiling produces more indirect light, increasing the efficiency of the skylight and allowing less glazing. Also best if north facing.

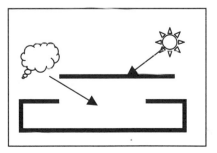

MONITOR OR DOUBLE CLERESTORY TOPLIGHT
Best if long axis is oriented east and west. Use passive shading on south side to prevent direct solar radiation into the space.

SIDE LIGHTING

Side lighting employs vertical fenestration (usually windows) to introduce natural light. Unlike top lighting, side lighting tends to introduce light that can be too bright relative to the room surfaces, sometimes causing glare. However, the desirable view provided by windows usually makes glare an acceptable side effect.

Many modern commercial windows employ low-e glazing. Low-e glazing employs two or more panes of glass, one of which is coated with a relatively clear material that reflects infrared energy while passing visible portions of the sun's energy. In any building with a cooling season, low-e glass is essential in minimizing solar heat gain. Reflective coatings can also be used; these make the building look mirrored while further decreasing solar penetration. Tinted glass can also reduce solar penetration and glare. Glazing selection is always a compromise between clarity and energy efficiency.

One way to increase both efficiency and clarity is to employ solar shading other than within the glass. Solar shading uses building elements to prevent direct solar radiation from entering the space during the cooling season. Overhung soffits, canopies, and awnings are the most common forms of external solar shading, while blinds, curtains, and shades are the most common forms of interior shading. Solar shading is difficult to design for east- and west-facing façades because preventing direct solar penetration very early or very late on a summer day is impossible without blocking the view. Interior shading devices should have a reflective surface to reflect unwanted light back outdoors. Dark shades prevent glare but absorb solar energy and become warm, heating the space. Adjustable exterior shading devices are probably the best means of shielding windows, but architectural and/or construction cost limitations may prevent their use.

An additional problem caused by side lighting is the limits of penetration into the space. Generally, the effect of the daylight is lost at a distance from the windows about 2.5 times the window's height. For example, in a room with windows having a maximum height of 8', the maximum useful penetration of natural light is about (8 x 2.5) or 20' (assuming, of course, that no walls are in the way). High windows increase the usable daylight area but can introduce glare.

Many modern buildings employ a light shelf to shade the lower part of the window, or view glazing, permitting clearer glass. The top of the shelf is reflective, intended to bounce light inward and onto the ceiling, which provides for deeper light penetration and improved interior light quality. The daylight glazing is generally darker or more reflective than the view glazing to prevent direct solar radiation and glare from a bright sky.

Sidelighting

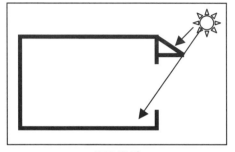

SOFFIT OVERHANG

AWNING

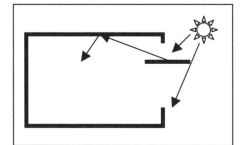

LIGHT SHELF

Sidelighting on east, south and west exposures can permit direct solar glare and heat gain. It is necessary to shade windows to prevent excessive glare and gain.

Overhang soffits provide a limited amount of shading and are best employed on the south façade (northern hemisphere) of the building.

Awnings or other extended shades offer additional protection and are generally needed on the east and west facades of the building.

A light shelf provides both shading and indirect lighting for the space, increasing the amount of daylight depth penetration. It is most effective on the south façade but can also be employed on the east and west facades.

Additional window shading material is generally needed on windows and sidelights, such as horizontal louver blinds, vertical louver blinds, solid shades, partially transmitting shades and draperies, and other methods. Soffit overhang

A light shelf is designed to scoop direct solar radiation into the room and onto the ceiling, where it becomes diffuse indirect light, one of the best types of light for both work and comfort. A light shelf can increase the depth of penetration of daylight by 100% or more, but only when it captures and redirects direct rays of the sun. A light shelf has limited benefit with diffuse light, as from sky without sun and on cloudy days. In general, light shelves work best on the south side of the building.

BASIC PRINCIPLES OF DAYLIGHTING DESIGN AND AWARENESS

While daylighting design can be relatively technical, you can use the following basic principles to develop designs that address daylighting opportunities.

1. Begin by planning the building such that every regularly occupied work or living space has access to a window, skylight, or other source of natural light. Give high priority to windows that provide a view. Remember that the effective daylighted area extends into the building only about 2 times the width of a window and about 2 to 2.5 times its height.

2. Minimize the size of the east and west sides of the building and maximize the south and north sides of the building. Because of the seasonally varying paths of the sun in the sky, it is difficult to design east- and west-facing windows. North-facing windows in the northern hemisphere present no solar heating problems, and south-facing windows are the easiest to protect with passive elements like overhangs, awnings, and light shelves.

3. If a large area of the building is not near a window, investigate top-light skylights in one-story buildings or the top floor of multistory buildings. Simple top-light skylights should occupy 3% to 5% of the total roof area in order to provide adequate levels of interior lighting.

4. Protect the interior from too much natural light—2.5 times or higher the level of ordinary electric light—by employing appropriate window glass, exterior shading devices, interior shading devices, or a combination of these.

5. Provide an electric lighting system and/or automatic lighting controls to permit harvesting of the energy savings. The best way is to dim the electric lights rather than switch them on and off. Modern fluorescent dimming systems allow daylighting controls and fundamentally energy-efficient fluorescent and compact fluorescent lighting.

It is often desirable to calculate the amount of light that will result from a design. While seldom required in residential design, lighting calculations are critical to the success of lighting designs in most nonresidential buildings — schools, offices, stores, and most other commercial and institutional building types. In this chapter, we describe the various ways lighting calculations can be performed and provide you with basic tools for predicting lighting results.

In modern design, it is common to talk about foot-candles of light (or *lux*, if working metric) rather carelessly. It is important to remember that the stated required number of foot-candles for a space generally refers to the average light level requirement measured in the horizontal plane at desk height. However, sometimes the criterion is for light only at the task or for light measured in the vertical plane (as for artwork).

BASIC THEORY

The science of lighting was invented over 300 years ago and was, of course, based on candlelight. The foot-candle is the amount of light striking a surface 1 foot away from a candle. The intensity of the light is 1 candela.

We measure light sources in two distinct ways. Most lamps are measured according to the total amount of light they radiate, while luminaires and directional lamps are measured by the intensity of the emitted light.

Lamps

The gross amount of light generated by a light source is measured in lumens. For instance, a candle generates about 12.5 lumens of light. Here are lumens for other common light sources.

Standard 60-watt incandescent lamp	890 lumens
Standard 18-watt compact fluorescent lamp	1200 lumens
Standard 4-foot-long T-8 fluorescent lamp	2850 lumens
Typical 100-watt high-pressure sodium streetlamp	9500 lumens
Typical 1500-watt metal halide lamp used for lighting athletic stadiums	165,000 lumens

Some light sources use energy more efficiently than others. Note that the 18-watt compact fluorescent lamp generates more light than does the 60-watt incandescent. The essence of energy-efficient lighting is using light sources like fluorescent lamps that generate light with much less power than incandescent lamps.

Lumens are basic data used in several types of calculations. This information is vital to designing the general or ambient lighting for a room.

Luminaires and Directional Lamps

Luminaires and directional lamps are measured according to the intensity and direction of light emitted from them. This is a complex process involving optical theory. However, some basic and useful points can be readily applied in everyday design.

As an example, consider a flashlight. An ordinary two-cell flashlight generates a beam of about 200 candlepower. But light is emitted from one end of the flashlight only—not in all directions, like a candle. The flashlight has the intensity of 200 candles, but in a very tight beam.

Candlepower values and distribution diagrams are used in most modern lighting calculations. The most basic calculation is called the *inverse square law*, as follows.

The illumination at a point x feet away from a light source of intensity C (candelas) is

$$\text{Foot-candles} = C/x^2$$

Shine the flashlight mentioned above onto a rock 10 feet away. The illumination in foot-candles is

$$200C / 100 = \frac{200}{100} = 2 \text{ foot-candles at the rock}$$

Initial Versus Maintained Light Levels

When lamps are new and luminaires clean, the lighting system is operating at its peak, called *initial lighting levels*. As lamps age and luminaires get dirty, light levels drop. The amount they drop depends on several factors, including the type of lamp and its age, the relative dirtiness of the environment, and how often lamps are replaced and luminaires cleaned.

Lighting is generally designed for *maintained light levels*. Factors that account for maintenance are part of all calculations. Assume, from now on, we are talking about maintained light levels unless stated otherwise.

PREDICTING LIGHTING RESULTS IN DESIGN

When designing lighting, you must make sure you have the proper amount of light. How many luminaires? How many watts? Which lamp type? Keep in mind that the acceptable light level ranges from about two-thirds to four-thirds of the target. This technical part of lighting design frustrates many architects and interior designers.

Predicting General and Ambient Light Levels

General and ambient light levels, the most common calculations of light level, are almost always average light levels in the horizontal plane. You can predict light levels for general and ambient lighting in three ways.

1. You can estimate the average lighting based on rough calculations, a procedure explained later in this chapter. While not very accurate, this method works well enough for many projects. As a minimum, it ensures that a design is not too far off.
2. You can perform lumen method calculations; these are complex but can be performed on a hand calculator. While you can learn lumen method calculations yourself, this level of expertise is not generally expected of architects and interior designers. The Illuminating Engineering Society of North America (IESNA) offers classes in this method, or you can teach yourself from the *IESNA Lighting Handbook*. This method is quite accurate for general lighting, but it does not work well if lighting is designed to be uneven.

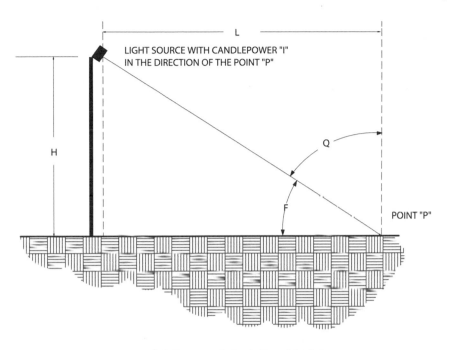

LIGHT SOURCE WITH CANDLEPOWER "I"
IN THE DIRECTION OF THE POINT "P"

Point Source Calculation Model

3. You can perform point-by-point computer calculations. These require considerable expertise using one of a number of relatively sophisticated programs that run on PCs (sorry, no Macs). Some of the programs are graphically oriented and may be of interest to architects and interior designers, especially those who calculate daylighting. However, most of the calculations are performed by lighting designers, engineers, and lighting sales companies. Computer applications are explained in Chapter 18.

Predicting Task Lighting and Focal Lighting Levels

Task light levels and highlights, such as the amount of light on a painting or retail feature display, are relatively hard to predict. In some cases, good data are lacking; in others, the calculations are tedious. Nonetheless, there are four useful ways to predict light levels for tasks and other highlights.

1. Use a guide published by the manufacturer of the luminaire you are planning to use. This is often the best way regardless of the knowledge level of the designer, especially for task lighting, such as lamps and undercabinet lights.

2. Use the inverse-square law to estimate the light level on a painting or retail display. This is relatively easy to do and an excellent way to estimate highlights for display lighting. The procedure is explained in more detail below.
3. Use a display lighting calculator program. This requires some lighting expertise, but the software is generally free from the lamp companies.

ROUGH CALCULATIONS FOR ARCHITECTS AND INTERIOR DESIGNERS

While it is no longer common for architects and interior designers to calculate lighting levels, they nevertheless produce basic lighting designs and perform lighting layouts. The following methods can be used with reasonable accuracy. Remember, however, that the results are only estimates and do not replace accurate calculations when they are called for.

The Watts per-Square-Foot Method

This method is extremely good for many space types. Simply multiply the room area in square feet by watts per square foot (see table on page 40). This tells you how many watts of either fluorescent or halogen sources you need to achieve recommended average lighting levels. By the way, the table is intended to work in conjunction with all North American energy codes as of 1 January 2000, but other restrictions may further affect your design.

This method works especially well if you follow these rules.

- Apply only to relatively ordinary spaces with white ceilings, medium tone to light walls, and a reasonable number of windows and other details. This method does not work well for dark-colored spaces or spaces with unusual shapes.
- Use common, everyday lighting equipment intended for the space being designed. Avoid custom designs and clever uses of lighting equipment.
- Make sure you understand the different effects of point sources, like incandescent or halogen lamps, and fluorescent lamps.

For example, the average overall proper light level for a classroom is about 50 foot-candles. Using the table, choose 1.2 watts per square foot of fluorescent lighting as the approximate amount of light needed. If the classroom measures 800 square feet, the total lighting power needed for this room is about (800 × 1.2) = 960 watts. If you plan on using luminaires with two 32-watt lamps each, you will need about (960/64) = 15 luminaires.

Watts Per-Square-Foot Method

Average light level desired and typical application	Watts per square foot of fluorescent, compact fluorescent or HID lights	Watts per square foot of incandescent or halogen lamps
2.5–5.0 fc Hotel corridors, stair towers	0.1–0.2	0.3–0.7
5–10 fc Office corridors, parking garages, theaters (house lights)	0.2–0.4	0.7–1.0
10–20 fc Building lobbies, waiting areas, elevator lobbies, malls, hotel function spaces, school corridors	0.4–0.8	1.0–2.0
20–50 fc Office areas, classrooms, hold rooms, lecture halls, conference rooms, ambient retail lighting, industrial work shops, gyms	0.8–1.2	Not recommended*
50–100 fc Grocery stores, big box retail stores, laboratories, work areas, sports courts (not professional)	1.2–2.0	Not recommended*

*Note: These levels are for general or ambient lighting *only*. It is not good practice to produce high light levels of general light using halogen sources. However, you can use halogen sources for accent lighting in these space types.

Another example: Consider the house lighting for a motion picture theater. The recommended light level is about 10 foot-candles. Because the lighting needs to dim over a full range, choose halogen lighting. The table shows you need about 1.0 watt per square foot. For a theater of 3000 square feet, you will need (3000 × 1.0) = 3,000 watts of lighting. You can choose between 60-watt downlights and 100-watt downlights. You will need (3000/60) = 50 downlights, 60 watts each, or (3000/100) = 30 downlights, 100 watts each. 6.2

A Very Simple Lumen Method

As in the above method, this method is limited in the kinds of lights and rooms it will work with. It works like this.

1. Divide the total number of initial lumens generated by the lamps by the area of the space.
2. Divide the result by 2 to obtain the approximate average light level in the room.

You can reverse the process if you want to find out how many lumens are needed to achieve a desired light level:

1. Multiply the desired light level by 2.
2. Multiply the result by the area of the room to obtain the total number of lumens needed from all lamps.
3. Divide the total lumens by the rated initial lumens of the lamp you wish to use to find how many lamps you need.

For instance, consider a private office of 150 square feet. Each room has four 2-lamp luminaires, each lamp having 2850 lumens. The total lumens in the room are (4 luminaires × 2 lamps each × 2850 lumens per lamp) = (4 × 2 × 2850) = 22,800. Divide by the area (22,800/150) = 152. Divide by 2 (152/2) = 76 foot-candles. (This is a bit higher than recommended. You can reduce the amount of light by 25% to about 57 foot-candles by removing one luminaire.)

Let's try the other way around. In the same 150-square-foot office, you wish to use a specific lamp (light bulb) that has 2200 lumens to achieve 40 foot-candles. Multiply 40 fc by 2 (40 × 2) = 80. Now multiply by the area (80 × 150) = 12,000 lumens needed. Next, divide 12,000 by the lumens per lamp you want to use, or 12,000/2,200) = 5.45 lamps. Round up to the next integer number of lamps (6). You need six single-lamp luminaires, three 2-lamp luminaires, two 3-lamp luminaires, or one 6-lamp luminaire.

CLASSROOM LIGHTING CALCULATION (RULES OF THUMB)
TRY TWO METHODS AND IF THEY GIVE SIMILAR RESULTS, YOU ARE PROBABLY CORRECT

USING THE WATTS PER SQUARE FOOT RULE OF THUMB
AREA = 960 SF
CLASSROOM (FROM CHART) = 0.8 TO 1.2 W/SF
PROVIDE 960 X 0.8 = 768 WATTS OF FLUORESCENT LIGHTING MINIMUM
PROVIDE 960 X 1.2 = 1152 WATTS OF FLUORESCENT LIGHTING MAXIMUM
WITH THREE ROWS OF FIXTURES 24 FEET LONG EACH = 72 FEET OF FIXTURES
768/72 = 10.6 WATTS PER FOOT OR MORE
1152/72 = 16 WATTS PER FOOT OR LESS

PER 4 FEET OF FIXTURE, BETWEEN 42.4 AND 64 WATTS
CHOOSE (1) F54T5HO LAMP PER 4' FIXTURE (54 WATTS) TOTAL OF 18 4-FOOT FIXTURES

SIMPLIFIED LUMEN METHOD
DESIRED FOOTCANDLE LEVEL – 50 FC
MULTIPLY X 2 =100
MULTIPLY BY AREA = 960 X 100 = 96000
USING F54T5HO LAMPS AT 5000 LUMENS EACH

NUMBER OF LAMPS REQUIRED = 96000/5000 = APPROXIMATELY 19-20
4-FOOT LONG FIXTURES

BOTH CALCULATIONS SUGGEST ABOUT 18-20 FIXTURES, SO THE DESIGN WORKS.

Classroom Lighting Calculation

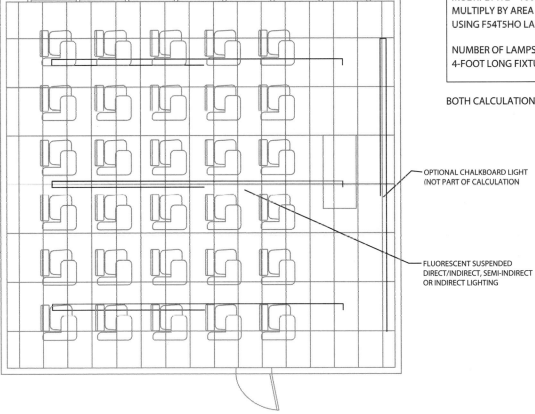

OPTIONAL CHALKBOARD LIGHT
(NOT PART OF CALCULATION

FLUORESCENT SUSPENDED
DIRECT/INDIRECT, SEMI-INDIRECT
OR INDIRECT LIGHTING

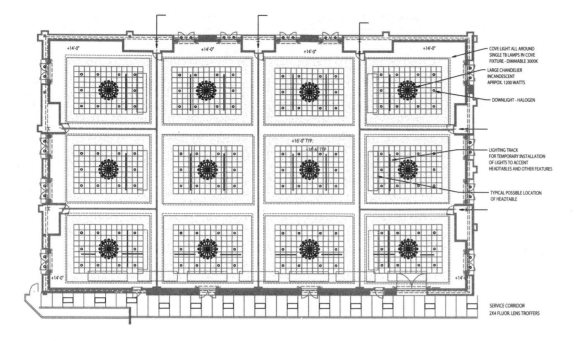

+14'-0"   +14'-0"   +14'-0"   +14'-0"

COVE LIGHT ALL AROUND
SINGLE T8 LAMPS IN COVE
FIXTURE - DIMMABLE 3000K

LARGE CHANDELIER
INCANDESCENT
APRPOX. 1200 WATTS

DOWNLIGHT - HALOGEN

LIGHTING TRACK
FOR TEMPORARY INSTALLATION
OF LIGHTS TO ACCENT
HEADTABLES AND OTHER FEATURES

TYPICAL POSSIBLE LOCATION
OF HEADTABLE

+16'-0" TYP.
+16'-6 TYP.

+14'-0"   +14'

SERVICE CORRIDOR
2X4 FLUOR. LENS TROFFERS

Hotel Ballroom Using Watts per Square Foot

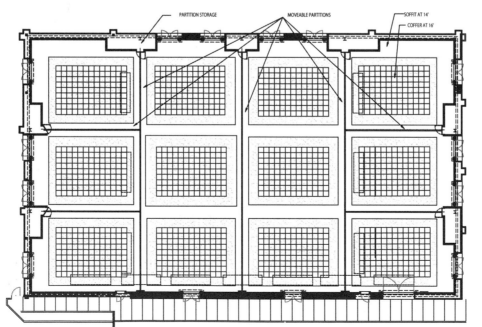

PARTITION STORAGE   MOVEABLE PARTITIONS   SOFFIT AT 14'
COFFER AT 16'

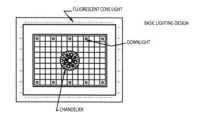

FLUORESCENT COVE LIGHT

BASIC LIGHTING DESIGN

DOWNLIGHT

CHANDELIER

The very simple lumen method works especially well in rooms with several types of lighting systems. Consider a hotel ballroom that has downlights, a chandelier, and a fluorescent cove light:

- Each ballroom section is 1200 square feet.
- The ballroom has 10 downlights, each with a 2000-lumen lamp.
- The ballroom has one chandelier with twenty-four 400-lumen lamps.
- The ballroom has cove lighting with (28) 3000-lumen lamps.

The very simple lumen calculation is

10 downlights x 2000 lumens	20,000 lumens
24 chandelier lamps x 400 lumens	9,600 lumens
(28) fluorescent lamps x 3000 lumens	84,000 lumens
Total	113,600 lumens
Divide by 2	56,800 lumens
Divide by 1200 square feet	47.33 foot-candles

Remember that 47.33 is an estimate—but you can be confident you will have 35 to 40 foot-candles with all lights on. Also note that if you turn off the fluorescent lights, you will still have at least 10 foot-candles, which is plenty for a social event such as a dinner or dance party. (In fact, this is exactly how the layering design method and preset dimming works.)

A Very Simple Point Method

In this method, you need to know the distance of a display light from the object being displayed. It works with individual spotlights only; it does not work for wallwashing or other forms of highlighting.

1. Square the distance from the light to the object.
2. Multiply the result by the desired light level (20–50 foot-candles for homes, hotels, and restaurants; up to 250 foot-candles for feature displays in stores and lobbies) to obtain the approximate candlepower.

Say you want to light a painting in a living room. Choose 50 foot-candles. Given the cathedral-style ceiling, the light will be 20 feet from the painting. Square this distance (20 × 20 = 400). Multiply by the foot-candle level (400 × 50 = 20,000 candlepower) to obtain the intensity of the light source you need. A lamp catalog lists the following 20,000-candlepower projector lamps.

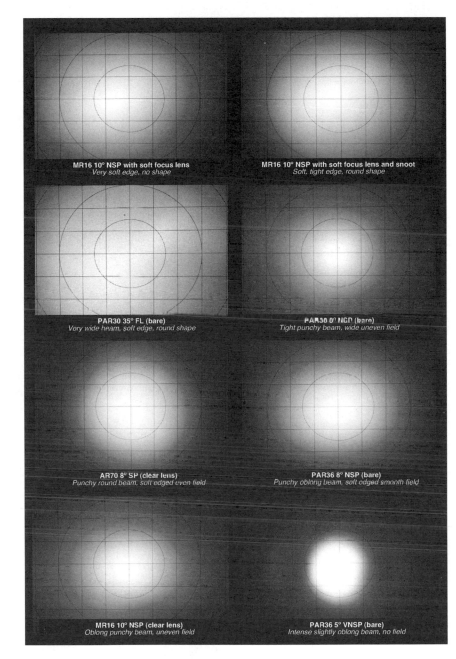

MR16 10° NSP with soft focus lens
Very soft edge, no shape

MR16 10° NSP with soft focus lens and snoot
Soft, tight edge, round shape

PAR30 35° FL (bare)
Very wide beam, soft edge, round shape

PAR30 0° NSP (bare)
Tight punchy beam, wide uneven field

AR70 8° SP (clear lens)
Punchy round beam, soft edged even field

PAR36 8° NSP (bare)
Punchy oblong beam, soft edged smooth field

MR16 10° NSP (clear lens)
Oblong punchy beam, uneven field

PAR36 5° VNSP (bare)
Intense slightly oblong beam, no field

Spots by Eight Lamps

Lamp	Candlepower	Beam
60-watt PAR38 IR line voltage spot	20,000	10 degrees
35-watt PAR36 halogen low-voltage spot	20,000	8 degrees
50-watt PAR36 incandescent low-voltage very narrow spot	19,000	6 degrees

The beamspread is a little harder to decide. This is where experience and a lamp guide come in handy. The PAR38 illuminates a circle about 4½ feet in diameter, the halogen PAR36 illuminates about 2¾ feet, and the incandescent PAR36 illuminates about 1¾ feet. (All of these values were taken from the lamp guide printed in a major luminaire catalog). You will choose the actual lamp based on the size of the picture.

Chapter 7

DOCUMENTING LIGHTING DESIGN

To communicate the lighting design intent to others, it is important to draw lighting in a manner generally recognized by interior designers, architects, engineers, and construction trades and to understand how and why lighting is illustrated the way it is. In this chapter, specific considerations for drawing lighting are presented.

DRAWINGS AND CONTRACT DOCUMENTS

Lighting documents are part of the process of developing *working drawings* or *contract documents*, which are the drawings that tell the contractor what to build. The law regulates who can prepare contract documents. Depending on the type of project and its location, an intermediate lighting plan may be used by others. It is common for the initial lighting plan to be drawn by an architect, interior designer, or lighting designer, but the drawing is then passed along to the electrical engineer or electrical contractor, who must add electrical circuits and other information to the drawing before it can be used for construction.

LIGHTING DOCUMENTS

A lighting design can be indicated in a number of ways:

- *On the architect or interior designer's plans:* The architect or interior designer develops plan drawings and related details, such as sections. Lighting can be indicated on either floor plans or reflected ceiling plans, making it unnecessary to develop separate electric or lighting plans. This method of indicating lighting is acceptable, but because lighting is constructed by different trades than the rest of the building, showing lighting on separate plans is generally preferred. Use this method to illustrate relatively simple lighting plans on minor projects, such as office tenant improvements.
- On the electrical plans: Whether developed by an architect, interior designer, electrical engineer, or contractor, the electrical plans use an architectural base plan (see below) and illustrate electrical information. In addition to lighting, information presented on such plans includes:

  –Lighting controls, such as switches and dimmers

—Receptacles, connections to equipment, location of panelboards, and other electrical information

—Telephone jacks, data outlets, fire alarm devices, and other data signaling and communications systems

In a complex building, electrical plans are often separated into *lighting plans, power plans,* and *signal plans* as well as legend sheets, detail sheets, and other drawings.

BASE PLANS

Floor Plans

A lighting design generally begins when the architect or interior designer develops a floor plan (or plans) for a building. The floor plan indicates the footprint of the building, the locations of walls, doors, and windows, and other details that aid in developing lighting drawings. Floor plans especially must be consulted for lighting that is not mounted to the ceiling, such as wall sconces, table and floor lamps, undercabinet lights, and lighting in bookcases, cabinets, and other built-in features.

Floor plans are useful as base plans because they permit lighting to be indicated with respect to walls, furniture, and other details that show up best on plan drawings. Many projects don't have reflected ceiling plans, so using the floor plan as a base drawing is sometimes the only choice.

Reflected Ceiling Plans

Reflected ceiling plans are used as the base drawing for most lighting plans because lighting is usually mounted on ceilings. Ceiling elements such as HVAC diffusers and grilles, sprinkler heads, and speakers are extremely important for coordination purposes. For complex ceilings with vaults or coffers, the reflected ceiling plan provides critical dimensions.

Floor Plan

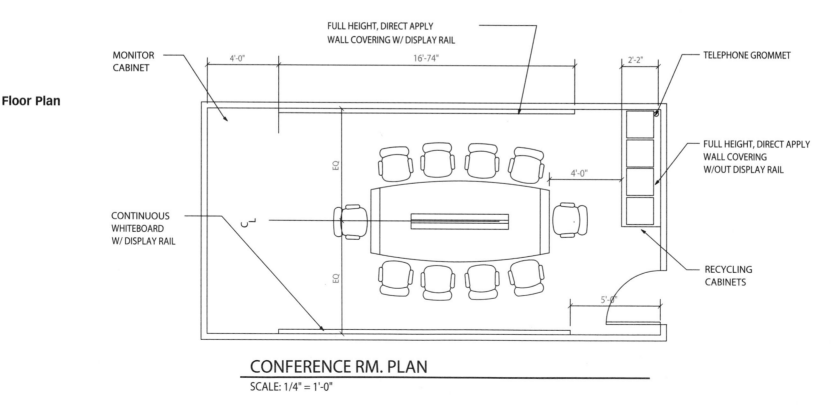

FULL HEIGHT, DIRECT APPLY
WALL COVERING W/ DISPLAY RAIL

MONITOR
CABINET

4'-0"   16'-74"   2'-2"

TELEPHONE GROMMET

FULL HEIGHT, DIRECT APPLY
WALL COVERING
W/OUT DISPLAY RAIL

4'-0"

CONTINUOUS
WHITEBOARD
W/ DISPLAY RAIL

EQ

C
L

EQ

RECYCLING
CABINETS

5'-0"

CONFERENCE RM. PLAN
SCALE: 1/4" = 1'-0"

Reflected Ceiling Plan

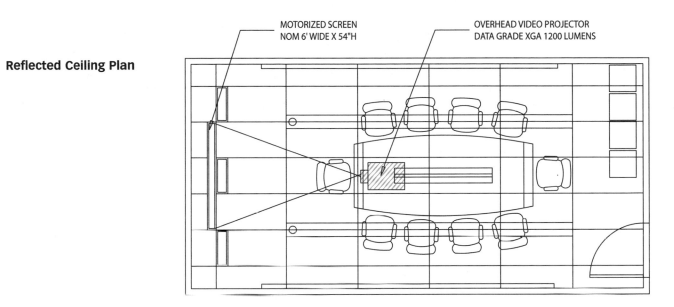

MOTORIZED SCREEN
NOM 6' WIDE X 54"H

OVERHEAD VIDEO PROJECTOR
DATA GRADE XGA 1200 LUMENS

CONFERENCE RM. REFLECTED CEILING PLAN

SCALE: 1/4" = 1'-0"

Electrical Plan

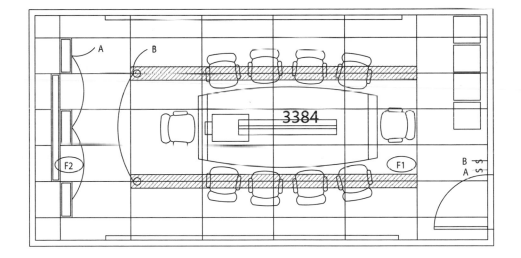

CONFERENCE RM. LIGHTING PLAN

SCALE: 1/4" = 1'-0"

Combined Ceiling/Floor Plans

CAD drawings make it especially easy to create custom base plans that incorporate elements of both floor and reflected ceilings plans. This is particularly true when designing spaces with complex layers of light. For instance, in a hotel lobby it may be desirable to have downlights and chandeliers on the ceiling, wall sconces, table and floor lamps, desk lamps, and undercabinet lights, all in the same space. A base drawing showing ceiling details plus a furniture and casework plan makes it easier to show the various kinds of lighting equipment in the right location. Using different layer colors helps differentiate ceiling elements from floor plan elements, making it easier to draw and check your work.

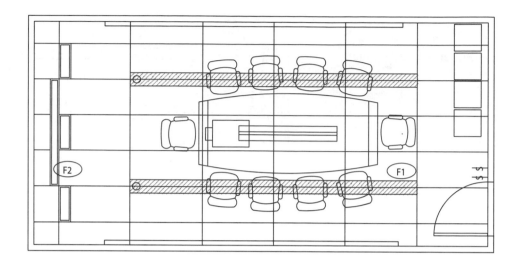

CAD LAYERS

SCALE: 1/4" = 1'-0"

CAD layers

Combined Ceiling/floor Plan

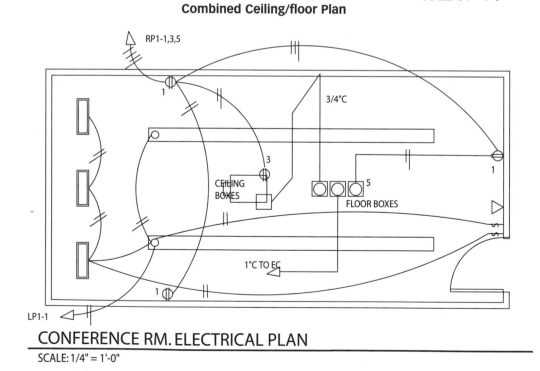

CONFERENCE RM. ELECTRICAL PLAN

SCALE: 1/4" = 1'-0"

CREATING A LIGHTING PLAN

A lighting plan begins with a base drawing that is usually made less obvious using lighter lines than the lighting symbols.

Lighting Symbols

Luminaires and other lighting equipment are generally indicated by symbols. This approach dates to manual drafting. Symbols indicate the type of luminaire by generic type, as follows.

In general, symbols are not to scale; in fact, they often appear much larger than scale so as to be easily seen on the plan. To draw lighting plans quickly and make them easy to read, these few standard symbols became commonplace. Drafters use templates to draw symbols of this type.

However, using CAD, you can choose to develop scaled symbols. These have the advantage of making the designer aware of potential interferences and aesthetic effects. It is smart to take full advantage of layer colors and plotting line weights so the smaller symbols are easily seen as lighting.

Lighting Tags

A lighting tag is an identifier that describes the specific characteristics of luminaires on the plans. The tag is drawn adjacent to a specific luminaire or group of similar luminaires. Tag identifiers can be alphabetical (*A*, *B*, etc.) or alphanumeric (*A1*, *F1a*, etc.) Some tags also show the luminaire type or wattage.

Historically, luminaire tags were listed in alphabetic order, with the most common luminaire on the project being type *A*, the next most common type *B*, and so on. On plans for complex projects like hospitals, luminaire types that are identical except for some small detail (such as a different number of lamps) would show as subtypes such as *AA*, *AB*, and so on. Note that this system is not hard and fast; the important point is for the tag to match the definition on the lighting schedule (see below).

More recently, and especially because of CAD, tags can be given greater meaning. In the following system, tags contain a substantial amount of information without becoming cumbersome.

⊢⊕	SCONCE OR LANTERN
⊛	TABLE OR FLOOR LAMP
○	RECESSED DOWNLIGHT
▣	RECESSED DOWNLIGHT IC HOUSING
⦶	RECESSED ACCENT LIGHT
⦶	RECESSED ACCENT LIGHT IC HOUSING
◐	RECESSED WALLWASHER
◐	RECESSED WALLWASHER IC HOUSING
⊙	PENDANT OR CHANDELIER
●	MONOPOINT ACCENT LIGHT
✛	STEP LIGHT
▯	FLUORESCENT TROFFER (2X4)
⊣⊢	FLUORESCENT STRIP LIGHTS
▭	FLUORESCENT WALLWASHER
▨▨	SUSPENDED FLUORESCENT UPLIGHT

Lighting Symbols

CONVENTIONAL WIRING SYMBOLS	
∮	SWITCH
∮3	THREE WAY SWITCH (SPDT)
∮4	FOUR WAY SWITCH (DPDT)
∮D	DIMMER SWITCH
∮D3	DIMMER THREE WAY SWITCH
∮D4	DIMMER FOUR WAY SWITCH
∮DLV	DIMMER LOW VOLTAGE RATED
∮DF	DIMMER FLUORESCENT
∮DOS	DIMMER OCCUPANCY SENSOR
∮OS	OCCUPANCY SENSOR SWITCH
SYMBOLS FOR ELECTRONIC DEVICES	
∮DM	DIMMER MASTER
∮DR	DIMMER REMOTE

Control Symbols

F   Fluorescent or compact fluorescent lamp luminaires

A   Incandescent lamp luminaires

H   HID luminaires

N   Neon or cold cathode lighting systems

X   Exit signs

FX   Exterior fluorescent or compact fluorescent luminaires

AX   Exterior incandescent luminaires

HX   Exterior HID luminaires

This system makes it easy to add and define new families. An exterior exit sign (rare but possible) might be XX1; an LED interior luminaire might be L-1. Sometimes types D are added for decorative chandeliers and lamps; creativity is fine as long as the tags match the lighting schedule.

Circuits

Illustrating circuits accomplishes two purposes.

1. The designer can communicate the intended switching or dimming groups by connecting lighting groups with lines or by indicating common control by letters.

2. The designer can indicate how the lighting is to be wired by showing specific connections to control devices, such as dimmers and switches.

Here is where the major difference between lighting design and electrical engineering must be understood. A lighting design does *not* have to indicate the exact wiring. The lighting designer clearly shows the desired switching or dimming groups but leaves the details of wiring, such as the number of circuits and the specific wiring between devices, to the engineer or contractor. An engineer's or contractor's *electrical drawing* must illustrate the circuits, wiring, and so on for the design to be constructed.

Switching and Dimming

Switches and dimmers are represented by symbols on the plan. A switch is usually indicated by a standard symbol, which may have subscript modifiers.

Dimmers and switches should be shown on the drawings at the intended location. In addition, their connection to the lights being controlled should be illustrated by a line or other obvious means. Here are a couple of examples:

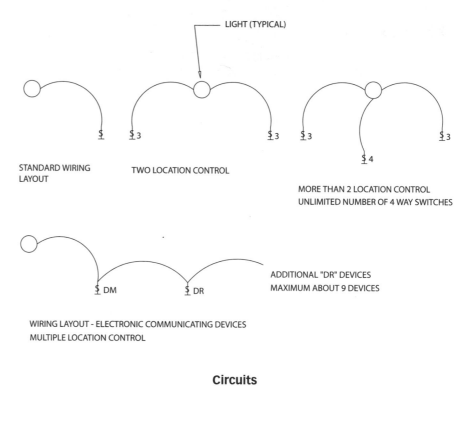

LIGHT (TYPICAL)

STANDARD WIRING LAYOUT

TWO LOCATION CONTROL

MORE THAN 2 LOCATION CONTROL
UNLIMITED NUMBER OF 4 WAY SWITCHES

ADDITIONAL "DR" DEVICES
MAXIMUM ABOUT 9 DEVICES

WIRING LAYOUT - ELECTRONIC COMMUNICATING DEVICES
MULTIPLE LOCATION CONTROL

Circuits

Details

Lighting details indicate how specific luminaires are to be installed in unusual mounting conditions. The main lighting plan should refer to the details, which may be included on the lighting plan sheet, on a separate drawing containing mostly details, or bound into a project book or manual. Here are some common lighting details:

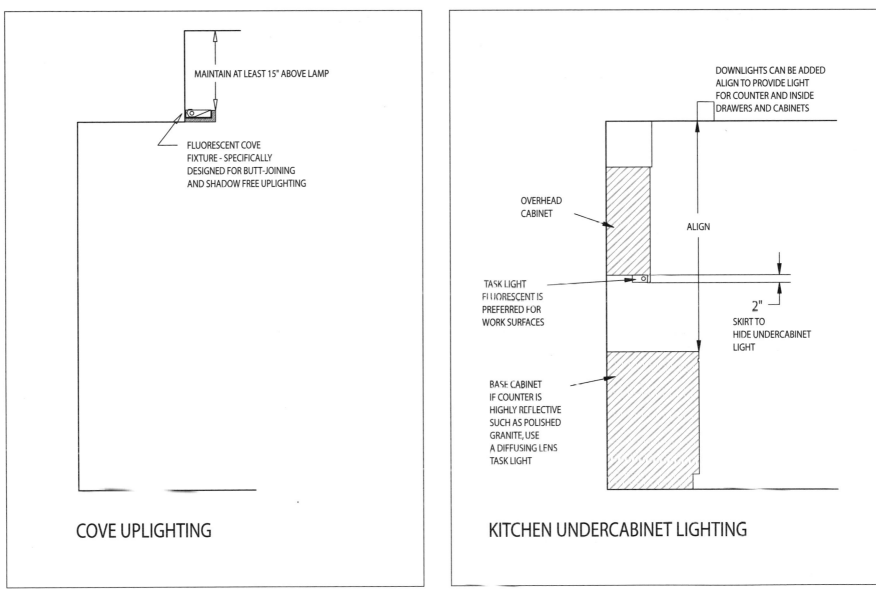

MAINTAIN AT LEAST 15" ABOVE LAMP

FLUORESCENT COVE
FIXTURE - SPECIFICALLY
DESIGNED FOR BUTT-JOINING
AND SHADOW FREE UPLIGHTING

DOWNLIGHTS CAN BE ADDED
ALIGN TO PROVIDE LIGHT
FOR COUNTER AND INSIDE
DRAWERS AND CABINETS

OVERHEAD
CABINET

ALIGN

TASK LIGHT
FLUORESCENT IS
PREFERRED FOR
WORK SURFACES

2"

SKIRT TO
HIDE UNDERCABINET
LIGHT

BASE CABINET
IF COUNTER IS
HIGHLY REFLECTIVE
SUCH AS POLISHED
GRANITE, USE
A DIFFUSING LENS
TASK LIGHT

COVE UPLIGHTING

KITCHEN UNDERCABINET LIGHTING

Cove Detail

Undercabinet Light Detail

LIGHTING LEGENDS AND SCHEDULES

Most lighting drawings include a legend and/or a schedule. The legend always appears on the drawings; a schedule may appear on the drawings or be included in a separate project book or manual. In some cases, the legend and schedule are combined.

Lighting Legends

The purpose of a lighting legend is to define each symbol. Historically, only a few symbol choices were used, so a classic lighting legend looked like this:

However, CAD drafting allows much greater detail, so more symbols can be used. With the older method, each luminaire was identified by a common sym-

LIGHTING FIXTURE SCHEDULE (WITH LEGEND)

TAG	SYMBOL	DESCRIPTION	VOLTS	LAMP	BALLAST	WATTS	MOUNTING	PRODUCT
A1		WALL SCONCE, ORNAMENTAL POLISHED BRASS LANTERN	120	3-25C10 CLEAR	N/A	75	WALL MOUNT TO BOX 6 -2" AFF TO CENTER	XYZ 123
A2		RECESSED DOWNLIGHT CLEAR ALZAK CONE 6" APERTURE	120	1-100A	N/A	100	RECESSED	XYZ 123
A3		RECESSED ACCENT LIGHT CLEAR ALZAK CONE 6" APERTURE	120	1-60PAR38SL	N/A	60	RECESSED	XYZ 123
A4		RECESSED WALLWASHER CLEAR ALZAK CONE 7" APERTURE ANGLED SPREAD LENS	120	1-100PAR38SL	N/A	100	RECESSED	XYZ 123
A5		PENDANT LIGHT CHROME STEM BLUE GLASS	120	1-100PAR38SL	N/A	100	RECESSED	XYZ 123
A6		MONOPOINT ACCENT LIGHT	120	1-50MR16FL	N/A	55	RECESSED	XYZ 123
A7		STEP LIGHT	120	1-25A	N/A	25	RECESSED	XYZ 123
F1		FLUORESCENT TROFFER (2X4)	277	2-F32T8/830	ELECTRONIC	58	RECESSED	XYZ 123
F2		FLUORESCENT STRIP LIGHTS	277	1-F32T8/830	ELECTRONIC	32	SURFACE MOUNT	XYZ 123
F3		FLUORESCENT WALLWASHER	277	1-CF40T5/830	ELECTRONIC	38	RECESSED	XYZ 123
F4		SUSPENDED FLUORESCENT UPLIGHT	277	1-F54T5HO/830	PREHEAT ELECTRONIC	61	SUSPENDED 18" BELOW CEILING	XYZ 123
X		EXIT SIGN SINGLE FACE	277	RED LED	ELECTRONIC	5	SURFACE WALL	XYZ 123
X1		EXIT SIGN SINGLE FACE	277	RED LED	ELECTRONIC	5	CEILING CANOPY	XYZ 123

Lighting Legend

bol and a tag. With the newer method, each luminaire can have a unique symbol instead.

If the symbol is defined as a *block* in CAD, some CAD programs permit assigning attributes and can aid in counting the number of each tag. This can be of great benefit when estimating the cost of a lighting installation.

Lighting Schedules

The purpose of a lighting schedule is to provide a specification for each tag or symbol. The specification should include all of the following information.

- Tag
- General description of the luminaire
- Lamp(s) to be used in the luminaire
- Finish
- Mounting
- Watts
- Manufacturer and catalog number

Additional information that may be included in a schedule:

- Picture or line drawing
- Detail references
- Ballast or transformer specifications
- Special characteristics, such as auxiliary components and lenses

LIGHTING SPECIFICATIONS

For commercial projects, lighting plans are usually accompanied by written specifications that appear in the project book or manual. Preferably, specifications are developed according to the Construction Specification Institute (CSI) system, in which lighting systems (including controls) are generally in sections numbered between 16,500 and 16,599. The electrical engineer on the project typically writes this section. Additional information about specifications can be obtained from CSI. Information about lighting specification integrity can be obtained from the IALD.

LIGHTING FIXTURE SCHEDULE

TAG	SYMBOL	DESCRIPTION
A1		WALL SCONCE, ORNAMENTAL POLISHED BRASS LANTERN
A2		RECESSED DOWNLIGHT CLEAR ALZAK CONE 6" APERTURE
A3		RECESSED ACCENT LIGHT CLEAR ALZAK CONE 6" APERTURE
A4		RECESSED WALLWASHER CLEAR ALZAK CONE 7" APERTURE ANGLED SPREAD LENS
A5		PENDANT LIGHT CHROME STEM BLUE GLASS
A6		MONOPOINT ACCENT LIGHT
A7		STEP LIGHT
F1		FLUORESCENT TROFFER (2X4)
F2		FLUORESCENT STRIP LIGHTS
F3		FLUORESCENT WALLWASHER
F4		SUSPENDED FLUORESCENT UPLIGHT
X		EXIT SIGN SINGLE FACE
X1		EXIT SIGN SINGLE FACE

Lighting Schedule

Here are the three major parts of a specification.

1. *A general part that introduces the topic* (in this case, lighting). It is common to state here requirements for code compliance, published reference standards, shop drawings, storing and protecting materials, and other nontechnical requirements for the lighting installation.
2. *A part concerning lighting materials.* The specific requirements and approved manufacturers of each lighting product type are discussed. Related topics, such as warranties, are typically included.
3. *A part concerning lighting installation.* The special installation requirements of the lighting system are discussed.

Today, architects, engineers, and interior designers generally utilize master specifications that are written in the CSI format and designed to be edited by the specifier for project requirements. These master specifications include carefully developed text, called *boilerplate*, that ensures the legal validity of the specification.

Color Temperature (Apparent Color of Scene)

| 1800K | 2200K | 2700K | 3000K | 3500K | 4100K | 5000K | 6500K | 7500K | 9000K | 12000K | 20000K |
| Red | Very warm | Warm | | Neutral | Cool | Cold | | Very Cold | | Icy cold | |

Plate 1-1 Color temperature

Primary and Secondary Colors of Light

Primaries
Red, Green, Blue

Secondaries
Magenta, Cyan, Yellow

Red, Green and Blue together produce
white light

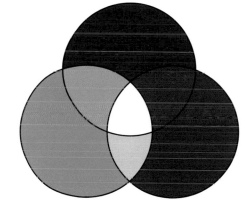

Real Light Sources

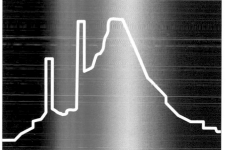
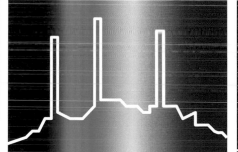
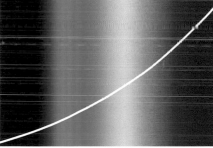
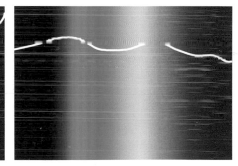

Fluorescent "Cool White"
Green and yellow dominant, warm
tones subdued

Modern Fluorescent "835"
All colors nearly equal, slight
warmishness

Incandescent ("Tungsten")
Warm colors dominant, blues and
greens subdued

Natural Light Summer Noon
All colors nearly equal,
slight bluishness

Plate 1-3 Color Spectra

Plate 3-1 *(right)* Transitional (Art Deco revival) Dining Room. Ambient lighting in cove, with decorative chandelier and recessed task and focal lights. Note light on table from recessed lights, not chandelier. *Photo: J. Benya*

Plate 3-2 *(below left)* Traditional Dining Room. Ornamental chandelier and sconces provide ambient light. Recessed focal and task lights. Note vivid table light and patterns on floor from recessed lights, not chandelier. *Photo: J. Benya*

Plate 3-3 *(below right)* Contemporary Dining Room. All recessed lighting provides task and focal lighting; ambient lighting is achieved by illuminating artwork and window treatments, which in turn provide some indirect light to the space. No decorative lighting—the art, including the table base, are the decorative elements in the space. *Photo: J. Benya*

Plate 8-1 *(far left)*   Modern Cathedral. The altar and throne are illuminated for television using focal lighting. Other focal lighting layers illuminate the large hanging sculpture. Wallwashing illuminates wood panels behind sanctuary. No decorative lighting. *Photo: Luminae Souter Lighting Design*

Plate 8-2 *(left)*   Historic North American Church. Concealed recessed lighting illuminates stage, lecturn, pulpit, and altar. No decorative lighting. *Photo: J. Benya*

Plate 8-3 *(far left)* Modern Bank. Downlights provide general and task lighting. Wallwashers provide focal lighting for mural over teller line. Ornamental sconces provide decorative and ambient lighting with additional ambient lighting from beams. *Photo: RMW Architects*

Plate 8-4 *(left)*   Airport Terminal. Many layers, including downlights, blue uplights, neon, and decorative pole lights. Other layers include sign lights (focal) and uplighting of globe. *Photo: J. Benya*

Plate 7-1 *(top)*   Kitchen, custom contemporary. White fluorescent luminaries provide task and general light. *Photo: J. Benya*

Plate 7-2 *(bottom)*   Kitchen, modern transitional, with decorative, task, focal, and ambient layers. Note lighting inside of glass-faced cabinets serves as a focal layer. *Photo: J. Benya*

Plate 7-3 *(top)*
behind headboa.
mented by task lig.

Plate 7-4 *(bottom)*   Tr
glow and ambient light—
and focal light is provided by

Scallops

The Decorative Layer

One way to think about decorative lighting is as the "jewelry of architecture." Like jewelry in dress, it serves no purpose other than to catch the eye and to make statements about style or wealth. Its primary purpose is ornament to the space, and it plays an extremely important role in interior design and themed environments. For instance, a crystal chandelier makes an important visual statement, but it can be used only in certain space types.

Decorative lighting includes chandeliers, sconces, lanterns, pendants, lamps, ceiling surface lights, and other traditional lighting types that are mostly decorative in nature. With the advent of themed design, some lighting fixtures originally designed to be utilitarian are now important decorative lighting vehicles.

Unfortunately, the majority of decorative lights emit light rather poorly, so it is increasingly common to avoid counting on the decorative light to suit a task lighting purpose. Many lighting designers, for example, add accent lights to illuminate the table (task lighting) in a dining room that already has a chandelier.

One Light, Two or More Layers

Too many lights—especially too many types of lights—can be visually busy. It certainly can add cost. A good lighting designer seeks to minimize the lighting design while maintaining the desired effects. One common design approach is to have one luminaire or lighting system provide two or more layers. Some common designs:

- *Use decorative lighting as ambient lighting.* Careful selection of decorative luminaires is required to prevent glare; luminaires with mostly uplight do an excellent job of providing both decorative and ambient lighting, whereas luminaires with bare lamps and other traditional elements are generally poor ambient light sources.
- *Use the same type of luminaire for focal lighting and task lighting.* Recessed adjustable luminaires and track lighting can be aimed at tasks as well as artwork.
- *Use decorative lighting as task lighting.* Table lamps, floor lamps, pendants, and other types of decorative lights make excellent task lights in some applications.

Only One Layer

General lighting is an approach whereby only one luminaire or group of similar luminaires is designed to provide all task lighting, ambient lighting, and other needs. This single-layer technique is used in many basic lighting designs for offices, classrooms, stores, and many other space types. General lighting tends to be inexpensive and easy to build and use, but it usually lacks the drama and style of designs with more layers.

TECHNIQUE

When designing a layer, one chooses from among basic lighting techniques. Each has qualities that can be varied, but the choice of technique is fundamental to the types of luminaires and the resulting quality of light in the room or space in question.

For many techniques, it is important to know the "Magic Triangle of Light." The proportions of the Magic Triangle are in a ratio of 1:4, with the short leg of the triangle (one unit) along the horizontal ceiling surface and the long leg of the triangle along the vertical wall surface. You will use the Magic Triangle to apply several lighting techniques correctly.

Here are lighting's basic techniques:

Downlighting

When downlighting, the intent is to illuminate the horizontal surface below the luminaire. Downlighting can be achieved with can downlights, troffers, industrial luminaires, or just about any luminaire aimed downward and having a directional light.

When downlighting, observe these key principles:

- Study how the downlight will strike the wall. Particularly with can downlights, the result is a shape of light called a *scallop* for its shape. Lights mounted too close to a wall tend to create a tall, thin scallop that is usually unattractive. Use the Magic Triangle as a starting point in deciding where to mount lights. For instance, if a wall is 8' high, then mount lights 2' away from the wall (8:2 = 4:1).
- Choose downlight beamspread according to ceiling height. In general, the higher the ceiling, the narrower the beamspread. This ensures a minimum of glare and maximum effectiveness. This is true whether you are using can downlights or linear fluorescent direct luminaires.
- Pick the luminaire according to the pattern of light on the floor. For instance, if you desire even downlighting, use luminaires with soft-edged light sources like fluorescent, compact fluorescent, and A-lamps. For pools of light, use directional sources like PAR lamps and low-voltage lighting.
- Check downlight shielding. Generally, the smaller the aperture and the higher the lamp above the aperture, the better shielded the luminaire.

Downlighting layouts need not be uniform, but they should be organized.

Uplighting

Uplighting involves illuminating the ceiling, often with the intent to provide indirect lighting by bouncing light back toward the space. While many luminaire types are designed for uplighting, uplight can also be created by turning downlight luminaires upside down. Uplighting is a good way to use decorative lighting like sconces and chandeliers.

When uplighting, consider the following:

- Ceilings to be uplighted should generally be white or off-white. It is possible to uplight a colored ceiling, but remember: The light will cast a color in the space. Uplighting a dark ceiling is inefficient. Uplighting windows and skylights is superfluous.
- Pools of light or stripes of light on the ceiling are generally annoying and unappealing. Uplights that don't produce a soft, even light may work, but such designs are risky.
- The distance from the uplight to the ceiling should be chosen carefully. As a rule of thumb, an uplight will illuminate the ceiling up to about 4 suspension lengths away. The Magic Triangle can be used to help predict ceiling uniformity.

Cove Lighting

Cove lighting is a form of uplighting that illuminates a ceiling from a cove on a side. Cove lighting can be mounted to a wall or along the sides of a coffer. Indirect lighting from a cove produces a much different effect than cove lighting from the center of the ceiling. Several key considerations for properly executing a cove design:

- Cove lighting is especially sensitive to the joints between light sources. When using fluorescent lamps, employ luminaires designed for cove lighting; their reflector shape eliminates socket shadowing. When using individual tungsten lamps, be sure to maintain at least one lamp spacing away from the cove's back wall.
- Make sure the lamp is level with the top fascia of the cove, or shadows will result.
- Stop coves short of end walls to prevent sharp cutoff lines.

Cove Lighting

Wallwashing

Wallwashing

Wallwashing involves illuminating a wall evenly. It is different from wall grazing, slot outlining, and accent lighting (see below). The intent of washing a wall is to provide lighting as evenly as possible, side to side and top to bottom.

Wallwashing is an excellent application of the Magic Triangle. Wallwash luminaires should be mounted about one-quarter of the height of the wall away from it. Spacing between wallwash luminaires varies from one-quarter to one-half of the wall height apart, depending on the luminaire. Good wallwashing requires high-performance luminaires to be efficient and effective.

Wallwashing tends to hide imperfections in a wall, but it flattens texture. Thus it is a good technique for gypsum wallboard walls, but it makes stone and brick look painted on. Wallwashing should be avoided if the wall surface is glossy or shiny because the surface will reflect the light source into the eye of the observer.

Wall Grazing

Wall grazing is a technique in which a wall is lighted with luminaires set intentionally close to the wall. The goal is to illuminate the wall as evenly as possible, usually by employing multiple narrow-beam, high-candlepower lamps closely spaced in a narrow trough at or near the junction of the wall. The grazing angle of the light reveals texture superbly; the technique is especially recommended for illuminating stone, brick, and other surfaces with interesting texture. Wall grazing can also be suitable for illuminating walls with a specular (shiny) finish— but be wary. Imperfect joints will be dramatically revealed. For example, a wall of mosaic tiles can be lighted this way, but every tile that is not perfectly flat will stand out.

Slot Outlining

Also a technique for lighting a wall, slot outlining places a continuous light source at the joint of a wall and ceiling. Usually a strip fluorescent light or luminaire designed for the purpose, a wall slot produces a bright upper wall that indirectly lights the space. The sharp edge of the dark ceiling and light upper wall outlines the shape of the ceiling and provides a strong line that emphasizes the architecture. However, this technique does not try to evenly light the wall. It should not be used to light artwork or murals.

Slot Lighting

Accent Lighting

Accent Lighting

Accent lighting is used to illuminate and highlight artwork or a retail display. Unlike other wall-lighting techniques, however, accent lighting is designed to illuminate the object on display only. An effective accent light is aimed at the center of the attraction using an angled luminaire mounted about 3' (or 1 meter) from the wall for every 2' (or 2 meters) that the center of the object is mounted below the light source. This produces a flattering light about 30 degrees from vertical, which is generally agreed best for art. (Other angles may appear better depending on the display, but this guideline is usually accurate.)

COMPOSITION

The creativity in lighting design is embodied in four main groups of decisions:

1. The choice of which layers to employ and which to avoid.
2. For each layer, the technique to be used and its execution.
3. Choice of luminaires, including both performance and appearance.
4. The balance of light as a function of lamps, luminaire locations, and their interaction with the space.

Good lighting designs bring together these decisions in harmony with the inherent design of the space. As with architecture and interior design, individual skill in lighting design increases with experience, critique, and practice. Simple single-layer designs are generally not as complex as multilayer designs, but it may be challenging to achieve a good composition with a limited amount of equipment. Energy-efficient lighting designs are especially hard to do because some layers (such as the decorative layer) will either need to do more than one job or be eliminated altogether.

In each of the following examples of dining rooms, note how the various spaces are lighted with all four layers, combining functions, in many cases, to minimize the number and type of luminaires in the design. The compositions speak for themselves.

DINING ROOM—TRADITIONAL OLD WORLD (SEE COLOR PLATE 3-2)

This design uses chandeliers and matching sconces for both decorative and ambient layers. Clear lamps produce sparkle and eye-level glow. There is no task lighting for the table, but task light is provided for the buffet using accent lights concealed in false rosettes. Accent lighting for busts, walls, and florals is also provided by accent lights in rosettes. The design maintains an old-world appearance via modern accents and convenience.

Dining Room—Historic (see color plate 3-1)

This design also uses a chandelier and matching sconces as decorative and ambient lighting, with the sparkle and eye-level glow expected of traditional lighting. Pinhole low-voltage accent lights produce task and focal layers of light with a minimum of intrusion. The illusion of a traditional space from the early twentieth century is almost perfectly maintained.

Dining Room—Contemporary (see color plate 3-3)

This design employs a chandelier strictly for ornament. Cove uplighting produces ambient light in the ceiling coffer. Recessed accent lights in the upper coffer ceiling illuminate the table; recessed accent lights in the lower ceiling by the walls illuminate the walls, buffet, artwork, and curtains. In this design, the chandelier is the eye-level glow and sparkle is caused by reflections and highlights on the table centerpiece.

CALCULATIONS IN LAYERS

You can design layers using calculations (see chapter 6). By allotting approximate lighting levels to certain layers, it is usually possible to achieve the proper amount of light without needing dimming to get the balance right. Here are some suggestions:

Ambient Lighting

Design ambient lighting to produce the overall desired atmosphere. For a bright and cheery room, ambient light levels of 20–30 fc are a typical target; for more dramatic rooms, lower ambient light levels should be chosen. In rooms where the mood varies between bright and dramatic, as in a kitchen, design for the higher level and dim to the lower level.

Task and Focal Lighting

Design task and focal lighting to meet design goals (typically 20–75 fc). If the ambient lighting layer contributes to the task, be sure to reduce the task light accordingly.

Decorative Light

Lighting for decorative-only effects should produce only a minor amount of light. For instance, consider a hotel ballroom. Assume you are using chandeliers, sconces, downlights, accent lights, and coffers with cove uplighting. The typical layers and illumination levels are:

Downlights	Task lighting for banquets	10–15 fc average
Cove lighting in coffers	Task lighting for meetings and cleanup	30 fc average
Chandeliers and sconces	Decorative	2–5 fc average
Accent lights	Focal lighting	Minimal

This layering scheme allows dimming and controls to achieve flexibility in room use.

Chapter 9

The preceding chapters provided an overview of the technical and operational factors involved in lighting design. Intelligently integrating those factors to achieve successful solutions is the heart of good lighting design. When faced with a lighting design problem, one could simply try a variety of hit-or-miss solutions in a trial-and-error approach, but this is clearly not an organized procedure. As is true of any design problem, a rational, efficient, and professional approach to problem-solving produces consistently good lighting design. What follows is a prescribed methodology that ensures good-quality, professional results for the vast majority of lighting design problems.

Good lighting design begins with identifying and solving visual functions and task-oriented issues. Contrary to the view of some in the design fields, lighting design is not an art. That view of lighting design implies a mystique connected to creating good lighting. But that mystique does not exist. Good lighting design can and ideally should be artful, in the same way that all design processes involve creative thinking and solutions. Experienced lighting design-

ers bring their richness of background to successfully enhance a room's ambience and spatial character.

A workable approach or methodology to solving lighting design problems is set in motion by identifying the functional issues, which are the seeing tasks to be performed in the space. That first step should be followed by the integration of appropriate lighting quantity (illumination level) with sensible lighting quality (visual comfort). Some rooms or spaces, due to their unusual use (such as a dance club or a church) or physical configuration (such as a domed or sharply sloped ceiling), demand that attention be paid to the aesthetic or sculptural aspects of lighting design from the start. But in the great majority of cases, it is best to put the issues of aesthetics aside until the functional issues are resolved.

As indicated at the close of chapter 1, there is no single or "correct" method for solving lighting design problems. Experienced professionals find a personalized method best suited to their own thought process and creative style. The sequential step process described below represents a workable process on which one can build a personalized methodology through repeated experience and experimentation.

SEQUENTIAL STEPS TO SUCCESSFUL LIGHTING DESIGN SOLUTIONS

Step 1: Determine Lighting Design Criteria

Before even thinking about a design, review and record the goals you expect your design to achieve. Some criteria involve lighting quantity and quality, which ensures that you design the lighting to produce the right amount of light. Other criteria, especially codes and standards, ensure the design meets regulatory standards. The following are generally considered the basic lighting criteria for a professional design.

Design Criteria: Quantity of Illumination

Standards for illumination are set by the Illuminating Engineering Society of North America (IESNA). Illumination is generally measured in the horizontal plane 30" above the floor. The units of illumination are foot-candles or fc (lumens per square foot) or lux (lumens per square meter). Foot-candles are still used in the United States, but in countries already converted to the metric system, lux is the proper measure.

The IESNA categorizes light level criterion recommendations based on complexity and difficulty of the visual tasks being performed in the space. They are:

Category A: Public spaces 3 fc/30 lux

Category B: Simple orientation 5 fc/50 lux

Category C: Simple visual tasks 10 fc/100 lux

Category D: Tasks of high contrast and large size 30 fc/300 lux

Category E: Tasks of high contrast and small size 50 fc/500 lux

Category F: Tasks of low contrast and small size 100 fc/1000 lux

Category G: Visual tasks near threshold up to1000 fc/10,000 lux

To choose an appropriate criterion level for each visual task, use these values or refer to the *IESNA Lighting Handbook*, 9th ed., for further explanation.

For instance, most office tasks are Category D, which means that the proper lighting level for this type of work is about 30 fc or about 300 lux. But some office work, such as accounting or map reading, may require 50 fc/500 lux or even 100 fc/1000 lux.

Points to remember about recommended criterion illumination levels:

- These are recommendations, not codes. However, specific lighting levels may be set by codes, such as life safety code and health code. For instance, NFPA 101 (Life Safety Standard) specifies 1 fc (10 lux) average along a path of emergency egress.
- The designer is expected to adjust the criterion level based on project needs. For example, if workers are old, the tasks are small, or the task involves low contrast, the designer may choose to set a higher level.
- The design criterion chosen is an average light level for task lighting. Some tasks may be lower and some higher.

The uniformity of lighting levels is also subject to IESNA recommendations. For interior lighting, IESNA generally recommends the following ratios of illumination:

Task proper: 67–133% of criterion value

Immediate surround: 33–100% of criterion value

Surround: 10–100% of criterion value

By designing light to maintain these relationships, the human eye will be in a constant state of proper adaptation and can respond quickly to visual stimuli.

Design Criteria: Quality of Illumination

Quality of illumination is an area of recent research and interest that was once believed to be an aesthetic issue. Now, guidelines for a number of specific quality issues can be addressed objectively. For each of the following, you should determine how important the criterion is and what you expect your design to achieve.

- Overall appearance of space and luminaires
- Color quality and appearance
- Daylighting integration and control
- Control of direct glare
- Reduction of flicker and strobe
- Uniformity of light distribution on task

- Brightness uniformity of light distribution on room surfaces
- Modeling of faces or objects
- Highlighting points of interest
- Control of reflected glare
- Shadowing (good and bad)
- Appropriate location of lighting for beneficial source/task/eye geometry
- Ability to produce sparkle/desirable reflected highlights
- Control and flexibility

Design Criteria: Codes

Five types of codes and similar regulations affect building lighting.

1. *Electric codes* are designed to assure that buildings are safe. These codes are enforced by building inspectors. The National Electric Code (NFPA 70) is used throughout the United States except in a few cities where local codes are used. The NEC has the following major effects on lighting:

   - It requires that electric wiring to lighting is safe.
   - It requires that luminaires listed for the application. *Listed* means tested and labeled by a testing company such as Underwriters Laboratories (UL).
   - It specifies and limits where lights can be placed in residences, especially in closets and around pools, spas, fountains, hydromassage therapy tubs, and other water appliances.
   - It limits lighting in industrial applications and other places where explosive vapors or other atmospheric considerations exist.
   - It limits the use of high-voltage lighting, especially in homes.
   - It restricts the use of low-voltage lighting systems, especially those with exposed cables and rods.
   - It restricts the use of track lighting.

2. *Building codes* are designed to assure that buildings are structurally safe. Their primary impact on lighting is that they require emergency lighting in commercial and institutional buildings to permit safe egress in the event of an emergency.

3. *Energy codes* are designed to ensure that buildings use a minimum of energy to operate. In general, energy codes have little impact on residential lighting but often place significant power restrictions on nonresidential projects (see Appendix B).

4. *Accessibility codes* are designed to ensure that buildings can be used by all persons, including those with handicaps and the mobility problems of aging. The Americans with Disabilities Act (ADA) requires sconces or other wall-mounted lighting equipment along the path of egress to project less than 4" from the wall if mounted below 80" or above 15" from the floor.

5. *Health codes*, in some states, require hospitals and nursing homes to provide minimum light levels at certain locations. Another type of law requires a protective lens or other covering for lighting in commercial kitchens and cafeteria food service areas.

Step 2: Record Architectural Conditions and Constraints

Record the architectural conditions that may control or affect lighting design decisions. The two conditions that most frequently affect lighting design are window location and size and the availability and size of plenum space. It is not uncommon for the structural system and/or its materials, ceiling heights, partition construction and/or materials, ceiling systems and their materials, and finish materials to have significant influence on lighting solutions.

As one enters the lighting design process, all of these factors must be surveyed and recorded. Personal observation should be the point of beginning. As-built drawings, when available, can also be invaluable. Discussion with building managers and maintenance personnel usually elicits firsthand knowledge of the property's problems and eccentricities. Regardless of the information-gathering methods used, record the data in an organized manner so it will be of optimum use later in the lighting design process.

In the case of new buildings still in the design phase, particularly when lighting design is given appropriate consideration early in the design process, lighting factors may influence building design decisions so that better and more economical lighting design results. Ceiling systems, the routing of pipes, ducts, and conduits in plenum spaces, and accommodating task/ambient lighting systems are among the many positive possibilities when lighting factors are taken into account early in the building design process. The building design team should include professional lighting design expertise from the start.

Step 3: Determine Visual Functions and Tasks to Be Served

Following are two ways to determine visual functions and tasks. In the case of a residential dining room, the primary visual task is the dining table, where seeing the food on the table and the faces of other diners is the first priority. An additional need is to see the items on a buffet when it is used as a serving station; third, a painting on a wall deserves accent lighting. While the corners of a residential dining room may not be lighted, a typical room of this size does not require perimeter lighting, assuming the luminaire(s) for lighting the table is selected to throw off adequate peripheral light.

A reception room, which might serve a small suite of business or professional offices, is typical of many office building settings. The only critical visual tasks are related to the receptionist's workstation, where conventional desk work and reading printed material in the file drawers must be accommodated. Working-level lighting in that area automatically provides a lighting accent in that corner of the room so that the attention of visitors is naturally drawn to the receptionist as they enter the room. The visual tasks in the remainder of the space call for ambient light for conversation and casual short-term reading. Rooms of this kind often have a visual feature such as framed artwork or a company logo that calls for focused accent lighting.

Using the criterion values from Step 1, record the required and desired levels of illumination for each room or space. Begin this process using the design criteria established in Step 1, understanding that light levels can be adjusted to mesh with the designer's personal judgment. In the corporate conference room, the primary visual task is the reading and note-taking performed by people sitting at the conference table; this requires about 50 fc. The selection of the luminaire(s) for lighting the table should take into account the comfortable lighting of the faces of the people sitting at the table. When a marker/presentation board is in use, its surface should be illuminated at about 30–50 fc. The perimeter space behind all four sides of the conference table requires ambient illumination of about 20–30 fc; this will also reasonably serve the visual needs of people pouring beverages and selecting refreshments from the credenza surface. The graphic material or artwork displayed on a wall should receive accent lighting of 20–30 fc; accent lighting of that kind in the relatively small confines of a single-function conference room will probably satisfy the need for perimeter lighting on that side of the table. The job of creating an attractively lighted credenza surface for beverage service deals more with ambience than level of illumination; this issue is discussed in Step 8 below.

In a boutique hotel lobby, several visual tasks must be addressed. At the building entrance, including the vestibule, there is a general need for ambient lighting throughout the space. The only critical visual tasks occur at the registration desk, where clerks and guests must read and write, and at the rear work counter, where clerks must read and make notes. In addition, major accent lighting is needed for the floral arrangement opposite the vestibule and for the registration desk so that new arrivals will spot it easily and quickly. A less critical accent is needed in the elevator niche, and the bell captain's desk needs a small task luminaire. The lounge area, like the reception area, requires only ambient light for conversation and casual short-term reading. Because hotels have a residential function, a residential ambience is desirable in the lounge area; while this is not a specific visual function or task, it must be addressed as an integral aspect of the lighting design solution. As indicated above in relation to the credenza surface in the conference room, the factors and techniques for creating desired ambience are discussed in Step 8, below.

Step 4: Select Lighting Systems to be Used

The basic elements of a lighting design solution are identified at this point in the process. Consideration should be given to all of the appropriate options for the case at hand. The location of the light source is critical. Should light come from above or at eye level (or occasionally from below)? Should the light be directed or diffuse? Should the light source be visible or hidden? The architectural conditions and constraints described in Step 2 often affect these decisions due to lack of plenum space, available ceiling height, or difficulty in getting power to particular locations. It is impossible to generalize about the effects of architectural conditions because each case is so individual. In the case studies that appear in chapters 10 through 15, the details of the architectural conditions are described, and the lighting systems selected for those studies take specific conditions into account. Keep in mind that most properly lighted spaces require at least two lighting systems.

Step 5: Select Luminaire and Lamp Types

Based on the lighting systems decisions made in Step 4, select luminaire and lamp types. The details of luminaire construction, shape, and dimension must produce the desired direction and concentration of light as well as fit the details of construction type and the materials with which they are to be integrated. Aesthetic compatibility often plays a major role in luminaire selection; shape, style, materials, and color must integrate with architectural quality as well as the details of interior finishes and furnishings. Lamp selection has its own set of criteria, of which lumen output, color rendition, energy code compliance, and lamp life are the major factors. It is not uncommon for lamp selection criteria to be the dominant factor in luminaire selection when the lamp qualities are critical for economic, code, or color factors. In the great majority of cases, luminaire and lamp selection is an interactive process in which the selection factors for both are considered as a unit. The case studies in chapters 10 through 15 describe the interactive nature of the process of selecting luminaires and lamps.

Step 6: Determine Number and Location of Luminaires

The most important element of this part of the lighting design process is getting light where it is needed for the visual functions performed in the space.

Accurate luminaire placement, required levels of illumination, and the avoidance of veiling reflections should all be accomplished. Then determine how many of each luminaire type is required. Often, several luminaire-lamp combinations are considered, so the number of luminaires will vary with the lumen output of each combination. In the great majority of cases in which luminaires are placed in, on, or suspended from the ceiling, they should be placed in an orderly pattern, creating an obvious visual geometry. Occasionally, in the case of irregularly shaped spaces or skewed furniture placement, a free-form or nongeometric ceiling pattern is appropriate. As discussed in chapter 6, for some generic situations, such as classrooms, training rooms, and large office spaces, rule-of-thumb formulas for the spacing of standard luminaires produce commonly accepted levels of general illumination for the intended room function. For most situations, consider each lighting design problem as an individual case and develop solutions specific to it. Here are a few "don'ts" to remember:

- When working with a suspended acoustic tile ceiling grid, don't begin the luminaire placement process until the grid layout is known and shown on the reflected ceiling plan.
- Avoid hot spots on walls created when luminaires are improperly placed too close to a wall surface. Don't place wallwashers (and track lighting, when it is used for wallwashing) too close to the wall or graphic material to be accented. For rooms with normal ceiling heights (8'–10'), the luminaires should be 2'-6" to 3'-6" away from the accented surface.
- Avoid placing track lighting where it will create direct and offensive glare for people using the space.

Chapters 10 through 15 include many illustrations of the factors involved in the placement of luminaires.

Step 7: Place Switching and Other Control Devices

This step in the lighting design process is primarily one of logic and common sense. User traffic paths, room usage, and user convenience should be your guides to good switching and control systems. Repeated experience and familiarity with controls technology create workable and user-satisfying solutions. Take into account the opportunities conveyed by the most recent developments in controls that automate energy management or user convenience functions.

Step 8: Aesthetics and Other Intangibles

To this point, all of the steps in the lighting design process address functional matters. However, it should be obvious to anyone concerned with lighting design that inherent aesthetic and psychological factors are of great importance to the success of lighting solutions. One can frequently observe well-designed spaces that have been made unsatisfying and unsuccessful with a poor lighting solution. Conversely, ordinary spaces can be made quite satisfying and successful through creative lighting solutions.

The aesthetic and psychological factors that must be considered in a complete approach to lighting design are, by their nature, intangible and difficult to categorize. Without exploring the depths of aesthetic and spatial theory, the following factors identify those intangible qualities that are necessary considerations in the lighting design process.

Size and scale are important design factors for all spaces. What is appropriate for a living room or a private office is not appropriate for a large and grand lobby or an auditorium. Ceiling height is of particular concern for lighting, where unusually tall spaces cannot rely on standard recessed or surface-mounted luminaires, as is so common with more conventional 8'–12' ceiling heights. The special qualities of residential spaces, in which familiarity and intimacy are normal expectations, have a great deal to do with the traditions of residential scale.

Construction systems are inherently tied to the size and scale of a building. Large buildings typically have large structural members. Large span buildings employ trusses or other large spanning systems such as space frames or arches. In general, the type and scale of luminaires and the type of lamps employed are directly affected when construction systems are exposed, as they sometimes are in all building categories. Typical examples are the exposed rafters in the cathedral ceiling of a large living room, the glass skylight roof over a shopping mall concourse, and the open-truss roof system over gymnasium or arena spaces. Residential buildings present a special case because they typically employ wood frame or ordinary construction, which is rare in nonresidential buildings; while this is not often problematic, large or open plenum spaces are usually not available, restricting the type and placement of recessed luminaires.

Materials and finishes, particularly those of a relatively permanent nature, such as stone, brick, and structural wood, play a significant role in luminaire and lamp selection. Special floor surfaces such as marble and terrazzo often require a particular light distribution and color rendition in order to display their unique qualities. An interior brick or stone wall may require a grazing light source as well as a carefully selected lamp color in order to show it off to greatest advantage. Although they are not common to residential interiors, suspended acoustic tile ceilings are an essential element of most nonresidential interiors, primarily due to the need to gain access to the plenum space above. It is impractical to tie down details of luminaire selection and placement until the suspension grid pattern and details are determined. The less permanent finishes and colors in an interior space, such as paint, draperies, furniture, and fabric, are typically determined after lamp selections are made, leaving the responsibility for satisfying color rendition of these elements to the architect or interior designer.

Design quality is the most elusive element of these aesthetic and psychological factors. Social norms and expectations play a role in lighting design solutions. Portable lighting (floor and table lamps) is commonplace and appropriate in residential interiors, while their widespread use in nonresidential settings seems out of place and is often impractical. Highlighting a decorative wall treatment or richly textured drapery can make the difference in creating a room that is aesthetically satisfying. In general, giving value and paying attention to how a space feels when making lighting design decisions is rewarded with successful lighting design results. Artfulness in lighting primarily means creating perceptible spatial quality. Certain kinds of spaces, such as churches, nightclubs, and grand reception rooms, seem to demand a special kind of atmosphere, much of which can be created with lighting. However, many less obvious spaces, such as living rooms, conference rooms, and restaurants, similarly benefit from thoughtful and creative lighting. To aid in accomplishing satisfying spatial quality, keep these few basic issues in mind when making lighting design decisions.

Creating ambience: Most room and spaces have a desired ambience, such as a living room that should be warm and inviting, an executive office that expresses competence and success, a health care setting that asserts efficiency and professionalism, and a hotel lobby that represents luxury. The desired ambience is usually an amalgam of the client's or user's wishes and the designer's vision of the space. Translating that desired ambience in lighting design terms is critical to successful lighting solutions.

Sculptural quality: The majority of spaces in which we live and work in are rectangular in plan and section and have normal ceiling heights. Unless spaces of this kind are significantly spatially modified through unique furnishings or equipment, the value of enhancing their sculptural quality through lighting techniques is questionable. But spaces that have intrinsic sculptural quality, such as a sensuous curved wall, a polygonal shape, or an arched or domed ceiling, demand lighting design solutions that enhance their unique shapes. Creating a gradation of light on a curved surface, using shade and shadow to

articulate complex angular relationships, and dramatically displaying of a collection of medieval armor are just a few examples of the kinds of solutions sought for these special spaces. Many techniques are available to the lighting designer; using them to advantage or enhancing spatial quality is one of the greatest challenges to the designer's creativity.

Techniques: Achieving the designer's aesthetic vision can involve techniques ranging from the simple to the complex. The desire for an inviting corner for conversation in a living room can be accomplished by creating eye-level glow through the use of a translucent shade on a table lamp. A small jewelry store may require an elaborate combination of hidden in-counter lamps, low-voltage eyeball luminaires, recessed downlights, and undershelf fluorescents. While the lighting design professional may have the knowledge and skill to use all of the available technology and techniques, the person with overall design responsibility must articulately direct that professional to the desired aesthetic result.

To summarize the eight-step process described above:

1. Establish design criteria.
2. Record architectural conditions and constraints.
3. Determine visual functions and tasks and required levels of illumination.
4. Select lighting systems to be used.
5. Select luminaire and lamp types.
6. Determine number and location of luminaires.
7. Place switching and other control devices.
8. Assess aesthetics and other intangibles.

One final step in the overall design process is not described above. That is because it occurs long after the first eight steps are accomplished. How does a designer know if his or her design efforts are successful? This applies to every aspect of architectural and interior design. Do the results of the finished project properly serve the users' needs? Do the space planning adjacencies work well? Do materials and finishes serve their intended function and wear well? Were furnishings properly selected for ergonomic comfort? Are the lighting design solutions functional, comfortable, and aesthetically pleasing?

Over the past two to three decades, a process called *post-occupancy evaluation* (POE) has been developed to tell designers whether or not what they thought would work well actually does. The POE concept is quite simple: Visit the completed project after it has been in use for some time and, through observation and discussion with its users, find out what works well and what doesn't. The POE process has two purposes for the lighting designer: first, to adjust what doesn't work well so it works better, and second, to learn from experience so successful elements can be repeated or enhanced and, obviously, to avoid or correct techniques that are not successful or workable. Particularly for lighting design solutions, the POE process is valuable because light itself is essentially intangible; the result can not be touched, but only experienced. A fair amount has been written about POE; this book's bibliography will lead you to learning more about its techniques and uses.

Now it is time to get to work and put this methodology to good use. The following six chapters focus on the typical lighting design problems encountered in each of the five major building use types that employ intensive use of lighting design and technology. The case studies present specific lighting design solutions, a rationale for each solution, and the design and construction details required to achieve the solutions.

As is true in all design experience, there are no "correct" or "right" or "perfect" solutions to lighting design problems. In most cases several, and often many, solutions can be successful. The designer should strive for workable solutions that meet the functional, aesthetic, and psychological needs of clients and users.

Chapter 10 RESIDENTIAL LIGHTING DESIGN

Residential lighting design has unique characteristics. There is a general expectation of personalization in both social spaces, such as living and dining rooms, and private spaces, such as bedrooms and studies. Some of these residential characteristics are comfortably translatable to nonresidential uses, such as small business reception rooms and private professional offices.

Because all of us, by definition, live in residential spaces and are accustomed to conventional residential lighting design solutions, it may be difficult to consider residential lighting from a fresh perspective. This has both positive and negative implications. Understanding most people's expectations of how residential rooms should be lighted is clearly an advantage; on the other hand, an inability to envision creative solutions because conventional lighting design techniques are so entrenched is a disadvantage.

As in all lighting design problem solving, the first step in creating good lighting design solutions for residential spaces is to identify the visual tasks that must be resolved. Because the visual tasks in residences are so commonplace,

they may be difficult to recognize and analyze from a fresh point of view. After the visual tasks are identified, the lighting design methodology spelled out in chapter 9 should be undertaken immediately. Do not assume that conventional residential lighting design techniques are the best or most appropriate, because conventional techniques are often improved upon by new technologies and product development. The most obvious example is the current availability of many new fluorescent lamps and luminaires for residential use.

Residential spaces are usually personal and often intimate in their use, and their lighting design solutions should respond to that aspect of their function. That personalization often relates directly to a desired mood or psychological response, such as a welcoming entrance foyer, an intimate conversation area, or a festive dining room. The other broad generalization that can be made about residential lighting is that critical visual tasks are usually limited to a few activities and spaces, such as food preparation in the kitchen, grooming in the bathroom, and sewing or desk work in a designated area of the residence.

Many conventions relate to residential lighting design, the most prevalent of which is the dominant use of incandescent lamps. With the growing variety and refinement of fluorescent lamps, little in residential lighting cannot be accomplished with fluorescents, but the conventional aversion to fluorescents persists despite their energy-saving advantage. Another entrenched convention in residential lighting is the widespread use of portable lighting — that is, table and floor lamps—which offers personal and immediate adjustability. While portable lighting has excellent nonresidential uses as well, its use is generally limited because personal adjustability is often discouraged in many nonresidential settings.

Residential lighting conventions include some generally accepted don'ts, most of which are related to avoiding a nonresidential ambience. For example, it is unusual to find an appropriate use for 2' × 2' or 2' × 4' recessed fluorescent luminaires in a residence despite their prevalent and appropriate use in many nonresidential settings. This is coupled with the inappropriateness of acoustic tile ceilings in most residential spaces. Despite these conventions, however, it is often worth one's time to question or rethink them on the principle that many design conventions have outlived their usefulness.

Codes and standards play a limited role in residential lighting. The most significant code impacts are caused by the National Electric Code. However, while energy conservation codes play a major role in all nonresidential facilities, they are generally not applicable to residences. (Note that California's energy code requires fluorescent lighting in kitchens and baths.) Despite this, it would be socially irresponsible to design residential lighting without attention to energy conservation. Limiting the use of incandescent lamps and employing energy-saving control devices are the two major techniques of responsible design. Similarly, Americans with Disabilities Act (ADA) requirements for lighting design have little applicability in residences, although the issue of switch and receptacle placement should not be overlooked.

Compared to other building types, residences have a predictable and relatively limited number of uses and functions. One can usually count on a living/family room function, dining and food preparation spaces, toilet/bathing/grooming functions, and sleeping/dressing accommodations. Homes may have an office, music room, or workshop, but it is unusual to have more than one or two of these special spaces in a single residence.

Residential projects can range from simple and modest to large, complex, and luxurious, with budgets to match. Both ends of this complexity spectrum present problems. Solving lighting design problems for modest residences with limited budgets is as challenging as designing the lighting for a huge house with several specialized spaces, complex control systems requirements, and an unlimited budget. The case studies presented in this chapter fall in the middle of the spectrum, tending toward the modest end. They are intended to be generic in nature, with the thought that the lighting design concepts and techniques presented may be useful in a great variety of floor plan configurations and functional requirements.

CASE STUDY **1**

Living Room Lighting

Most living rooms require flexible lighting design solutions because they serve a broad variety of changing functions. The lighting in a typical living room should comfortably serve small group conversation, larger social gatherings that include casual eating and drinking, and more solitary activities such as reading, music listening, and TV viewing. Somewhat less typically, a living room may have a desk or home office corner, a place for card or board games, a major library collection, or an art collection to be prominently displayed.

The visual tasks in living rooms range from basic and simple to complex and highly technical, depending on the size and intended purpose of the room. It is usually safe to assume that ambient illumination levels in all areas of the room are always great enough to comfortably accommodate personal navigation through the space. The typical living room shown below, which is of ample but moderate size and furnished to serve several functions, presents the following visual tasks to be accommodated:

1. *Ambient lighting* for conversation and social functions. Illumination levels may vary from as little as 7–8 fc to 25–30 fc depending on the desires of people involved. More specifically, critical or extended-period visual tasks are not expected to be performed under these lighting conditions.

2. *Task lighting* for extended-period visual tasks. In this case, the only task planned for is reading in two locations.

3. *Focal light* is required for the large floor-to-ceiling bookshelves on the east end of the *south wall* and the *north end* of the *east wall*, as well as for graphic material anticipated on the *west side of the south wall*, the center wall area of the *north wall*, and above the fireplace mantel.

4. *Lighting for television viewing.* TV viewing presents unusual lighting requirements because the rest of the lighting in the living room is unwanted and detrimental for this purpose. If TV viewing is an expected function, the lighting design solution should accommodate it.

The lighting solution shown below addresses the visual tasks in the following manner:

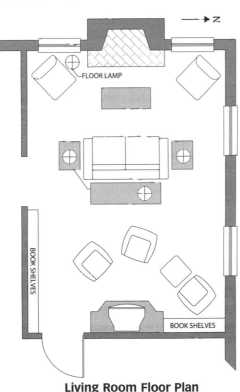

Living Room Floor Plan

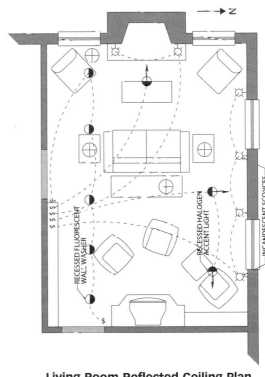

Living Room Reflected Ceiling Plan

1. The need and desire for ambient lighting is met by several lighting elements. The sconces on the north wall provide a blanket of light for that side of the room, the intensity of which can be adjusted by the controlling dimmer switch. The portable lighting adds to the quantity and effectiveness of the ambient lighting, with three table lamps and the floor lamp contributing primarily to the conversation area at the west end of the room. The sconces and the floor and table lamps, if their baffles and shades are translucent, can also add much eye-level glow, a desirable quality if a sense of sparkle or warmth is sought. While their contribution is secondary to those mentioned above, the five wallwashers and three accent luminaires represent still another element of ambient light. The many luminaires in the room (14 fixed and 4 portable), call for many ways of adjusting the quality of ambient light by selecting those to be turned on as well as by adjusting their output through dimmer controls.

2. The primary reading chair is positioned in the northeast corner of the room, where the adjacent sconce should serve as an adequate light source. The chairs in the northwest and southwest corners of the room can also serve as reading chairs, with the former receiving light from the adjacent sconces and the latter having a floor lamp nearby. Depending on the users' habits, an additional floor lamp can be placed adjacent to the primary reading chair.

3. Focal lighting requirements are met with the five recessed wallwashers directed toward the south wall and the three adjustable accent luminaires directed toward the wall above the fireplace mantel, the center area of the north wall, and the shelving/cabinetwork unit at the north end of the east wall.

4. Television viewing presents lighting problems in multipurpose spaces such as living rooms. When TV is viewed in a room or space used primarily for that purpose, creating appropriate lighting is simply accomplished. In this example, many of the luminaires could create unwanted reflections on the TV screen. The only luminaires that will not adversely affect TV viewing are the wallwashers facing the south wall. If the sconces on the north wall are dimmed for low output, their negative effect could be quite minor. Adding a floor lamp in the northeast corner of the room would balance the lighting of the room during the viewing period.

Because flexibility in lighting is essential in living rooms, most lighting should be controlled with dimmer switches. With dimmers, the lighting of the room can be adjusted to achieve just the right quality for any occasion

Luminaire and lamp selections should be based on the following considerations:

Sconces: direct-indirect ratio, task (reading) light for adjacent chairs, degree of eye-level glow and/or sparkle.

Wallwahsers: recessed or surface mounted, spread of light (depending on graphics, if known).

Table lamps: direct-indirect ratio, diffuse shade, degree of eye-level glow and/or sparkle.

Floor lamp: direct-indirect ratio, task (reading) light for adjacent chair, diffuse shade, degree of eye-level glow and/or sparkle.

Lamp selection in all cases can be compact fluorescent or incandescent, with wattage based on personal preference.

The design quality or style of the selected luminaires will be determined primarily by the quality or style of the architectural and interior design detailing and materials, from traditional cut glass (sconces) and fringed shades (portables) to contemporary woods, plastics, and metals to high-tech materials. This element of luminaire selection is difficult to articulate because it deals with the elusive elements of aesthetics, style, and taste. Only long experience in a trial-and-error process over the course of many projects will inform the designer in making intelligent aesthetic decisions.

CASE STUDY **2**

Dining Room Lighting

Ambience is vital in dining room lighting. The creation of mood and personal atmosphere must be at the top of the lighting design criteria list, second only to satisfying the visual tasks to be performed in the room. In addition, the desired ambience is subject to change; it is not uncommon to expect a dining room to be bright and formal on one occasion, intimate and romantic on another, and festive yet casual on still another.

The visual tasks in the great majority of dining rooms are basic and relatively simple. For the typical dining room shown below, they are as follows:

1. First and foremost, provide light at the table so diners can see their food as well as the faces of the other diners.

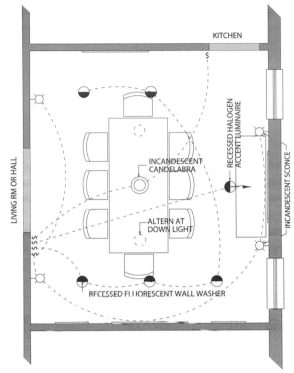

Dining Room Reflected Ceiling Plan

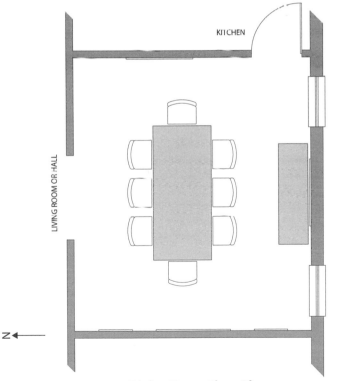

Dining Room Floor Plan

2. When the buffet is used for serving, provide enough and appropriate light for the server to comfortably perform the task.

3. Assuming that the major wall surfaces will display graphic material (paintings, posters, photographs), focal lighting on these materials is necessary for appropriate visibility.

4. Ambient lighting is needed for the periphery of the room to avoid the feeling of dimly lighted and empty spaces surrounding the table.

The lighting design solution shown above addresses the visual tasks in the following manner:

1. A pendant is suspended over the center of the table for the primary visual functions. A table of this size, 7' to 8' long, requires only a single pendant, but two or even three could be used. Its mounting height, best at about 5'

AFF, is low enough to accent the tabletop and the diners' faces but high enough to be comfortably out of their line of vision. The light distribution should be determined in conjunction with the other lighting in the room so as to create the quality of ambient light desired. Finally, the pendant can be opaque or translucent depending on the desire for sparkle and eye-level glow.

An alternate solution for lighting the dining table is shown on page 77 with a dotted line. While pendants are a good and reliable technique, the alternate solution of using recessed accent lights near each end of the table also provides a desirable result, including reflected light from the tabletop softly illuminating peoples' faces.

2. Wall sconces are placed on both sides of the main entrance to the room as well as on both sides of the buffet on the south wall. They provide ambient light on the north and south sides of the room in addition to the eye-level glow sconces generally produce. The specific quality of that eye-level glow depends on the design and materials of the selected luminaire. The sconces adjacent to the buffet can provide task light on the buffet surface for serving functions. Because sconces are more visible than ceiling-mounted luminaires, it is good practice to study elevations of walls containing sconces so that good visual composition of those walls is not left to chance.

3. The recessed wallwashers are placed to give visibility to graphic material on the two major (east and west) walls. The west wall is long enough (13^) so that three luminaires are needed to provide adequate coverage if multiple graphics are intended. If a major display of graphic materials is intended for all wall surfaces, including the two sections of the north wall, a track system should be considered for the north, east, and west walls; this would provide maximum flexibility in lighting the graphic works.

4. Specific ambient lighting for the periphery of the room is not required because the three systems described above more than adequately serve that task. The indirect component of the pendant can provide reflected light from the ceiling surface; the sconces can provide an area of light on the north and south sides of the room; and the wallwashers can reflect light from the east and west walls. Obviously, these luminaires must be selected with their ambient light contribution in mind.

Because ambience is so important in dining rooms, all luminaires must be controlled by dimmer switches so that a great variety of combinations of lighting intensity can be used to create the desired mood for every occasion.

Luminaire and lamp selections should be based on the following considerations:

Pendant: direct-indirect ratio, spread of light, degree of eye-level glow and sparkle.

Sconces: direct-indirect ratio, directional to buffet surface, degree of eye-level glow and sparkle.

Wallwashers: recessed or surface-mounted, spread of light (depending on graphics, if known).

The design quality or style of the selected luminaires must be determined by the quality or style of the architectural and interior design detailing and materials, from traditional crystal and cut glass to contemporary natural woods to high-tech materials and techniques. It would be quite unusual for the room's detailing and materials to be determined by the lighting design solution, including the selection of luminaires. This element of luminaire selection is the most difficult to articulate because it involves the elusive elements of aesthetics, style, and taste. Only long experience in a trial-and-error process over the course of many projects will inform the designer in making intelligent aesthetic selections.

CASE STUDY **3**
Small Kitchen Lighting

With the possible exception of a home office, day-to-day kitchen functions present the most demanding lighting design solutions of all residential rooms and spaces. Kitchens are workplaces where the critical nature of visual tasks is compounded by the dangers associated with sharp tools, scalding liquids, and burning-hot pots and utensils. The typical small galley kitchen shown below shows most of the functional lighting issues found in all residential kitchens without the complexities of informal dining and the social interaction found in many larger kitchens.

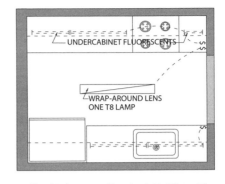

Small Kitchen Reflected Ceiling Plan

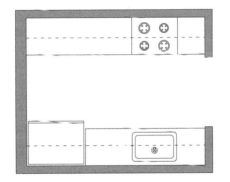

Small Kitchen Floor Plan

All of the primary visual tasks in the kitchen occur at the counter level, including the work counter surfaces, the sink, and the cook surface. A secondary task involves adequate visual access to cabinets and shelves above the countertop level. While providing visual access to cabinets below the countertop level is also important, kitchen lighting solutions that address that task are rare.

The kitchen requires a modest level of ambient light for general use. Because refrigerators and ovens usually feature an internal light source, tasks related to those kitchen elements are usually not a concern. Avoid casting shadows on the work surface; without strong task lighting aimed directly on the surface, the kitchen's ambient or general lighting source likely will place kitchen users in the position of casting their own shadow on the work counter, making their work difficult.

The lighting solution shown above addresses the visual tasks in the following manner:

1. The task lighting, except for that on the cook surface, is accomplished with the use of undercabinet fluorescent luminaires that illuminate all counter and sink surfaces. Many, if not most, wall cabinets are made with a front lip or fascia to visually conceal the luminaire, providing a smooth and uninterrupted line at the bottom of the cabinet. Exhaust hoods over stoves usually contain their own light source; this automatically addresses the need for task lighting on the cook surface.
2. Ambient light and light for the wall cabinets is easily accomplished with a 1' X 4' ceiling-mounted fluorescent luminaire featuring a wraparound plastic lens. Typically, luminaires of this kind are designed to hold two 4' long lamps; these lamps provide more than the needed level of ambient light, but not so much that they cast a shadow on the work surface when the undercabinet luminaires are on. A decorative alternative to the ceiling-mounted fluorescent fixture may be desired; many well-designed luminaires (fluorescent, halogen, and incandescent) are available that solve this lighting problem while presenting a less utilitarian appearance.

Standard (nondimming) switches placed at the entrance to the room are most appropriate in this situation. The light contained in the cook surface hood has its own switch.

Luminaire and lamp selections should be based on the following considerations:

Undercabinet fluorescents: direct light focused on the surface, concealed source to avoid glare, cover lens to avoid dirt and grease accumulation

Ceiling-mounted fluorescent: centrally placed for even distribution, wrap-around lens to provide direct light as well as side light for wall cabinets

In selecting lamps, pay attention to color rendition; many standard fluorescent lamps make food look unappetizing. Lamps at 3000K, 80+ CRI are strongly recommended.

The design quality or style of the selected luminaires will be primarily determined by the quality or style of the architectural and interior design detailing and materials. Kitchens usually contain standard manufactured equipment (refrigerators, ranges, dishwashers, compactors); the inherent contemporary appearance of these items limits the aesthetic range of luminaire selections. Even kitchens with a traditional design quality cannot easily incorporate a luminaire appropriate for a period room. Despite this, a broad range of appropriate luminaires for all sizes and design styles of kitchens is available.

CASE STUDY **4**

Lighting the Larger Kitchen

The typical small kitchen of the previous case study illustrates the basic lighting issues found in all kitchens. But many kitchens incorporate functions that go beyond those of that small kitchen to the point where they become the activity center of the residence. The most frequent use of a kitchen space, after food preparation, is informal dining. The larger kitchen also is often a space for personal and social exchange, where food preparation and conversation are expected to flow in an uninterrupted manner. It is not uncommon for the kitchen to be the hub of all family and social activity such that all living, dining, and kitchen functions flow together in the space. The kitchen shown below is a modestly sized space that permits more than one person to participate in food preparation, incorporates a small informal dining corner, and provides the opportunity for social interaction with family and guests.

The visual tasks performed in this kitchen are obviously more complex than those in a small kitchen. The increase in complexity is seen in each area of this larger space. The need for strong task lighting on all work surfaces is constant, but the island work surface requires a different lighting design solution. The need for ambient lighting goes far beyond comfortable navigation of the kitchen space to demand an ambience conducive to social interaction. The informal dining corner, while not requiring the flexibility of mood expected in a more formal dining setting, still relies on lighting to establish a separate space for eating and to create an atmosphere conducive to dining conversation. Finally, the west wall is an ideal location for graphic material, which requires focal light.

The lighting design solution shown below addresses the visual tasks in the following manner:

Task light: Three areas in this kitchen require task lighting.

1. The perimeter work counter/desk surfaces, which are primarily lighted with undercabinet fluorescent luminaires, as in the typical small kitchen of the preceding case study, plus the single recessed downlight directly above the sink.

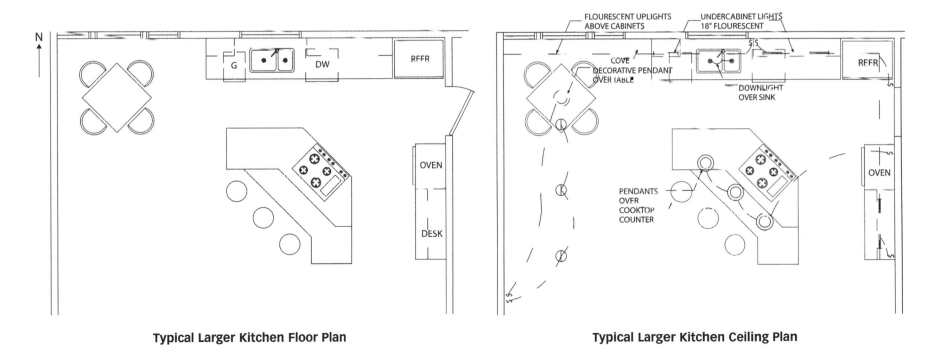

Typical Larger Kitchen Floor Plan   **Typical Larger Kitchen Ceiling Plan**

2. The island counter surfaces for work and casual dining, which are lighted with three small pendants. While two pendants would be adequate, three were selected for the sake of aesthetics and scale. These luminaires should be placed to enhance conversation between those seated at the counter and those working in the kitchen.

3. The dining table, simply resolved with the use of a single pendant scaled to the size of the table. This luminaire should be placed to enhance the dining experience, as was the dining room pendant described in the dining room case study. The collateral task of illuminating items stored on shelves or in cabinets above the work counters is accomplished by the room's ambient lighting, as in the small kitchen case study.

Ambient light: The primary technique for providing ambient light is fluorescent uplights above the wall cabinets and a cabinet bridge above the windows and the door opening along the north and east walls. An evenly dispersed, shadowless light is achieved in the areas adjacent to these two illuminated lines. All four pendants in the room were selected to provide some uplight as well as lateral light cast through their translucent glass shades. They are an important element in the room's ambient light quality in addition to their contribution of eye-level glow and decorative potential. The focal light directed to the west wall adds significant ambient light to that area of the room. Seen in their totality, the fluorescent uplights, the pendants, and the west wall's wallwashers present a complex and well-orchestrated combination of ambient sources.

Focal light: The anticipated graphic material on the west wall is illuminated by the three evenly spaced recessed wallwasher luminaires.

Maximum benefit from the pendant luminaires is obtained by installing dimmer controls. All of the other luminaires are best controlled by standard (nondimming) switches; in addition to being unnecessary, dimming fluorescents is generally expensive. Note that the fluorescent uplights that provide the basic navigational light for the room are controlled by three-way switches at the room's two points of entrance.

Luminaire and lamp selections should be based on the following considerations:

Undercabinet fluorescents: direct light to the work surface, concealed source to avoid glare, cover lens to avoid dirt and grease accumulation; lamps selected for appropriate color rendition in food preparation.

Downlight above sink: basic recessed luminaire with shallow baffle; narrow-beam halogen PAR lamp, 50 to 90 watts.

Island counter pendants: direct-indirect ratio, spread of cast light, degree of eye-level glow, and ambient light contribution; incandescent, halogen, or compact fluorescent lamps selected for appropriate color rendition.

Dining table pendant: same considerations as for the island counter pendants, with adjustment in luminaire size to reflect the single fixture rather than the series of three above the island.

Fluorescent uplights: standard two-lamp fluorescent strip lights, concealed from view, with the lamps separately switched from other luminaires so different levels of ambient light can be achieved; T lamps with an electronic ballast.

Recessed wallwashers: basic luminaire with directional baffle to focus on west wall; 50- to 100-watt halogen lamps.

In selecting lamps, pay attention to color rendition; many standard fluorescent lamps make food look unappetizing. Lamps at 3000K, 80+ CRI are strongly recommended.

The design quality and style of the selected luminaires will be primarily determined by the quality and style of the architectural and interior design detailing and materials. The pendant luminaires require special attention because they are the only visible luminaires in the space; they could play an important decorative role in establishing the aesthetic character of the room. In contrast to the small kitchen in the preceding case study, the room presented here serves many functions beyond food preparation and has fewer limitations placed on luminaire selection.

CASE STUDY 5
Bathroom Lighting

The visual tasks performed in bathrooms are usually basic, predictable, and primarily functional. While ambience and aesthetics are an issue in lighting any space, they are secondary considerations in most bathrooms. Large and customized bathrooms, some of which can include huge whirlpool baths and exercise areas, can require nonstandard lighting solutions; otherwise, task light for grooming and shaving at a mirror and ambient light for showering, bathing, and short-term reading are the only lighting requirements.

The task lighting at the mirror should have certain attributes. First, it should provide enough light for detailed inspection of skin and beard. As a rule of thumb, use 50 to 60 watts of fluorescent per lavatory or 150 to 200 watts of incandescent or halogen per lavatory. Second, the lighting effect should be essentially shadowless to avoid difficult seeing conditions and to provide a flattering view of the face. Third, the selected lamp should provide color quality that is flattering to skin tones; lamps at 3000 K, 80+ CRI are recommended.

The ambient lighting needs are much more variable. Often, the light emitted from the mirror luminaire(s) is adequate for ambient purposes, particularly if the shower curtain or door is transparent or lightly translucent and the toilet is adjacent to the mirror. Despite this, bathroom shapes, configurations, and fixture locations can sometimes severely limit the mirror luminaire's ability to provide adequate ambient light. Regardless of configuration, and if budget permits, a recessed luminaire rated for shower, spa, or bath use in the shower/tub area ceiling and a luminaire above or adjacent to the toilet are always appreciated.

The basic bathroom shown below presents the visual tasks described in the preceding paragraphs. The lighting solution addresses those visual tasks in the following manner:

1. The grooming/shaving tasks performed at the mirror above the lavatories are addressed by the placement of a fluorescent or halogen bath bar luminaire adjacent to the sides of the two grooming mirrors; this is a common and widely accepted lighting solution for residential bathrooms. Several good lighting solutions for the grooming task are available; see an alternative solution in chapter 12 (Case Study 14).
2. Ambient lighting for the tub and toilet areas is reasonably addressed by the lighting above the lavatories. Despite this, a wall sconce in the toilet area will brighten the room and provide light for reading when desired. While it is not shown, a recessed and lensed downlight in the tub area is generally helpful and sometimes necessary if an opaque or close-to-opaque shower curtain or door is installed. In residential situations, the designer rarely knows in advance the type of shower enclosure that will be used; if the budget permits, specific lighting for the tub/shower area is usually welcome.

Standard (nondimming) switches are most appropriate in bathrooms. Desired lighting levels are best adjusted in the choice of lamps.

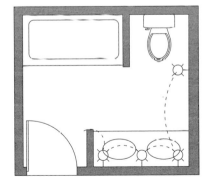

Typical Bathroom Floor Plan

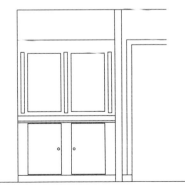

Elevation of Lavatory/Mirror Area

Luminaire and lamp selections should be based on the following considerations:

Bath bar: of appropriate length, to be placed directly adjacent to the sides of the two mirrors

Sconce: primarily direct light focused on toilet area; avoid eye-level glow and sparkle

Downlight: for shower area, recessed with lens, rated for shower/bath use

Design quality or style is relatively limited in most bathrooms. The presence of moisture places immediate restrictions on luminaire selections. While the room's materials and detailing will influence selections, the range of materials, finishes, detailing, cabinetry, and plumbing fixture color(s) will impose further limitations. Selecting from this relatively narrow band of available luminaire products still requires the same kind of intelligent aesthetic and design judgment that must be applied in all lighting design projects.

CASE STUDY **6**
Bedroom Lighting

Two broad generalizations can be made about the design of bedrooms, including their lighting:

1. They should be conducive to sleep.
2. They should be a quiet refuge from the more active or social parts of the residence.

Minimal bedrooms may serve only as a place to sleep and change clothes. More typically, bedrooms also serve as a place to read, watch television, or write a letter or do homework at a desk. When bedrooms are shared, they often serve as a place for intimate relationships. Larger bedrooms may incorporate a sitting/conversation area, a work corner for desk work or sewing,

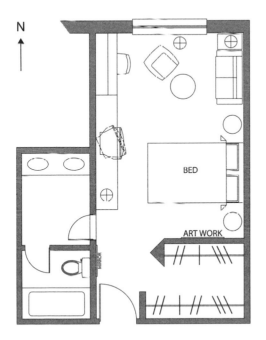

Master Bedroom Floor Plan

and/or an exercise area. Consequently, bedroom lighting must often serve diverse functions, creating different ambiences, while simultaneously serving the separate needs of two users. The bedroom shown below is planned to serve several functions: sleeping, changing clothes, reading in bed, watching television, doing desk work, intimately conversing, and reading in the large lounge chair. Although it is fairly modest in size, this bedroom requires a lighting solution for several functions.

The visual tasks to be resolved in this case are:

1. *Task light:* In the bedroom proper, three visual tasks must be accommodated: reading in bed, seeing tasks at the desk, and reading in the lounge chair. In the walk-in closet, clothes must be seen in reasonable detail and with color accuracy. Adjacent to the walk-in closet is a full-length mirror, which requires carefully positioned light. The bathroom is where the critical visual tasks of grooming and shaving take place; these were addressed in the preceding case study.
2. *Ambient light:* Ambient light is needed for several visual functions, including changing clothes, conversing in the sitting area, and watching television in bed or from the sitting area. The bath/toilet compartment also requires a modest level of lighting for bathing and short-term reading.
3. *Focal light:* The major art/graphic work(s) anticipated on the south wall require focal lighting. While others work may be hung elsewhere in the room, one can reasonably assume that their importance is minor and that the ambient light in the room will be adequate for seeing them.
4. *Television viewing:* As described in Case Study 1, television viewing presents unusual lighting requirements that often conflict with the room's other lighting needs. If television viewing is an expected function, the lighting design solution for the room as a whole should be adjustable, with minimal effort, for those periods.

The lighting solution on page 86 addresses these visual tasks in the following manner:

1. Bedside lighting is provided by wall-mounted swing-arm luminaires; ideally, they should be selected to limit the amount of light that will spill over to the other side of the bed so as not to disturb the bed partner. A good and often-used alternative to swing-arm sconces is two recessed reading luminaires placed in the ceiling above the conventional position for reading in bed. The undershelf fluorescent provides excellent light for desk work. The floor lamp adjacent to the lounge chair should be selected to provide good

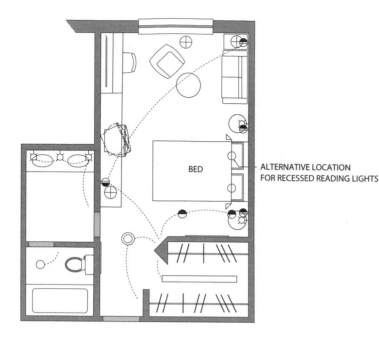

ALTERNATIVE LOCATION
FOR RECESSED READING LIGHTS

Master Bedroom Reflected Ceiling Plan

reading light and with personalized adjustability in mind. A basic downlight positioned in front of the full-length mirror can adequately serve the dressing function. The ceiling-mounted fluorescent in the walk-in closet provides plentiful light for seeing and selecting the hung apparel. The grooming/shaving tasks in the lavatory area are satisfied by three vertically placed luminaires, which provide even and relatively shadowless light for these tasks and maintain a residential scale and character for the space.

2. Ambient light needs are met by several lighting sources. The downlight in front of the full-length mirror, switched immediately adjacent to the entry door, provides basic navigational light as one enters the room. The two table lamps are strategically placed to provide soft lighting and eye-level glow in the two areas of the room that do not have task-oriented luminaires. All of the task sources (bedside, desk, and lounge chair) can be selectively switched on and off to contribute to the room's quality of lighting, includ-

ing additional eye-level glow from the bedside sources, if desired. The wall-washers focused on the south wall make an additional contribution to the room's ambient light. A basic dropped-lens downlight in the bath/toilet compartment provides appropriate light for the limited functions in that area.

3. The recessed wallwashers are positioned to give a lighting accent to the anticipated art/graphic work(s) on the south wall.

4. Depending on where the viewers are positioned to watch television, unwanted light sources should be switched off to avoid reflections. Low-level output from the several other light sources can provide a desired dimmed quality.

The diversity of lighting needs and sources in this room requires an equally diverse approach to switching. As noted before, the navigational light provided by the downlight in front of the full-length mirror requires a switch adjacent to the entry door. The three-way switching of the two convenience receptacles, one convenient to the table lamp adjacent to the television and one in the far northeast corner of the room, allows for a warmer ambient light for the whole of the room and is controllable at its source as well. The National Electric Code (NEC) requires at least one switched receptacle in every bedroom. Except for the recessed wallwashers, which are switched near their source, all other luminaires are switched directly at their source.

Luminaire and lamp selections should be based on the following considerations:

Swing-arm sconce: focused reading light, easy personal adjustability, degree of desired eye-level glow, compact fluorescent for low heat output. The alternative solution for two recessed downlights obviously calls for narrow beam distribution; ideally, a low-voltage luminaire should be employed for maximum beam control.

Undershelf fluorescent: narrow profile for ease of incorporation, visually concealed lamp.

Downlight at mirror: deep baffle, medium beam, compact fluorescent.

Portable floor lamp: focused reading light, easy personal adjustability, compact fluorescent for low heat output. Eye-level glow is questionable in this location.

Closet fluorescent: ceiling mounted with design detail consistent with the bedroom's decorative detail.

Bath bar: of appropriate length, and placed directly adjacent to the sides of the two mirrors.

Table lamps: ambient quality, degree of eye-level glow, design characteristics consistent with the room's interior detail, compact fluorescent.

Bath/toilet downlight: recessed downlight with dropped lens for maximum diffusion, compact fluorescent.

Lamp selection is important for color consistency throughout the bedroom (a color shift can occur when entering the master bath) as well as for color rendition in a space that should tend to visually soft qualities rather than crisp and hard lines. K and CRI values are not recommended here because the desired ambience of bedrooms varies so greatly.

The design quality of the selected luminaires must be determined by the quality or style of the architectural and interior design detailing and materials, from traditional silk shades to contemporary natural woods to high-tech materials. It is rare for the room's detailing and materials to be determined by the lighting design solution, including the selection of luminaires. This aspect of luminaire selection is difficult to articulate because it deals with the elusive elements of aesthetics, style, and taste. Only long experience in a trial-and-error process over the course of many projects will inform the designer in making intelligent aesthetic decisions.

Chapter 11 OFFICE AND CORPORATE LIGHTING DESIGN

As our work world becomes increasingly service-oriented, more and more people work in office or workstation environments. In addition to the buildings we classify as office buildings, most nonresidential buildings have a significant office area or function.

Because office environments have become so pervasive, typical lighting design solutions in these settings have become simplistic and formulaic in nature. The prevalence of the speculative, multi-tenant office building has been a major factor in the growing reliance on generic solutions because they must accommodate ever-changing tenants. Most of the design elements of these buildings, including their lighting systems, are geared to serving a great variety of tenants as well as those that regularly move from office space to office space. Hence the almost universal use of lay-in acoustic tile ceilings, which permit the easy relocation of 2' X 2' and 2' X 4' recessed fluorescent troffers and access to ceiling plenum spaces for installing and servicing mechani-

cal and electrical equipment. Rarely is this the best lighting design solution for even the most undemanding office design.

In most work environments, productivity and efficiency are high-priority goals, and lighting design solutions are expected to support them. More specifically, visual tasks should be easy and comfortable to perform; fortunately, the growing trend is to increase employee satisfaction in most workplaces, and lighting should contribute to a visually and psychologically satisfying environment. The use of formula lighting solutions provides less than positive results in most work spaces in terms of both user productivity and user satisfaction. Nonstandard and creative solutions *can* be economically applied in many office settings.

The practicalities of the speculative or multi-tenant office building do place stringent limitations on the approaches to lighting design that can be successfully employed. Clearly, the rapid turnover and subsequent reconfiguration of tenant spaces demand maximum flexibility and little that is custom-designed, save for reception, conference, or high-level executive spaces in which the company's image is important.

For office spaces designed for more permanent occupancy, such as company-owned business buildings and institutional facilities, the approach to lighting can and should be different. While access to plenum space remains essential, the other elements that affect lighting design decisions can be addressed with greater flexibility. Appropriate and accessible ceiling systems other than lay-in acoustic tile ceilings do exist. Drywall soffits can be employed more freely. Although sconces and other wall-mounted luminaires are used in multi-tenant buildings, they and other fixed and customized lighting solutions are more practical in owner-occupied buildings.

The relationship between the ceiling system and the lighting system is always critical. In the great majority of office settings, mechanical and electrical equipment and distribution lines are not exposed, primarily because the finished appearance of a suspended ceiling is desired. Typically, office space ceiling heights range from 8' 6" to 9' 0". In small and/or private office spaces, ceiling height can be comfortably reduced to 8' 0", but in any space larger than a conventional enclosed room, 8' 6" should be the minimum ceiling height. The height of the plenum varies considerably depending on the design of the building's structural system. Typically, in high-rise office buildings, they are about 2' 6" from finished ceiling to the underside of the floor above. It is convenient to have a roomy plenum that does not restrict luminaire type or placement, but the tendency is to keep the plenum at a minimum in order to keep the building volume (and therefore cost) as small as possible. While small areas in an office suite can use a drywall or other nonaccessible ceiling, access to mechanical and electrical services is of great importance. Although general schematic lighting design solutions can be conceptualized before the ceiling system is selected, no concrete lighting design decisions can be made until that selection is made. That architectural decision is best made collaboratively with the lighting designer. Even the specific positioning of the ceiling system as it relates to fixed walls and building core elements is best made collaboratively. More specifically, the final positioning of luminaires cannot be assigned until the final ceiling system details are determined.

In the majority of office settings, 2' X 2' and 2' X 4' grid systems are used. The grid itself can range from the common, low-cost T to visually more discreet (but also more costly) fine-line grids. Myriad tile patterns, textures, and colors are available, as are 1' X 1' tiles that employ a hidden spline installation system that offers an almost tileless appearance. However, this hidden tile approach is not only relatively expensive but accessibility to the plenum for repairs or ceil-

ing/lighting reorganization is difficult and costly. Further, achieving the original tileless appearance is difficult once it has been disturbed.

Variations to the basic lay-in acoustic tile ceiling are limited, but several are viable, even when budget constraints are important. Snap-on aluminum slat systems come in a great variety of colors and finishes. Vertically positioned acoustic baffles present another option, again available in a variety of materials and colors. Suspended or floating panel solutions have been employed, especially in settings requiring a dramatic effect. Translucent or luminous ceilings, employing both plastic and textile surface materials, have been quite successful in many situations requiring diffuse ambient light. While nonstandard ceiling systems may not always be appropriate, they should be given design consideration whenever possible.

Most design problems respond to many viable solutions. Design students see this regularly in studio classes, when 10 or 20 students each present a different solution to the same design problem. But there is one *best approach* to solving most office lighting design problems, and that is the use of the *task/ambient concept*, whereby a generally low level of ambient illumination is employed for most of the space and strategically placed task lighting luminaires concentrate work-level illumination where critical visual tasks are performed. The task/ambient concept is best because it provides the optimum visual or seeing conditions in the work setting *and* it conserves energy best by providing high-level illumination only where it is needed. This concept is applicable not only in office work situations but also in kitchens (both residential and commercial), health care facilities (as in medical exam rooms and nursing stations), and many retail situations where the lighting task is to draw the customer's eye to specific merchandise.

Of course, some office spaces, such as lobbies and break rooms, do not require task lighting. Likewise, in some office spaces, such as training rooms, visual tasks are performed but the task/ambient approach is inappropriate. But generally, when designing lighting in places where people work, look first to the task/ambient approach for good, workable solutions.

Most office settings house a variety of visual tasks and therefore present a number of lighting design problems. The obvious starting point in solving these problems is with the visual tasks related to the desk, which sometimes means an open or freestanding desk but more often these days means a low-partitioned workstation. Each of these situations presents different lighting design problems. The private office presents additional visual tasks and conditions beyond those at the desk. Reception areas typically require one lighting condition for the receptionist and another for waiting visitors. The primary visual task in a conference room is at the conference table surface, but other activities often occur in conference rooms that require additional lighting solutions. This list of office lighting functions and settings could go on to include presentation rooms, exhibit areas, filing centers, training rooms, and more. Regardless of the number of office lighting design problems you encounter, remember that the design solution process begins with identifying the visual tasks related to each function and setting.

It is important to note that office lighting design, as is true of many lighting design problems, is often a compromise between ideal practice and the practical limitations of budget, the lay-in ceiling system, and effective standards of the marketplace. This means that commercial real estate tends to control what is used to light office buildings. In most office buildings, one or two luminaires are identified as building standards. Tenants (and their architects and interior designers) are discouraged from using anything else, unless the tenant is unconcerned with cost. In office settings in other building types, for practical reasons of budget and constructability, the same design constraints tend to apply.

Beyond the identification of visual tasks, use the design methodology, which is fully described in chapter 9, to complete the lighting design process. Despite the primary design focus on employee productivity and the human factors that are part of productivity concerns, don't forget that most people spend more waking hours in their work environment than anyplace else. This fact demands that an intelligent approach to all workplace environments also gives high priority to the human, social, and psychological aspects of those environments. While this is true of all design aspects of workplaces, lighting design plays an important and integral role in the final design result.

Most of the lighting design concerns in office settings focus on employees, who typically spend many hours there each day. In many business and professional offices, important attention must also be paid to the needs of visitors—clients, customers, colleagues, vendors. Usually, visitors' access is limited to reception spaces, conference or presentation rooms, and private offices. In some cases, visitors perform specific visual tasks, such as reading and writing in a conference room or reviewing paperwork at a desk. Often, the design intentions in these visitor-accessible spaces include fostering a positive company image that the lighting design solution is expected to support. This may mean highlighting an unusually textured or reflective wall surface, displaying artwork or company products, dramatizing a ceremonial conference room, or showing off the richness and elegance of a chief executive's office. Creating image effects of these kinds is a frequent task of the lighting designer.

Designing office spaces requires consideration for computers and other office equipment. Computers are everywhere; it is rare to find a workstation without one. Unwanted reflections on CRT screens range from annoying to disturbing. Employing the use of parabolic louvers for fluorescent troffers has become a common and partially successful solution. Indirect ambient lighting, which is rapidly gaining favor, is a more successful technique for avoiding unwanted reflections. Personally adjustable task lighting combined with relatively low-level ambient lighting (assuming that parabolic louvers or indirect lighting techniques are employed) provides the best solution for this pervasive problem.

This unique office-related problem adds weight to the argument for employing task/ambient solutions. The quality of ambient light should not be taken for granted; providing adequate illumination for the casual tasks of personal navigation and conversation does not fully solve the ambient lighting problem. Uniform low-level ambient light, particularly if indirect luminaires are the exclusive source, yields a lifeless and undesirable visual environment. People need both variety and spatial definition in their work environments, and uniform low-level lighting does not create visually satisfying spaces. Variations in ambient lighting levels and highlighting wall surfaces at visual termini should be considered and appropriately incorporated to create visually alive and satisfying environments.

Complying with energy codes has become a major criterion in all workplace lighting. The primary result is the pervasive use of full-size and compact fluorescent lamps. The expanding development of fluorescent technology has created products that can address all of the needs of workplace lighting, from subtle effects to dramatic creations. HID and low-voltage lighting can assist in office facilities, but the bulk of lighting solutions is accomplished with fluorescents.

The case studies presented in this chapter represent five of the most common office spaces and functions. The examples shown are relatively small in order to make the lighting design issues easily understood. These lighting design issues are fundamental and can be translated to larger settings and to varying functional conditions and situations.

CASE STUDY **7**

Reception Room Lighting

Reception rooms in office and corporate settings are usually the point of entry to a place of business or professional or institutional office. Typically, the reception room is a place for visitors to be greeted and acknowledged, or perhaps to wait to be seen and served. As is the case in all entrances, it is also a symbolic place that creates the first impression of a given environment—one that conveys a professional, corporate, or institutional image and sets the stage for the remainder of the interior space.

Reception rooms range tremendously in size from a few seats and a glass vision panel through which visitors speak to a greeter who works in an adjacent space to a waiting area with dozens of seats and an open reception desk with one or more greeters. The point of reception can vary from a simple desk that serves only as a point of greeting to a receptionist's workstation requiring a large work surface, files and storage space. Many business and institutional office reception rooms have an element of display—perhaps a simple logo highlighted on a wall, an extensive display of products, or certificates, awards, or current work. In general, major entrances, including lobbies and reception areas, present an important opportunity to use lighting to express image and similar ideas.

A few basic visual tasks are served in most reception rooms. Some concentration of light should focus on the reception station in order to visually guide first visitors to it. Task light at the reception desk should be geared to the receptionist's work functions, from a simple reading of paperwork to additional functions such as filing or proofreading. Ambient light is needed for general navigation throughout the space at a level appropriate for personal conversation and the casual reading of a book or magazine. Focal light may be needed to visually accent a company logo, a display of company-related material, or other art/graphics works.

The floor plan in the figure at right indicates a modest-sized reception room, one that might be appropriate to a small or medium-sized law or other professional firm or that could be the entrance to a department within a large corporate or institutional office.

1. The workstation configuration indicates that this receptionist requires task light for concentrated paperwork, filing, retrieval of paperwork, and other typical desk-related functions, including work at a desktop computer. If thoughtfully selected, that task light can also serve as the concentration of light needed to direct visitors to the receptionist when they enter the room.

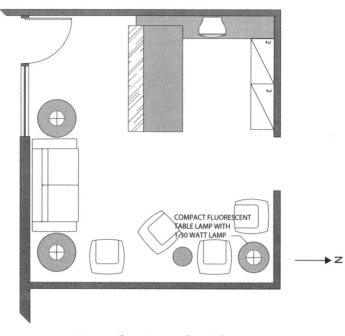

COMPACT FLUORESCENT TABLE LAMP WITH 1-30 WATT LAMP

Reception Room Floor Plan

2. The seating area requires a modest level of ambient light to serve the typical casual visual tasks of a waiting room—primarily personal conversation and short-term magazine reading.
3. The logo on the west wall requires focal light. While framed art or graphic work might be placed on other wall surfaces, it is assumed here that it does not require focal illumination.

The lighting solution shown in the following figure addresses the visual tasks in the following manner:

1. *Task light* at the receptionist's workstation is met with four downlights that concentrate light on the primary work surface and on the file drawers when they are open. This heavy concentration of light on the workstation also serves to direct visitors to the receptionist when they enter the room.
2. The *ambient* light component is resolved with four recessed downlights in the central area of the room and three table lamps that are directly related

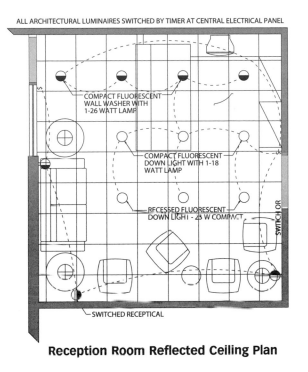

Reception Room Reflected Ceiling Plan

to the waiting area seating. The table lamps, because of their scale and placement at eye level as well as their association with residential lighting, provide a personal and welcoming touch to the room. The wallwashers focused on the west wall and the table lamp seen through the entrance door sidelight contribute to the ambient light in the entrance area.

3. The *focal light* required to highlight the company logo is handled simply with two recessed wallwashers placed about 3' from the west wall and focused on the logo area.

Note that the ceiling grid does not start with a full 2' tile in any corner of the room. The grid, while symmetrically placed in the room, is manipulated to allow the best placement of the recessed luminaires.

Because the reception room is critical in setting the tone of the overall interior environment, the optimum level of illumination should be determined when the room is first put into use and not adjusted day to day. For this reason, a single switch is used to control all luminaires, architectural and portable. In situations of this kind, switching may be best operated on a time clock with a manual override because personal control is not necessary and may even be detrimental.

Luminaire and lamp selections should be based on the following considerations:

Downlights: depth of baffle, light distribution spread compact fluorescent (18 and 23 watts)

Table lamps: size/scale of lamp/shade combination, direct-indirect ratio, translucency of shade (some eye-level glow desired, but avoid major reflections in CRT screen), compact or circle line fluorescent (30 watts)

Wallwashers: recessed high hat, light distribution adjusted to area desired for logo, compact fluorescent (26 watts)

The only luminaires that have significant aesthetic impact on the space are the three portable table lamps; their selection should be closely coordinated with the interior design color, finishes, and furniture selections.

CASE STUDY 8

Private Office Lighting

The traditional private office conveys an element of status as well as positive acoustic separation for its occupants. Despite the growing use of open, nonprivate workstations for all levels of office tasks and management, the private office is still widely used where customs of status and/or visual and acoustic confidentiality require it. This case study addresses the issues of the modest-size office designed for its primary occupant and a maximum of two or three visitors. It is a place for concentrated desk work and conversation. The larger, status-oriented executive office is dealt with in Case Study 9.

The lighting requirements of the private office shown in the figure below are typical of most rooms of this type. The freestanding desk is the primary focus of task light, with the north wall credenza, serving as a secondary work surface, requiring adequate task light. People's faces on both sides of the desk should be comfortably illuminated for conversation. Some private offices have graph-

ic material on their walls—a tack board, work-related material, or fine artwork—that requires focal light. Here, the south and west walls are otherwise unused and could accommodate several kinds of graphic materials. With so many visual tasks to be served, it is assumed that additional light sources will not be required for ambient light in this relatively small room.

The lighting shown in the figure below addresses the visual tasks in the following manner:

1. *Task light* for the freestanding desk is accomplished with two 1' X 4' recessed fluorescent luminaires that provide relatively shadowless light and avoid disturbing veiling reflections. This type and placement of luminaires has for many years been a widely accepted approach to lighting a single desk in a room. There are other workable solutions for lighting a freestanding desk, two of which are shown in Illus. and Illus. Alternate scheme *a* indicates two 1' X 4' pendant fluorescent uplights that provide a wash of task-level light on the desk. Alternate scheme *b* indicates a task/ambient approach in which a single 1' X 4' pendant fluorescent uplight provides a wash of ambient-level light in the desk area: this is supplemented by a portable adjustable swing-arm desk luminaire lamped with a compact fluorescent.

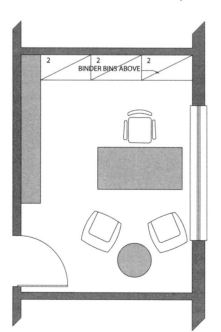

Small Private Office Floor Plan

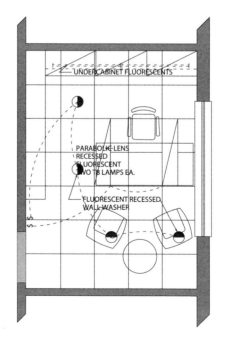

Small Private Office Reflected Ceiling Plan

2. The *secondary task light* on the credenza top is produced by two 4' under-cabinet fluorescent luminaires. Because these luminaires are so close to the work surface, a modest lamp output provides a more than adequate level of illumination. This undercabinet source serves two additional purposes. First, it helps illuminate the contents of the lateral file drawers, which are also lighted by the two recessed 1' X 4's. Second, it provides eye-level glow behind the desk user in a room that is otherwise lighted only from the ceiling. If the shelf or binder bin above the credenza does not have a fascia to hide the luminaires, it is aesthetically desirable to detail and provide one.

3. *Focal light* for anticipated graphic material or artwork on the south and west walls is achieved with two wallwashers focused on each wall. Reflected light from the wallwashers also adds desirable ambient light to those two edges of the room, which might otherwise feel a little underlighted In contrast to the concentration of light in the two work areas.

Switching is accomplished in a direct and conventional manner at the point of entry to the room. Dimming is not required. Note that the undercabinet luminaires are switched from the wall directly below the wall cabinets.

Luminaire and lamp selections should be based on the following considerations:

Recessed 1' X 4's: direct light focused on desk, small-cell parabolic louver lens, two 48" lamps per luminaire

Alternate scheme a: The two recessed 1' X 4' fluorescents are replaced with two indirect pendant 1' X 4' fluorescents suspended at 7' 0" AFF and containing two 48" fluorescent lamps.

Alternate scheme b: The two recessed 1' X 4' fluorescents are replaced by a single 1' X 4' fluorescent, as in alternate scheme *a*, and a swing-arm desk luminaire lamped with a compact fluorescent.

Undercabinet fluorescent: direct light focused on credenza top, light source concealed to avoid glare, one 4' lamp per luminaire.

Wallwashers: recessed, spread of light adjusted to materials to be illuminated (if known), compact fluorescent lamps (26 watts).

Luminaire design characteristics and style should be consistent with the architectural and interior design qualities of the room, including materials, color, furniture, and detailing. In this case, the only significantly visible luminaires occur in the two alternate solutions. In alternate scheme *a*, the visible luminaires are the two pendant fluorescents over the freestanding desk area, and even they can (and probably should) be selected to be anonymous and not draw visual attention. In alternate scheme *b*, the visible luminaires are the single pendant fluorescent and the desk lamp; again, the pendant should probably not draw visual attention, but the desk lamp selection should be closely coordinated with all of the interior design color, finishes, and furniture selections.

CASE STUDY 9

Lighting the Large Executive Office

The large executive private office serves two functions in addition to those of the more typical (and smaller) private office described and shown in the previous case study. First, its larger size accommodates more visitors or guests; second, it imparts an aura of prestige, status and importance to its occupant. Some executive offices are immense, often containing a large conversational area and a sizable conference table in addition to a large desk and credenza for its primary user and a few pull-up chairs at the desk. For the purposes of this study, a more modest and typical executive office has been selected.

The lighting requirements for the executive office shown in the following figures are typical of those required for most offices of this kind and size. The one critical requirement for task light (1) is at the desk, where concentrative work occurs regularly. The credenza on the east wall provides a secondary work surface that also requires adequate task light (2). Ambient light (3), for navigation and short-term reading, is required for the conversation area as well as the central space in the room. Focal light (4) should be provided for the large open expanse of the south wall and for the tall bookshelves near the north end of the east wall. While the west wall may have some graphic material, it is assumed that this will be of less importance than the work on the south wall because of the seating in front of it; it will be adequately lighted by the ambient light at that end of the room.

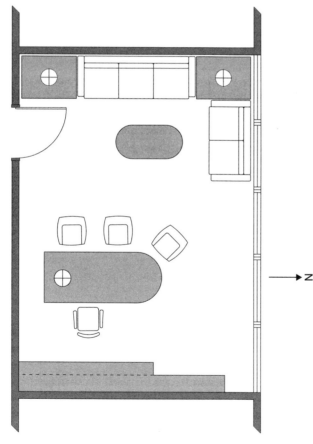

Large Executive Office Floor Plan

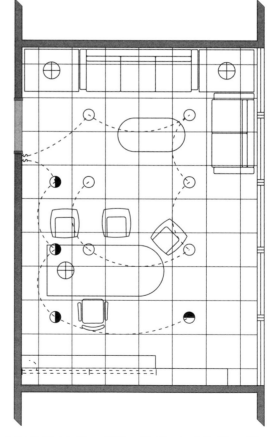

Large Executive Office Reflected Ceiling Plan

The lighting solution shown in the preceding figure addresses the visual tasks in the following manner:

1. *Task light* for the freestanding desk is provided by the swing-arm portable table lamp placed on the desktop. Its simple and direct adjustability permits the user to place high-level illumination directly on the paperwork at hand. Luminaire and lamp selection can be highly individualized to the style and preferences of the user.
2. *Task light* for the credenza work surface is provided by a typical undercabinet fluorescent luminaire that blankets the work surface with working-level illumination and creates desirable eye-level glow behind the primary desk. The light source itself should be concealed from view.
3. *Ambient light* is provided by two very different sources. The six downlights cover the central area of the room. Their illumination level should be adjustable to accommodate a variety of desired moods. In addition to the downlights, the table lamps on the end tables at either side of the three-seat sofa provide an alternative kind of ambient light as well as eye-level glow for the west end of the room.
4. *Focal light* for the south wall graphics/fine artwork is provided by the three equally spaced wallwashers placed about 3' from that wall. In addition, the single wallwasher focused on the east wall bookcase provides better visibility of the bookcases' contents while giving greater visibility to the bookcase unit itself and adding the special warmth that a display of books generally brings to a room.

Switching is accomplished in a direct and straightforward manner. All of the ceiling-recessed luminaires are switched at the entry door, with the downlights on dimmer control in order to adjust room ambience. The undercabinet fluorescents and the three portable desk/table lamps are switched at their source.

Luminaire and lamp selections should be based on the following considerations:

Desk lamp: maximum adjustability and ease of adjustability, high-level work illumination, lamp type and wattage best selected by individual user.

Undercabinet fluorescent: direct light focused on credenza top, light source concealed to avoid glare.

Downlights: beamspread/distribution, adequate baffling, lamped with compact fluorescents.

Table lamps: base and shade scaled to room and furniture, translucent shade for eye-level glow, compact or circle-line fluorescents.

Wallwashers: recessed, spread of beam adjusted to materials to be illuminated (if known), compact fluorescents.

Luminaire design characteristics and style should be consistent with the architectural and interior design qualities of the room, including materials, finishes, color, furniture, and detailing. In this case, the three portable luminaires are important to the room's decorative qualities and should be selected as much for their role as furniture and accessories as for their lighting quality. In other words, they are best selected with the furniture, with appropriate consultation from the lighting designer. Often, luxurious executive offices are treated as personally as a living room, where the personal wishes of the occupant dominate every design decision.

CASE STUDY **10**

Conference Room Lighting

Conference rooms generally serve a limited range of functions where a group of people meet for verbal exchange. While some conference rooms can accommodate scores of people for large-scale presentations, more typically they contain a central table of a size that permits personal eye contact, conversation, and a limited amount of reading and note-taking. Conference rooms are frequently used for presentations, from a simple personal talk to a group of presenters to the deployment of a variety of electronic media.

A few basic visual tasks are performed in most conference rooms. The primary visual task is reading and writing at the conference table. Good lighting of the faces of those seated at the table is also important. Personal presentations that include graphic material such as diagrams and charts require focal light on those items. While conference rooms require comfortable navigational ambient light, consideration should be given to adjusting it for video, PowerPoint, and other electronic presentations. A less critical consideration is providing comfortable task light for a surface from which beverages and food are served.

The conference room shown in the following figures are typical of many modest-sized conference rooms, including their lighting requirements. As indicated in the previous paragraph, the primary lighting requirement (1) is to provide

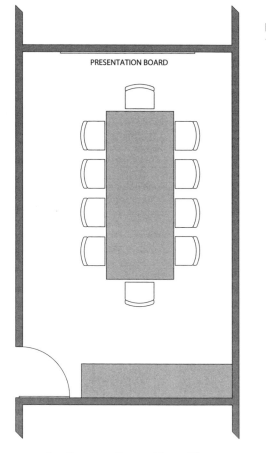

Conference Room Floor Plan

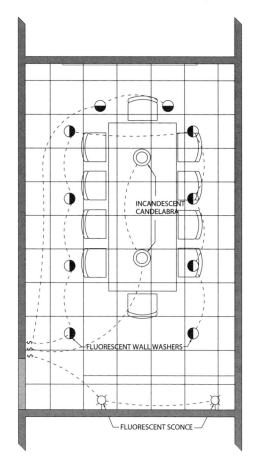

Conference Room Reflected Ceiling Plan

appropriate task light for reading and writing at the conference table. That light source should also provide appropriate illumination of the faces of those seated at the table. The presentation board at the north end of the room (2) requires strong focal light when it is in use. The credenza surface (3), used for beverage and casual food service, requires modest task light. The perimeter of the room (4) behind the chairs must receive sufficient ambient light.

The lighting solution shown in the preceding figure addresses the visual tasks in the following manner:

1. *Conventional task light* at the conference table is accomplished with two incandescent candelabras placed symmetrically on either side of the center line of the conference table, lamped to provide about 30 fc at the tabletop.
2. *Focal light* for the graphics/presentation wall is achieved with recessed wallwashers placed 4' o.c. While many types of wallwashers can be used in a situation of this kind, MR-16 luminaires have been selected in order to maximize coverage and precise focusing.
3. *Secondary task light* for the credenza surface is provided by a pair of fluorescent sconces.
4. *Ambient light* for the perimeter of the room is accomplished by the fluorescent uplights, which not only provide adequate task light for the conference table but also create a more than adequate wash of soft light for the perimeter of the room. When the wallwashers for the walls and the second

ary task light for the credenza are on, they supplement the ambient light for the room's perimeter.

Each of the three groups of luminaires are separately switched at the room's entry door.

Luminaire and lamp selections should be based on the following considerations:

Fluorescent uplights: narrow distribution band to concentrate task light on table

Low voltage downlights: controlled narrow beam, well baffled for inconspicuousness

Wallwashers: evenness of distribution, inconspicuous appearance

Lamps shall have similar K and CRI values in order to present a unified (nondramatic) visual environment.

Luminaire design characteristics and style should be consistent with the architectural and interior design qualities of the room, including materials, color, furniture, and detailing. In this case, the only significantly visible luminaires are the pendant fluorescents. Depending on the overall design characteristics of the room, those pendants could be selected to be visually dominant or unobtrusive.

CASE STUDY 11

Open Office Lighting

Lighting the workstation areas of office settings is one of the most common building design challenges. As discussed in some depth in the introduction to this chapter, several factors must be considered and integrated in creating these lighting design solutions. To briefly recount these factors, they are:

User needs for visual comfort and productivity, utilizing task/ambient lighting concepts for optimum visual conditions, including minimizing CRT reflections.

Construction practicality and economy, including built-in flexibility, access to mechanical and electrical systems, and development and use of building standards.

Energy codes that limit energy consumption, which again strongly suggests the use of task/ambient concepts.

In most cases, open office areas do not involve major visitor traffic, making public image of limited concern and allowing the lighting design solution to focus on user needs.

The relatively small open office area shown in the following figure presents most of the typical lighting design considerations in work settings of this kind. Of prime importance is high-quality task lighting for each station. Comfortable, low-level navigational lighting is needed throughout the space. Adequate seeing conditions for placing or finding written material in the filing cabinets is required, as is eye-level glow and the lighting of people's faces at the two stations with visitors' pull-up chairs. Lighting for anticipated graphics/artwork/bulletin board on the east wall is required. Ambient daylight is available along the western third of the space.

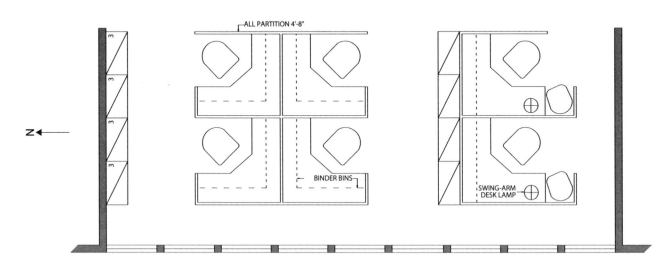

Open Office Floor Plan

The lighting solution shown in the following figure addresses the visual tasks in the following manner:

1. *Task lighting* is accomplished primarily with two undercabinet luminaires per station, except for the two stations with visitors' chairs where swing-arm desk lamps are used adjacent to the chairs to provide eye-level glow as well as illuminating faces when there is a personal exchange.

2. *Ambient lighting* is accomplished primarily with five pendant strips of uplight fluorescents, which provide an even wash of low- to moderate-level light for most of the space. The five 4' lengths of these fluorescent luminaires closest to the window wall should be separately switched and controlled by an automatic timer shut-off in order to conserve energy when daylighting will provide adequate ambient light. In addition, the focal light-ing of the north, east, and south walls contributes to the ambient light for those edges of the room.

3. *Focal lighting* for the north and south walls is accomplished with fluorescent wallwashers adjacent to those walls; these provide an even wash of light. The longer and more prominent east wall is illuminated with individual wall-washers placed 4' o.c., providing greater opportunity to adjust both the quality and level of lighting for graphics, artwork, and other visual material.

All task lighting is controlled at its source by the employees at the workstations. All other switching should be controlled at a nearby panel box because personal choice is not at issue. The wallwashers for the east wall should be controlled by dimmers in order to adjust the lighting level. As noted above, the fluorescent uplights closest to the window wall should be controlled by automatic timer shut-off.

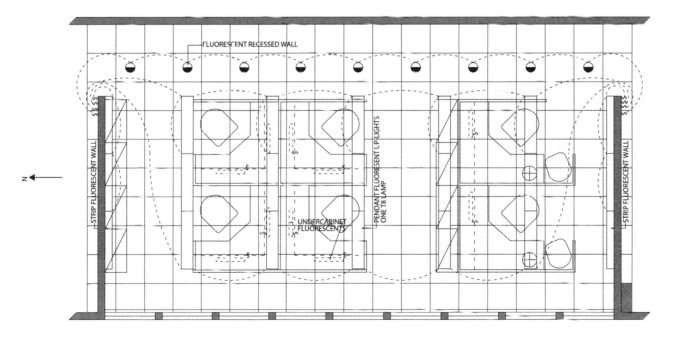

Open Office Reflected Ceiling Plan

Luminaire and lamp selections should be based on the following considerations:

Undercabinet fluorescents: direct light directed to the work surface, concealed source to avoid glare, adequate in length to illuminate the entire work surface, easy-to-reach switch; ideally detailed so the entire luminaire is concealed from view.

Swing-arm desk lamp: adjustable to provide good task light on work surface, translucent shade for eye-level glow and the illumination of both people engaged in conversation; can be portable or fixed to desk or panel surface.

Pendant fluorescent uplights: maximum distribution and illumination of ceiling surface; note that ceiling height must be adequate for at least a 1'-6" suspension of the luminaire.

Fluorescent wallwashers: recessed, adjacent to the surface being illuminated, engineered for maximum wallwashing effect.

Halogen wallwashers: recessed, basic luminaire with directional baffle to focus on east wall, 50- to 100-watt lamps.

The design quality and style of the selected luminaires will be primarily determined by the quality and style of the architectural and interior design detailing and materials. While the pendant fluorescents are highly visible, in most situations their visibility is best minimized by selecting a color/material that blends with the ceiling. The desk lamps, while not visually important to the room as a whole, should be carefully selected to create the desired ambience for conversation.

Chapter 12 HOSPITALITY LIGHTING DESIGN

The hospitality business involves serving people and giving them enjoyment. From restaurants to hotels, resorts, and even theme parks, facilities are designed with the intent of transporting guests from the world of the ordinary to a special time and place.

Lighting design for hospitality projects is, along with retail lighting, the most demanding. Many of the spaces are designed to be visually interesting or intriguing; others are highly themed, more like stage sets than rooms. It is generally important to create drama and sparkle to enhance the effects of the space.

One of the challenges of hospitality lighting is to create adequate task light while achieving the necessary style, theme, and drama. For some demanding tasks, such as gaming tables in a casino, where illumination levels must be high and glare control is critical for players, dealers, and video surveillance cameras. It is important to identify the visual tasks, design illumination for them, and then work the task lighting into an overall program of lighting design that meets the requirements of the project. Lighting designs for these projects employ layered lighting designs out of necessity; the ambient light is the apparent light source, while concealed architectural lighting often provides the task illumination.

A classic hospitality lighting problem is the illumination of tabletops in restaurants. Diners must be able to read menus and see their food, but not at the expense of atmosphere. Designers often spotlight each table, install a table lamp on the adjacent wall, or hang a pendant over the table. But because tables move, many restaurateurs prefer candles or battery-powered table lamps, neither of which work as well but provide greater versatility and maintain the atmosphere. The choice requires thoughtful discussion with the people who will eventually operate and manage the restaurant.

Most hospitality facilities are designed specifically for apparent use; a hotel lobby will always be a lobby, and a restaurant will remain a restaurant. Flexibility is needed rather in exhibition halls, ballrooms, meeting rooms, and conference centers, where rearranging seating, partitions, and lighting schemes is important. In general, hospitality facilities are not renovated without a relatively complete replacement of lighting systems, so the long-term flexibility of lighting with respect to reconfiguration is minimal.

Most hospitality designs rely heavily on decorative chandeliers, sconces, pendants, table lamps, floor lamps, and other highly styled lights that play a critical role in interior design. Because of this, decorative lighting is commonly part of the furniture, fixtures, and equipment (FF&E) budget and specified by the interior designer, whereas architectural lighting in the same space is part of the construction budget and specified by the architect, engineer, or lighting designer. Coordination among professionals is critical in these spaces because the actual lighting design is a combined effort.

A variety of ceiling types is used in hospitality spaces, ranging from ordinary acoustic tile and gypsum wallboard to decorative and ornamental ceilings. Some spaces may not have a finished ceiling at all, as when the character of a loft or club is desired. Ceilings are critical to lighting, and it is important that proposed lighting designs be checked against the ceiling system for compatibility. Especially in hotels and other large spaces, the ceiling can become a platform for a multitude of building functions; lighting systems should take precedence to make sure the lighting works properly.

Some hospitality spaces, such as conference centers, hotel ballrooms and exhibition halls, and restaurants and bars with stages are designed with both architectural lighting and performance lighting systems. Performance lighting systems are often simple, employing track lighting and separate dimming channels to permit dramatic illumination of a solo performer, small group, or keynote speaker. A few spaces require more complex theatrical systems; these designs generally call for professional entertainment lighting assistance. But a professional lighting designer or an enlightened engineer, interior designer, or architect can execute many designs.

Because of the huge variation in options, viable designs are myriad. But, as with offices, the best solution to a particular problem generally flows from the interior design or interior architecture, which sets the style and mood of the space. *Layered lighting* is best because it builds the design on the decorative lighting selections that are of necessity present from the beginning. The challenge of the lighting design is to add task, focal, and ambient light in a manner that completes the illumination of the space without the design appearing too busy or contrived.

This suggests the following overall approach to the problem. First, allow the interior designer or architect to develop the concept completely, including his or her own impressions of the proper lighting. Then identify all of the visual tasks. Take into account both guests and employees, remembering that sometimes the two groups have different needs. Next, determine whether or not the decorative lighting provides task illumination and add it for the tasks not properly illuminated. Repeat the process for focal lighting.

The hardest part of layered lighting for the hospitality interior is determining to what extent ambient light must also be added. For example, in traditional spaces the decorative lighting consists mostly of ceiling-mounted chandeliers, pendants, and ceiling lights. Traditional chandeliers tend to glare, so a good lighting design often dims these lights and adds hidden ambient light, such as cove light, to compensate for their deficiencies. In more contemporary designs, the chandeliers can be designed to deliver mostly uplight, in which case additional ambient illumination may not be required.

Task and focal lighting can also be difficult. The interior design may prevent lights from being located in necessary spots. Stringent interior styling may limit the number of choices. Even if budget is not a limitation, style and design may prove difficult challenges. After all, the electric lamp is a little over a century old, and architecture and interior design is much older and more entrenched.

As a result, modern hospitality lighting tends to be a mixture of decorative lighting and architectural lighting, with architecturally neutral lighting techniques like cove lighting, accent lighting and downlighting playing a major role in providing task, focal, and ambient lighting. Energy codes apply to hospitality spaces; the ability to employ fluorescent lighting in nondescript architectural lighting permits the traditional luminaires to use incandescent lamps and still meet the energy code.

In fact, overall compliance with energy codes has become a major challenge for designers of hospitality projects. For instance, a crystal chandelier cannot be replicated by a fluorescent source—at least not yet. The twinkle quality of an incandescent filament and the natural warming of incandescent lights when dimmed are critical to creating atmosphere and mood. The layered approach to lighting design is essential here. Conserve wherever possible so the overall building design complies with the code.

A significant percentage of the hospitality industry is hotels and motels, and designing the lighting for guest quarters requires a thoughtful combination of residential and commercial lighting techniques. Most energy codes do not limit lighting in guest quarters (although they do apply in corridors and lobbies). Because the design is repeated dozens of times in each property, designers often must use inexpensive, low-maintenance, energy-efficient products that are durable yet appear homelike to the guest. Such decisions require thinking as a guest—for instance, guests are more apt to dislike a compact fluorescent table lamp than an incandescent one because they probably do not have compact fluorescent lamps at home. Few guests appreciate the energy efficiency of the compact fluorescent; most see the fluorescent lamp as a cost-cutting move by the hotel and take offense. (A few guests know that compact fluorescent lamps are costly and steal the lamp!)

The case studies in this chapter represent four typical spaces and functions. The examples are relatively basic in order to make the lighting design issues easily understood. These issues are fundamental and can be translated to other settings and to varying interior designs and styles.

CASE STUDY 12

Restaurant Lighting

Perhaps the most important attribute of lighting in a restaurant is its ability to create character or ambience. This goal generally goes hand in hand with the interior design of the restaurant, which often is intended to express a particular mood or theme. The lighting design is based on answers to the following questions:

Is the restaurant themed? This means that the restaurant's interior design is almost theatrical, such as a seafood restaurant meant to look like a fisherman's wharf or a beef house meant to look like an old-time English country restaurant. In a themed restaurant, the tendency is to use a lot of themed decorative lights, such as lanterns, pendants, and chandeliers. A current style in restaurant design is to use custom glass chandeliers or other exotic lighting techniques in trendy designs.

Is the restaurant for families, groups, or couples? While couples tend to prefer a romantic atmosphere, groups and families prefer more general light. In other words, candlelight dinners, which use dramatic lighting techniques, should be reserved for fine dining, and the more general the menu, the less dramatic the lighting should be.

Is the restaurant for dining or for fast food? Fast-food restaurants can employ low-cost fluorescent lighting, but the finer the dining, the more important it is to use incandescent or halogen lighting. The fast-food restaurant looks right with a relatively high level of even illumination, while the fine dining restaurant should have layers of lighting and contrast between task and ambient illumination levels.

The primary visual task in lighting a restaurant is the dining table. In a fine dining restaurant, traditional designs still use candles, but electric illumination can do a much better job without ruining the ambience. Typically, a dining table is illuminated with a low-voltage spotlight. A low-wattage MR16 or PAR36 lamp is generally used. The light is concentrated on the table for both functional and dramatic reasons.

In a family-style restaurant, general lighting evenly illuminates the tables, the seats, and the whole area. Pendant lights over the tables are both logical and traditional, but their light should not be carefully controlled.

The secondary visual tasks in a restaurant may include:

- The hostess or *maître d'hôtel* station
- Waiter stations
- Access to rest rooms, service areas, and the kitchen
- Cashier
- Displays such as featured dishes or desserts
- Serving lines, salad bars, and dessert bars
- Bars for beverages

Each of these must be illuminated at an appropriate level. Some are very important, such as a beverage bar, which is generally expected to be attractive as well as lighted for the tasks of making drinks—and, of course, consuming them.

The challenge of most restaurant designs is to use architectural lighting to ensure proper lighting and to introduce decorative lighting as needed to ensure that it is in the right place and reinforces the theme or style of the restaurant. A good design approach is to use sconces, chandeliers, or pendants to create eye-level glow.

The final task of lighting is to create or reinforce style, ambience, or aesthetics. Restaurants are among the few places where lighting can show off and make a powerful statement. From ornate and attractive luminaires to washes of color and special effects, restaurant lighting can be a terrific venue in which to use light itself as a design medium.

In the figures at the top of page 107, the restaurant is a traditional dining room and bar. We have decided that it should be a fine dining restaurant catering to couples and small parties. The primary task, table lighting, is addressed in two ways:

1. By a table lamp at each fixed table. The lamp is attached to the table and power is fed from the wall. This lamp also provides eye-level glow.
2. By low-voltage pin spots on the other tables.

Low-voltage pin spots also illuminate the waiter station, the bar top, and the back bar top. The principal task layer is complete. The design challenge remains to provide focal lighting, ambient lighting, and decorative lighting—keeping in mind that table lamps are already part of the design.

To provide focal lighting, adjustable accent lights illuminate the back bar and bar wall, which is the only major vertical surface in the space. To maintain the table lamp theme, lamps similar to those on the tables are located along

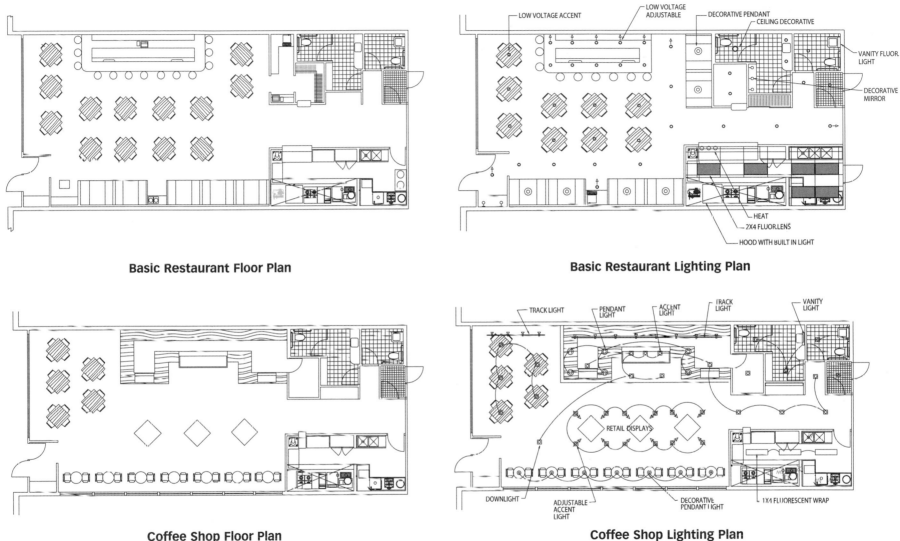

Basic Restaurant Floor Plan

Basic Restaurant Lighting Plan

Coffee Shop Floor Plan

Coffee Shop Lighting Plan

the bar top. Fluorescent lights are built into the back bar to uplight the bottles on the bar.

To illuminate the hall leading to the rest rooms, recessed downlights keep the area dim and dramatic. Inside the rest rooms, downlights illuminating the vanities and toilets also appear dramatic and mysterious, yet provide enough light for the space.

A preset dimming system is generally recommended for restaurants because different light levels are needed for day, evening, and night—and cleanup. A preset system ensures that the settings are consistent no matter who pushes the button.

In the figures directly above, the same room is designed as a coffee bar. Instead of fixed tables and banquette seating, movable tables are intermixed

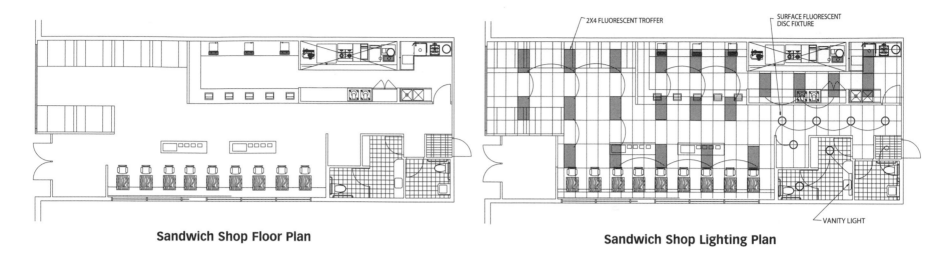

Sandwich Shop Floor Plan

Sandwich Shop Lighting Plan

with movable displays. This floor plan is similar to the design used by a popular chain of coffeehouses. The key to the design is recognizing that the task of lighting the bar counter is the most important because this restaurant is also a retail store. The back bar has a menu board that must be lighted.

The design uses themed ornamental pendant lights over the counter for task light, decorative light, and eye-level glow. The distinctive color and shape of the light attract passersby through the window. The pendant lights can be compact fluorescent or incandescent depending on energy concerns.

Providing both task light and focal light, a lighting track located over the bar work area illuminates the back bar and the menu board and highlights displays on the back bar wall. Downlights over the tables and floor displays provide task light. Lighting for the rest room hall and restrooms is more ordinary, with a downlight for the hall, vanity lights over the sinks, and decorative ceiling drums over the stall area. This design can use a great deal of fluorescent lighting and still look the same.

A simple dimming system should be used to change the overall brightness of the shop between day and night. A day setting, which is often brighter and

cheerier, will drive away those looking for a more dramatic space in the evening.

In the figures above, the restaurant is now a fast-food house with a serving bar. This plan is similar to that used by a chain of sandwich houses. Pendant lights are used over the fixed seating, both for task illumination and for eye-level glow. Because they are in front of the windows, they also help attract passersby. With careful selection, these pendant lights can be compact fluorescent as well as incandescent.

As in the coffee shop, the sandwich bar/counter is the primary task area. Because this is a fast-food facility, low-cost fluorescent troffers provide general illumination throughout the bar area and most of the restaurant. This yields enough light to obviate the need for additional focal light for the menu board. Likewise, simple lighting is used for the rest rooms both to save money and to maintain a modest appearance.

Dimming controls for this use might not even be needed. The bright light desired by day also serves as a beacon to attract customers at night. Consider this decision carefully; a more dramatic night setting may be desirable if it suits business better.

CASE STUDY 13

Hotel Lobby Lighting

A hotel lobby gives a first impression about the hotel. Style, appearance, and aesthetics are dominant considerations. Decorative lighting is usually critical in the success of a hotel lobby, even for a modest hotel.

The lobby also presents a few visual tasks. The most important is generally the illumination of the desks, including registration, concierge, and bell station.

The front desk employs computers, which makes the lighting design as challenging as for a computer workstation. Relatively high light levels must be provided locally, while the balance of the lobby must be warm, friendly, and welcoming.

Other visual tasks in a lobby generally involve seating areas, where casual reading and socializing occur.

In the following figures, a hotel lobby includes all of these elements. The style is a traditional design using chandeliers, table lamps, and gentle lighting details featuring warm-toned light.

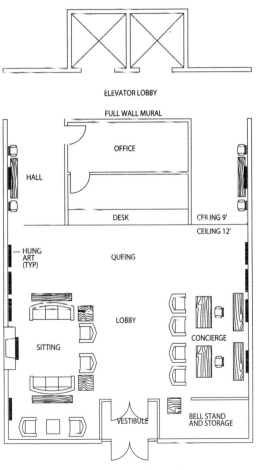

Hotel Lobby Floor Plan

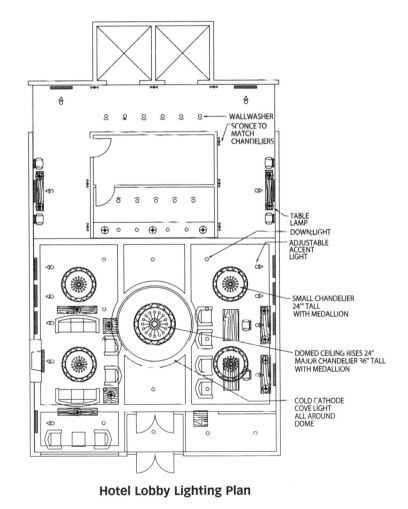

Hotel Lobby Lighting Plan

Most of the lighting for this type of space is traditional and is generally chosen by the interior designer or architect. The center of the ceiling is dominated by an overscale chandelier. Smaller chandeliers are used on each side of it, and matching sconces are used on the walls near the entry and behind the front desk. Table lamps provide task lighting and eye-level glow for the space.

Many would think this space was properly illuminated by traditional nonlayered design. However, the main tasks would actually be poorly illuminated because chandeliers, sconces, and table lamps tend to diffuse light, with a resulting lack of task illumination and drama. The following architectural light sources are added:

- Downlights over the desks, especially the transaction surface
- Undershelf task lights for the desk work surfaces
- Cove lighting for the main ceiling dome, even though a chandelier is in it
- Accent lights for artwork on the walls
- Downlights throughout the main space for drama and task light for reading

A dimming system might be added to enhance the drama of the space. Most interiors require additional illumination during the day because people coming in from outside are adapted to bright light; dimming by night creates a warmer and more dramatic space.

CASE STUDY 14

Guest Room Lighting

This example is representative of most new ordinary guest rooms in hotels throughout the world, especially in North America. The room is a simple rectangle without a suspended ceiling, and finishes applied to the walls and ceiling. This generally precludes ceiling-mounted and recessed lighting in the bedroom area. However, the toilet and entry usually feature a slightly lower dropped ceiling, permitting ceiling lights in these areas only.

The hotel guest room must be designed to convey a residential feeling, but it must also be easy to maintain and should not be easily broken or damaged. Because ceiling-mounted lights can't be used in the bedroom, table lamps and wall-mounted lamps are common solutions. Usually the challenge is to provide enough lamps with enough light output to satisfy the tasks.

The visual tasks in most guest rooms are obvious and relatively simple. As in the typical guest room shown here, they are as follows:

- Provide light at the bathroom vanity for shaving, makeup, and bathing.
- Provide entry hall illumination adequate to illuminate the path and, usually, the closet or clothes storage area.
- Provide light by the side of each bed. Other than the bath vanity light, inadequate illumination for bed reading is the most common complaint about lighting by hotel guests.
- Provide light for the desk or worktable.
- Provide light for the reading chair.
- Provide ambient lighting if needed for the rest of the room to avoid it seeming dimly lighted.

Cost is usually a significant concern in hotel design because each light is then multiplied by dozens or even hundreds of rooms. Better hotels sometimes add the following separately lighted tasks:

- A separate shower light, which tends to permit a more attractive vanity light
- A separate closet light, often turned on by a hinge switch or motion sensor
- A night light for the toilet room

Older rooms, premium rooms, and suites often have suspended ceilings and are therefore not limited by the typical constraints of ceiling structure. In these cases, residential lighting techniques are generally preferred; consult chapter 10.

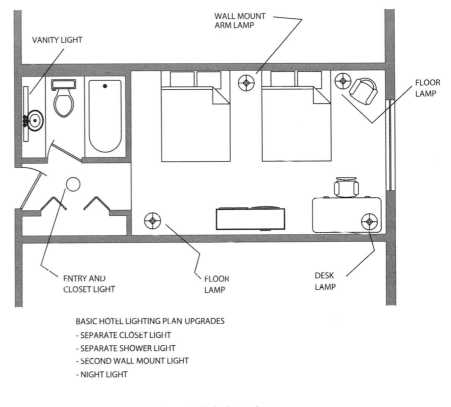

BASIC HOTEL LIGHTING PLAN UPGRADES
- SEPARATE CLOSET LIGHT
- SEPARATE SHOWER LIGHT
- SECOND WALL MOUNT LIGHT
- NIGHT LIGHT

Guest Room Lighting Plan

The lighting design solution shown here addresses the visual tasks in the following manner:

1. A vanity light mounted above the mirror illuminates the entire bathroom. It is probably a good idea to use at least two 4' fluorescent lamps in a surface-mounted lensed luminaire. Many hotels still prefer to construct a light box over the vanity, often with a lens or eggcrate louver, which tends to require two lamps.
2. A ceiling surface luminaire is mounted in the entry. It distributes light widely, which is especially needed to illuminate the closet.

3. A lamp is mounted on the wall between the beds. This lamp usually has two separate bulbs and shades, permitting light for either or both beds. This lamp is usually portable, but plugged into the wall.
4. Table and floor lamps are located near each task.

Switching is usually kept as simple as possible: a switch at the entry door for the hall light and a switch just inside the bathroom door for the vanity light. All other lights are switched at the lamp. A better switching layout might be used, such as a three-way switch for the hall light at the bedside. A master lighting switch at the entry door is sometimes also used to encourage guests to turn off all lights when leaving, but most hoteliers believe that guests don't understand this feature and fail to use it effectively.

The interior designer typically chooses all luminaires, the style of which should be consistent with the interior design and finishes. Light-colored finishes and light linen or plastic shades are strongly recommended to prevent the room from seeming dark.

For an energy-efficient design, use T-8 fluorescent lamps and an electronic ballast for the vanity light and compact fluorescent lamps in the ceiling light and all portable lights. Some premium hotels use only incandescent lamps in the guest rooms and expect housekeeping personnel to change bulbs. However, with the rising costs of energy and wages, many three- and four-star hotels now use compact fluorescent lamps extensively.

CASE STUDY 15
Hotel Ballroom

A ballroom in a hotel is a multipurpose room; it serves as a banquet hall, exhibit hall, convention hall, meeting room, recital room, theater, showroom, classroom, reception hall, church, studio—and, on occasion, it actually serves as a ballroom. The types of events are limited only by the size of the room and the height of the ceiling. Most ballrooms can be divided into segments in which several uses can occur simultaneously.

It is not possible to identify all of the potential visual tasks, nor is it possible to illuminate all of them correctly. The best approach is to determine the visual tasks common to ballroom functions and to make both permanent and flexible provisions to illuminate them. Permanent lighting is generally needed to support the following tasks:

- IESNA Category D tasks throughout the space. The D task is typical office paperwork. By providing general lighting of 30–40 fc, it is possible to use the room as a meeting room, conference room, or classroom without adding portable or special lighting.

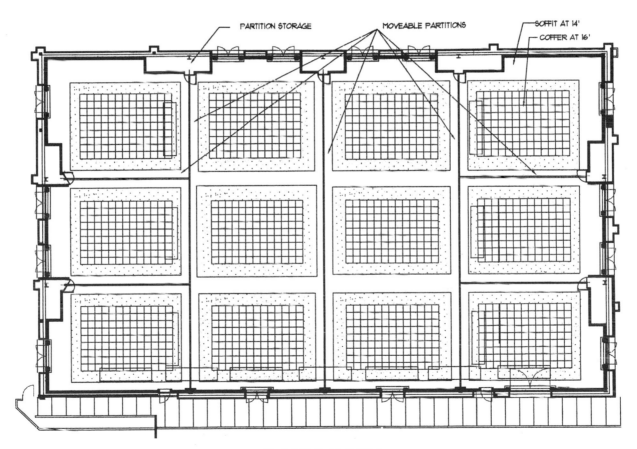

Hotel Ballroom Plan

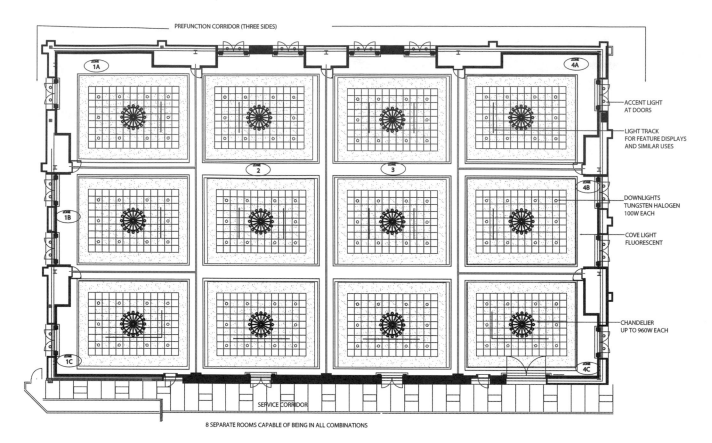

PREFUNCTION CORRIDOR (THREE SIDES)

ACCENT LIGHT
AT DOORS

LIGHT TRACK
FOR FEATURE DISPLAYS
AND SIMILAR USES

DOWNLIGHTS
TUNGSTEN HALOGEN
100W EACH

COVE LIGHT
FLUORESCENT

CHANDELIER
UP TO 960W EACH

SERVICE CORRIDOR

8 SEPARATE ROOMS CAPABLE OF BEING IN ALL COMBINATIONS

Hotel Ballroom Ceiling

- By providing IESNA D lighting levels, you also provide ambient and general illumination for trade shows, exhibits, and other uses of the room to which task or focal lighting, if needed, can be added.
- IESNA Category B tasks throughout the space, which is 5–10 fc, generally with good glare control and excellent aesthetics. This permits the use of the room for dining and formal events, such as receptions, banquets, and dancing.
- A dimmable house lighting system that can provide up to 5 fc of controlled illumination (preferably downlighting) for audience seating and audiovisual note-taking lighting.

In addition, a good design permits the installation of temporary or portable lighting equipment to illuminate head tables, speaker podiums, exhibits and displays, performance groups and stages, and other occasional special tasks. In modest designs, this equipment might employ track lighting or canopy monopoints. In larger professional establishments, such as a 1200-room convention hotel in a major city, permanent wiring and rigging for theatrical lighting may be necessary.

The design of a specific hotel may require additional task lighting. For instance, lighting for entry and exit doors, lighting for artwork, and other special tasks should be identified.

In the preceding figures, a hotel ballroom includes all of these elements. The style is Old Southwest, which suggests a traditional design using wrought-iron chandeliers and sconces. This ballroom is divisible into eight adjacent rooms. The structural system produces logical bays with a repeating ceiling pattern. The diverse tasks lend themselves naturally to the layered lighting approach.

LAYER 1: AMBIENT/GENERAL LIGHTING

The most difficult part of designing ballroom lighting is to determine an ambient layer or general lighting system capable of providing at least 25–30 fc. The three most common methods are:

1. Create ceiling coffers with cove lighting. This method is architecturally neutral and permits the use of switched or dimmed fluorescent general light and regular linear fluorescent lamps.
2. Employ chandeliers with a major (often concealed) uplight component. This method also permits the use of fluorescent uplight, although the less efficient compact fluorescent lamps must be employed.
3. Increasing the light output of chandeliers and downlights to reach the required light levels. This method tends to cost the least, but it is the most inefficient use of energy.

Our design is to employ ceiling coffers with a fluorescent cove lighting system using T8 lamps. We can choose either 2700K or 3000K lamps, depending on the ambient quality we want to achieve. The system uses cove light fixtures, and it can be dimmed or switched. It produces about 30 fc.

LAYER 2: DECORATIVE

The chandeliers are needed for interior design and authenticity. Using an over-scale chandelier with many low-wattage incandescent lamps is typical; the total watts of chandelier lighting should not exceed 1 watt per square foot. Our design assumes 960 watts of chandeliers in each 1400 square-foot ballroom bay. We estimate that the design will produce about 5 or 6 fc.

LAYER 3: TASK

Downlights serve many of the tasks, and their tendency to create dramatic spaces is an aesthetic bonus. Incandescent or halogen downlights are used, designed to produce 8–10 fc of average light. By using A-lamp downlights, broader and more even light is provided; use of PAR downlights tends to pool light which can be more dramatic and often better for house lighting.

LAYER 4: FOCAL

Track lighting is located 6–10 feet in front of where a head table, speaker podium, or similar common key location would be set up in the room. This layout is tricky, because this key location must be identified for every combination of partition settings.

CONTROLS

Usually, ballrooms have full-fledged dimming systems that permit each group of lights in each bay to be dimmed independently of other bays and lights. Some ballrooms even have control rooms where the architectural dimming controls can be managed from a console that also controls theatrical lighting. In simpler ballrooms, a preset dimming system permits the choice of four or more scenes, or off, in each partitioned space. These systems have separate control circuits for each layer.

The dimming and control system must be designed and circuited so that it can operate the lights correctly in each partition setting. Modern dimming systems have partition switches that automatically reconfigure the dimming system depending on the partition arrangement. In addition, the dimming system is usually connected to an emergency generator source; in the event of a power failure, some lights will automatically come to full brightness relatively quickly under emergency power.

Chapter 13

HEALTH CARE/INSTITUTIONAL LIGHTING DESIGN

Health care facilities are challenging for the lighting designer because of the wide variety of tasks performed and the constant change and evolution. Perhaps even more challenging is meeting the lighting needs of a wide range of ages, from newborn infants to seniors. With an increasingly aging population, lighting must be designed with the visual difficulties of an active elderly population in mind. Further, because of the emphasis on health, there is an increased awareness of photobiological issues such as Seasonal Affective Disorder (SAD), circadian rhythms, and ways in which lighting design can be either beneficial or problematic.

The greatest challenge is probably to provide competent, energy-efficient, and cost-effective lighting that does not contribute to the institutional appearance traditionally attributed to hospitals and doctors' offices. Low-cost fluorescent lighting systems are increasingly less acceptable, and most new hospitals, senior living facilities, and clinics now require lighting design that exceeds the quality standards of office buildings and hotels.

Unlike in hotels, theme and style are generally not important. Most hospitals, clinics, and medical offices employ a standard palette of interior finishes that appear modern, clean, and simple, if not a bit bland. Contemporary architectural and decorative lighting systems are easily incorporated, giving the lighting designer a relatively wide choice among lighting fixtures that use fluorescent and compact fluorescent sources. Other than a few codes and standards, lighting design can be creative as long as the visual tasks are properly addressed.

Senior living and care centers are different because they are more like hotels or apartment buildings. A strong theme might be used for interiors to set the facility apart from its competitors. Portable lighting, like floor lamps and table lamps, reinforces a residential theme. After all, seniors want to live in a home, not an institution.

Health care facilities include a number of spaces in which demanding visual tasks are important. Operating rooms and laboratories spring to mind, but an even larger number of procedure rooms and special spaces exist where lighting requirements are equally critical. Most operating rooms and some procedure rooms, such as dentists' offices, employ specialized task lights that are usually specified by health care equipment specialists and supplied by equipment companies rather than lighting companies. But the examination lights in patient bedrooms and many other places are part of the general lighting design.

Health care facilities feature spaces where specific aspects of lighting must be controlled especially well. For instance, in radiological suites, low levels of indirect lighting are preferred to prevent exposing X-ray film to light. In nurseries, newborns' eyes must be shielded from direct light. In magnetic resonance imaging (MRI) suites, lighting must be designed to prevent radio frequency interference (RFI). In dental procedure rooms, lighting should have high color temperature and high CRI to enable accurate color matching of crown work.

The majority of health care facilities require conventional lighting as well— for offices, cafeterias, hallways, meeting rooms, lobbies, waiting rooms, and similar spaces that are also found in buildings of conventional usage. Most of these spaces appear to have no special lighting requirements. However, unlike in office buildings, where you can assume that most building users are working-age people with normal eyesight, health care facilities have a high population of patients who are older or have disabilities, and it is important to remember that older eyes and most vision defects benefit from higher light levels. The key is to increase lighting levels over office building standards, but not so much as to cause glare or discomfort.

Daylighting is highly desirable in health facilities for several reasons. Other than energy efficiency, its primary benefit is the strengthening of circadian rhythms, which has been shown to aid the healing process and, in older persons, to aid in overall health and vitality. Another important attribute of daylight is color rendering, which can be useful in dental procedure rooms and other spaces where color matching is critical. Remember, however, that the color-rendering properties of daylight are generally lost when modern glazing systems are used.

The use of decorative lighting in health care historically has been minimal and reserved almost exclusively for waiting rooms. However, modern designers often use traditional and decorative lighting, including chandeliers, sconces, pendants, and floor and table lamps as part of an overall scheme to deinstitutionalize the feel of the institution. Given that the cost of maintenance is a major concern, compact fluorescents should be used with decorative lighting in health care settings whenever possible.

Most ceilings in health care institutions use acoustic tile. Tile permits easy access to the ceiling plenum; with the number of services above the ceiling—plumbing, sprinklers, heating, venting, and air conditioning (HVAC), medical gases, data lines—access is a primary concern. Hard ceilings like gypsum wallboard are rarely used because they require access panels that detract from the appearance of the ceiling and add cost. Unusual ceiling types are uncommon because of cleanliness and health concerns.

Flexible lighting designs are rarely used in health care facilities because lights are not often changed or relocated, with the exception of surgical and exam lights and lighting for art collections, gift shops, and a few other minor areas. To the contrary, a good health care design is fixed, durable, and uses energy-efficient light sources that last a long time. Fluorescent lamps are preferred; a good design uses just a few lamp types, which simplifies stocking and replacement.

Some health care facilities lend themselves to general lighting. Ignoring portable and fixed examination and surgical lights, the following spaces tend to require general illumination: treatment and exam rooms, toilets, working corridors, operating and surgical rooms, scrub-down rooms, kitchens, storage rooms, intensive care suites, procedure rooms, and laboratories. This is because of the relatively large portion of the space in which tasks may occur and, in some cases, the potential for interference with procedures and emergency response.

But a large number of spaces in the health care setting can employ layered lighting principles. Because layered lighting permits decorative lighting, it is easy to incorporate simple and effective decorative lighting and still meet overall illumination and energy requirements. This approach works best in offices, lobbies, waiting rooms, patient corridors, nursing stations, and libraries. In fact, a trend in health care design is to introduce decorative lighting as a key element in interior design, serving to deinstitutionalize adding sparkle, color, and accent to these spaces.

A major benefit of layered lighting is in allowing different lighting levels by day and night. The general lighting within the nursing environment by day should probably be bright, providing both ample task lighting and a daytime sense of activity. At night, however, bright lights can interfere with the sleeping cycle of patients; by extinguishing ambient lights and dimming task lights, a comfortable night environment for both nurses and patients can be created. The patient bedroom is an especially complex lighting problem. Most of the time, the lighting of the patient room should be as residential as possible. This is particularly important in birthing suites and senior living quarters, where the usual intent is for the space to look and feel like a home. Soft ambient light permits easy movement about the room, and task lights permit reading in the bed and in nearby chairs. At night, a very low light level permits nurses to check on patients but does not interfere with sleep. But during an examination of the patient, high light levels throughout the bed area can be energized at the flick of a switch.

Codes can play a limiting role in health care design. Health care design regulations, which vary by state in the United States (and elsewhere), require certain foot-candle levels in various facility types. For instance, in Oregon, the laws regulating senior care facilities specify foot-candle requirements for various rooms and spaces. In California, hospitals and senior care facilities are regulated by the Office of the State Architect, whose requirements must be met. It is good practice to contact the regulating authorities before proceeding with a design.

The Americans with Disabilities Act (ADA) specifies critical requirements for lighting, especially in limiting wall-mounted light projections to 4" unless the light is 80" or more above the floor. Furthermore, because the focus of the ADA is accessibility, the health care designer should consider every aspect of lighting carefully, keeping in mind the limited eyesight and mobility of many facility users. For instance, locate easy-to-use light switches where they can be reached by people seated in a wheelchair.

The case studies in this chapter represent three of the most common spaces and functions. The examples presented are relatively basic in order to make the lighting design issues easily understood. These lighting design issues are fundamental and can be translated to other settings and to varying interior designs and styles.

CASE STUDY 16

Patient Room Lighting

This example represents current trends and issues in private patient care rooms. The ceilings in the bedroom and the bath are acoustical tile, and the finishes are typical for health care facilities, including vinyl wall coverings.

As in a hotel guest room, a residential feeling is desirable, but this space features significantly more demanding tasks and related issues. Ceiling-mounted and wall-mounted lights can be used everywhere. Table lamps and hotel-like wall-mounted arm lamps are generally not wanted because of interference with patient beds, IV stands, privacy curtains, and crash carts.

The visual tasks in the patient bedroom include the following:

- The patient must have task light for reading in bed.
- Doctors and nurses must have examination light that provides a great deal of illumination all around the patient.

- The patient needs light at the bathroom vanity for shaving, makeup, and bathing.
- The patients needs lighting at the shower or tub.
- Medical personnel need light at the nursing sink and other work areas.
- Guests should have light at the desk and reading locations.
- Medical personnel need a night-light that permits access to the patient without disturbing sleep.
- Patients, medical personnel, and cleaning personnel need ambient lighting in the rest of the room both for cleaning and for visual comfort.

The lighting for the patient bed area is a key decision. A luminaire that is entirely recessed in the ceiling may be used, or a wall-mounted luminaire, or a combination of wall and ceiling luminaires. Because this lighting system serves three tasks (patient reading, medical examination, and ambient room light), some of the lights will serve two or three independent functions. These lights are highly specialized and designed specifically for the health care market. However, sometimes the designer can employ other solutions.

Patient Room

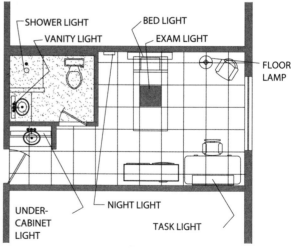

BASIC PATIENT ROOM (SINGLE BED PRIVATE ROOM)

OPTIONS
- INTEGRATED BED LIGHT/EXAM LIGHT WALL MOUNTED
- INTEGRATED BED LIGHT/ EXAM LIGHT CEILING RECESSED MOUNTED

Patient Room Lighting

The lighting design solution shown here addresses the visual tasks in the following manner:

- A wall-mounted two-function patient bed light and a ceiling-mounted exam light are traditional selections that allow some flexibility in choosing the bed light system, which provides downlight for reading and uplight for ambient light. Both lights are switched with relays connected to the bed management system.
- The overhead exam light is a 2' X 2' fluorescent with two 32-watt lamps.
- A table or floor lamp provides task light for the guest chair. This lamp is far enough away from the bed to not interfere with medical activity. It is probably compact fluorescent in keeping with the energy efficiency and relamping standards needed for a hospital.
- A wall-mounted fluorescent task light illuminates the desk.
- A wall-mounted fluorescent vanity light illuminates the vanity and mirror area and provides general illumination in the toilet room.
- A separate shower light provides shower stall lighting.
- An undercabinet fluorescent task light illuminates the work area near the entry.

- A compact fluorescent night-light located out of the patient's line of sight illuminates the floor near the bed.

Switching is as simple as possible. There is a switch at the entry door for the task light and switches just inside the bathroom door for the vanity light and shower light. The exam light is switched on the wall near the patient bed. There is a switch on the wall above the desk; the lamp by the chair has its own switch. The combination up- and down-light over the bed is controlled by the bed control system, which is connected to the lighting system with relays.

Style is usually a secondary decision, as most hospital finishes are modern and neutral. The patient wall light offers an opportunity to introduce color and style, although most of the products on the market look out of date, and grace the interior with the finest faux walnut vinyl fascia.

An energy-efficient design using T-8 fluorescent lamps in most of the luminaires is essential, as are compact fluorescent lamps in the shower light, night-light, and floor lamp. Dimming could be of benefit in some of the lighting to improve the ability to create a restful environment.

CASE STUDY 17
Examination Room Lighting

Examination rooms are found in hospitals, clinics, and other medical and dental facilities. They are general-purpose rooms, so some of the principles that apply to them can also be used for some types of treatment and therapy rooms. Usually the ceilings are acoustical tile, and the finishes are typical for health care facilities, including vinyl wall coverings.

An examination room generally has an exam bed or chair, depending on the facility and practice. Illuminating this is the primary task of the lighting design. While specific procedures may require a special high-intensity light, such as a dentist's light or surgical light, most exam rooms utilize overhead lighting. For general medical practice the visual tasks may be less demanding, with lower light-level requirements. In most rooms, however, it is preferable to have adequate light for more demanding examinations, which suggests a lighting level of 100 fc or more. Because medical tasks may involve the sides of the body as well as the upper surface, overhead lights should be set slightly to the side of the patient bed or chair, suggesting at least two overhead lights rather than one for overall examinations.

In addition to the examination site, exam rooms often feature a counter where medicines or treatments are prepared; a high light level is desired there as well. This counter is typically beneath an overhead cabinet, so undercabinet lights are an obvious choice.

Finally, exam rooms sometimes include a desk surface for writing in patient records and prescription pads. This desk can have a more conventional or residential-style lamp or task light, which can help warm or personalize the room.

The lighting design solution shown in the following figures addresses the design requirements in the following manner:

This design uses two ceiling-mounted recessed troffers. This low-cost, conventional selection provides ample light for all exam purposes. Two-level switching of three lamp fixtures (two switches, one for the center lamp and one for the outer lamps of each luminaire) or dimming provides flexibility in

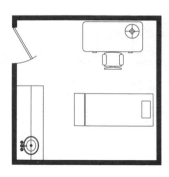

Exam Room Plan

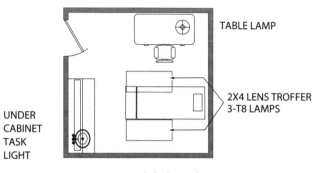

TABLE LAMP

2X4 LENS TROFFER
3-T8 LAMPS

UNDER CABINET TASK LIGHT

Exam Room Lighting Plan

light levels. An undercabinet light for the counter surface illuminates the task to over 100 fc with a single T-8 lamp.

A table lamp provides task light for the desk. In keeping with energy efficiency standards, it is probably compact fluorescent. The style can vary with the interior design.

Switching is as simple as possible. There are two switches (or a dimmer) at the entry door for the task lights and a switch just above the counter for the undercabinet light. The desk lamp has its own switch.

CASE STUDY 18

Classroom Lighting

Classrooms are the primary design problem for schools, but they also are found in office buildings, corporate headquarters, hospitals, and many other building types. Classrooms vary in their lighting requirements as more become electronic.

A traditional classroom is still common for the majority of primary, secondary, and higher-education classrooms. The invasion of computers is not as critical in designing classrooms as once thought. Traditional concerns for illumination of deskwork and vertical surfaces still take priority. The modern challenge is to provide high-quality lighting and low-energy use while remaining within the budget. Daylighting is especially important; recent studies have shown that daylighted classrooms contribute to improved learning as measured by standardized tests.

From a lighting standpoint, there are two special types of classrooms:

1. Rooms in which the classic arts, especially painting and sculpture, are taught and practiced
2. Rooms in which computer arts and sciences are taught and practiced

A conventional classroom is designed with tasks throughout the space. In addition to tasks performed at classroom seats, visual tasks occur at the chalkboard, bulletin boards, and other vertical display surfaces as well as in special study areas. General illumination typically is used to ensure adequate illumination throughout the classroom, with particular attention paid to lighting systems that produce relatively high vertical surface illumination and, if possible, ceiling illumination for comfort and balance of brightness. Most traditional tasks are considered properly illuminated with 30–50 fc of electric lighting.

The design shown in the figure at the right is a classroom design that employs direct-indirect fluorescent luminaires specifically designed for classrooms. It is simple and works well, illuminating ceiling and wall surfaces while producing 40–50 fc evenly throughout the student desk area. The use of daylight dimming or other control strategies is important in classrooms, both to save energy and to enable flexibility.

The classic arts classroom is different. In addition to a higher lighting level (50+ fc), this classroom has critical needs with respect to the color of the light. Arts classrooms are often illuminated with a 5000K white light source, using

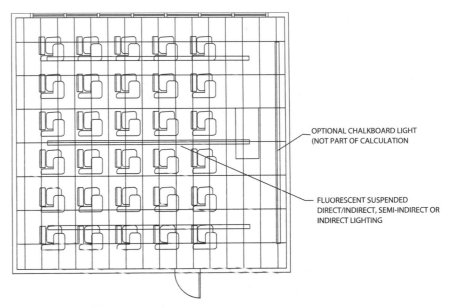

OPTIONAL CHALKBOARD LIGHT (NOT PART OF CALCULATION

FLUORESCENT SUSPENDED DIRECT/INDIRECT, SEMI-INDIRECT OR INDIRECT LIGHTING

CLASSROOM LIGHTING CALCULATION (RULES OF THUMB)
TRY TWO METHODS AND IF THEY GIVE SIMILAR RESULTS, YOU ARE PROBABLY CORRECT

USING THE WATTS PER SQUARE FOOT RULE OF THUMB
AREA = 960 SF
CLASSROOM (FROM CHART) = 0.8 TO 1.2 W/SF
PROVIDE 960 X 0.8 = 768 WATTS OF FLUORESCENT LIGHTING MINIMUM
PROVIDE 960 X 1.2 = 1152 WATTS OF FLUORESCENT LIGHTING MAXIMUM
WITH THREE ROWS OF FIXTURES 24 FEET LONG EACH = 72 FEET OF FIXTURES
768/72 = 10.6 WATTS PER FOOT OR MORE
1152/72 = 16 WATTS PER FOOT OR LESS

PER 4 FEET OF FIXTURE, BETWEEN 42.4 AND 64 WATTS
CHOOSE (1) F54T5HO LAMP PER 4' FIXTURE (54 WATTS) TOTAL OF 18 4-FOOT FIXTURES

SIMPLIFIED LUMEN METHOD
DESIRED FOOTCANDLE LEVEL = 50 FC
MULTIPLY X 2 =100
MULTIPLY BY AREA = 960 X 100 = 96000
USING F54T5HO LAMPS AT 5000 LUMENS EACH

NUMBER OF LAMPS REQUIRED = 96000/5000 = APPROXIMATELY 19-20
4-FOOT LONG FIXTURES

BOTH CALCULATIONS SUGGEST ABOUT 18–20 FIXTURES, SO THE DESIGN WORKS.

Classroom Lighting Plan

either natural daylighting or 5000K fluorescent lamps to simulate natural light. Color rendering at 5000K is more or less neutral, and artists are effectively free to make visual choices about color without concern for the color bias of most electric light sources.

An arts classroom may use industrial fluorescent luminaires that provide effective and efficient illumination with mounting heights of 10' to 16'. (A different lighting system might be used if the mounting height is above 16' or so.) The T-8 lamp system permits the use of 5000K lamps as well as more common 3000K, 3500K, or 4100K fluorescent lamps.

The electronic classroom is different as well. Computer displays can be affected by room light, so computer workspaces often require highly con-trolled lighting. Computer images projected onto screens are particularly sensitive to room lighting. The general nature of computer classrooms is a highly controlled lighting environment, with two or more layers of light and controls that permit optimizing the lighting system for specific teaching situations.

Another example of a nonconventional classroom is a graphic arts classroom in which students work on computers and interact with overhead video projections created by the instructor. The lighting design employs low-voltage track lights to illuminate the work surface; dark surfaces everywhere else prevent light inadvertently falling on screens and projections. Separate dimmers for the student work area and chalkboard area permit flexibility between video projections by the instructor and live chalkboard instruction.

Chapter 14 LIGHTING FOR STORES

Stores use—and their operators appreciate—lighting more than just about any other building type. In most cases, brightly lighted stores are more successful and desirable than dimly lighted ones. Lighting in stores not only illuminates products for sale but also plays a major role in store design and style, or theming.

The first and, some say, most important role of lighting in store design is to attract the eye. Lighting naturally does this through the brilliance and sparkle of lighting systems, but the effect is especially significant in a store. For example, in the design of a grocery store, the brilliance of ordinary fluorescent lights attracts the eye and tells shoppers that the store is open for business. In the visually competitive world of the mall, more dramatic lighting effects, such as moving lights, colored lights, and attractive luminaires, must be used to attract the attention of shoppers. Store windows constitute such an important opportunity that lighting them is an art form unto itself and akin to stage set lighting.

The second most important role of lighting in stores is to illuminate the merchandise. The most successful store designs provide illumination for all of the merchandise before highlighting feature displays. This Is true whether the store is designed to appear bright, using general illumination, or dramatic, using track or other types of display lighting.

The third most important job of lighting in stores is to excite the shopper. Excitement is part of the theme of the design, and the role of lighting may be substantial. Some ways in which to excite the shopper include:

- Dramatically lighting merchandise, especially feature displays
- Using luminaires whose strong style reinforces the theme of the architecture
- Using architectural lighting techniques like cove lighting and wallwashing to reveal or reinforce elements of the interior design or architecture
- Employing highly specialized lighting techniques such as fiber optics, theatrical lighting, neon, color-changing lights, and moving lights to energize the space or produce spectacular lighting effects

The fourth most important role of lighting in stores is to illuminate the work of storekeeping, including stocking, cleaning, and point of sale. For example, a classic solution to many store designs is to use highly styled pendant luminaires at the point of sale. This technique ensures adequate light for sales work, reinforces the store's theme, and functions as a wayfinder for shoppers.

The fifth and final role of lighting in stores is to reinforce the shopper's sense of value and price point. This has proven to be a delicate balance. For example, in a discount store, the lighting must appear inexpensive, or the shopper may feel out of place. Many grocery stores use bare-lamp strip lights, both for economy and to suggest that the store is competitively priced.

Recent research has found that daylighting dramatically increases sales when used in stores. If the store design allows, consider adding daylight via simple skylights or more complex architectural expressions. Remember to use many smaller skylights, just as you would use many luminaires rather than one big one.

A major difference between stores and other building types is that the merchandise often is displayed in the vertical plane rather than the more typical horizontal plane. As a result, lighting solutions must avoid concentrated downlight—unless, of course, the specific task is in the horizontal plane. General fluorescent downlighting is sufficiently diffuse to create good vertical light, but downlights using incandescent, compact fluorescent, or HID lamps tend to concentrate downlight too much.

Stores are regulated quite heavily by energy codes. In 2001, power density limits for grocery stores and big-box retail stores were about 1.5 watts/square foot (w/sf). The limits for other store types depend on the merchandise, with the highest permitted for jewelry stores and the like. The following examples are designed to meet energy codes in most states.

CASE STUDY 19
A Small Boutique

A large percentage of retail lighting is for small and medium-sized stores. In most cases, the store has a rectangular floor plan and is located in a row of similar-sized stores along a street or in a mall.

In most smaller stores, shelving displays are rarely ceiling-high, except at the walls. Instead, displays in the center of the store are often short shelving, freestanding merchandise, or flat gondola displays. The focus of the store design depends largely on the type of store. In the three examples below, you can see how the store layout and function affect task locations and lighting design.

The lighting design approach in a small store is especially important for store image and appeal. Basic, inexpensive fluorescent lighting and high light levels convey cost-consciousness. Decorative lighting fixtures, especially those with colored glass or other distinctive qualities, tend to give the store an identity. Dramatic architectural and track lighting give the store a sense of mystery

and quality. It is critically important to choose the right image in lighting as well as other aspects of store design.

In general, lighting controls should primarily consist of a time clock with manual override switches.

Most energy codes allow additional power for specialty stores and boutiques through customized calculations. From a basic allowance of about 1.8 w/sf for general merchandise, it is possible to have up to 5 w/sf for jewelry stores and stores selling china and other fine goods.

The design shown in the following figure is for a shoe store, but it could also be for any medium-priced store selling general merchandise, such as gifts and cards, clothing, or housewares. The design style is bright and cheery, so a non-dramatic general lighting approach is used. To keep the store from looking inexpensive, the design calls for an upscale suspended fluorescent lighting system, with some highlighting and a few pendant luminaires for theme reinforcement. The general lighting system uses T-8 lamps and electronic ballasts, and the wallwashers and pendant lights employ compact fluorescent lamps. A few MR16 IR display lights are used in the store window and on the vertical panel behind the point of sale to illuminate posters and key displays. Pendant lights hang over the point of sale to help the shopper find the cashier.

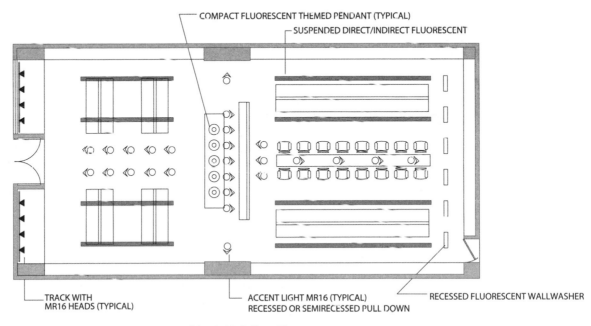

COMPACT FLUORESCENT THEMED PENDANT (TYPICAL)
SUSPENDED DIRECT/INDIRECT FLUORESCENT

TRACK WITH
MR16 HEADS (TYPICAL)

ACCENT LIGHT MR16 (TYPICAL)
RECESSED OR SEMIRECESSED PULL DOWN

RECESSED FLUORESCENT WALLWASHER

Store Lighting Plan

CASE STUDY 20

A Small Supermarket

Quite a few tasks must be illuminated in a grocery store, most of them involving the display of merchandise.

- The freestanding and wall-mounted shelving fixtures for dry and canned goods. The shelving fixtures are used to create aisles in most grocery stores. Sometimes the top shelf, although out of reach, is also used for display.
- The freestanding gondolas for displaying fresh produce.
- The wall displays for produce, many of them refrigerated and, in some cases, with built-in misting systems.
- Similar wall displays for meats and dairy.
- Aisle end displays.
- Specialty self-serve areas like bakery, wine, pharmacy, and floral
- Specialty service counters like coffee bar, deli, and ethnic foods
- Refrigerated and frozen cases
- Checkout

Because grocery stores contain so much to illuminate, most employ efficient, low-cost general lighting systems, such as fluorescent strip light, industrial fluorescent, or HID luminaires or troffers, in a space with a relatively high ceiling (14'–16') or, increasingly, with no ceiling and exposed structure at 18' or more. This lighting system illuminates many of the shopping tasks, primarily merchandise in the aisles. Direct lighting systems generally work best because they tend to punch light into the aisles better than diffuse or indirect lighting systems do.

In most stores, a different lighting system is used for the produce area, especially for highlighting the gondolas. One popular approach is to highlight the gondolas with track lighting, as if the produce were a sculpture gallery. Other successful designs include hanging decorative pendants or stylish fluorescent luminaires over the gondolas. For example, in the marché style, industrial shaded lamps are effective and appealing.

Another important task is lighting the produce and dairy shelves, generally at the walls of the store. A fluorescent valance light is usually used, often supplied with the display equipment. Similarly, for lighting the refrigerated cases, special built-in luminaires are almost always the solution.

Bakery, wine, floral, deli, and other departments often demand an individual architectural and lighting theme. Instead of the general lighting system, a unique lighting or ceiling solution is often employed—frequently a dropped acoustical tile ceiling that permits the use of recessed troffers or pendant lights. This is a common opportunity to develop a theme using lighting, as when a ribbed glass pendant light is installed over a bakery counter.

In the illustration below, the store has a themed style, with distinct produce, bakery, wine, pharmacy/toy, and checkout areas along with the traditional aisles.

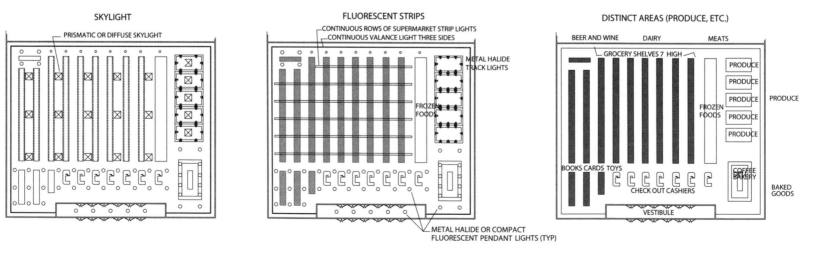

A Small Supermarket

It has an acoustical tile ceiling at 14'. The general lighting system employs fluorescent strip lights and provides task and ambient light throughout the store.

The high efficiency of the strip lights produces abundant vertical and horizontal illumination. If the store has windows, the general lighting system is visible from a considerable distance, informing potential customers that it is open for business.

The themed aspect of the design is achieved via the pendant luminaires that illuminate the specialty departments. Different lights are used in each department to create department identity. In the bakery, ribbed glass pendants hang over and around the shelving; in the wine area, white glass modern pendants hang over the wine racks; and over the pharmacy and checkout, larger industrial-style pendant lights are hung close to the ceiling to provide area illumination. In the produce area, track lighting is used to dramatically illuminate the produce gondolas, and fluorescent valance lights are used to illuminate the produce in refrigerated misting wall fixtures.

For lighting control, provide switches or time clocks for alternating luminaires so lighting levels can be reduced to save energy during stocking, closed, and low-traffic hours. A more advanced design would use dimming throughout all areas, permitting lower light levels from sunset to sunrise.

For the general lighting system, select standard T-8 lamps and electronic ballasts. For the pendant lights, choose compact fluorescent lamps or low-wattage metal halide lamp. For the track lighting over the produce gondolas, the energy-efficient choice is metal halide, although halogen lamps would also work. The tricky part is choosing a color temperature and making sure that the lamps' color matches fairly closely. For a warmer store, especially in a cold climate, 3000K might look best; in a warm climate, people prefer cooler light sources, and 4100K works quite well.

Adding daylight to a grocery store can be easy, as long as the store is a single-story structure. When skylights are placed in the ceiling as if they were light fixtures, natural light illuminates most of the store by day, allowing the electric lighting system to be dimmed or turned off. Daylight in the produce area is even higher than in other areas, because there are more skylights. Avoid skylights over the checkout, however; they can interfere with readers and other electronic tasks. A store where skylights cover about 5% of the ceiling area and lighting controls are used to turn electric lights off has a green, or environmentally thoughtful, design.

CASE STUDY 21

A Gallery

A gallery is a cross between a museum and a store. As in a museum, the lighting should display art objects in their best light. But as in any store, the lighting design should compete for the view of the potential customer and create an atmosphere that is visually and psychologically appealing.

The main lighting task is to illuminate the merchandise throughout the gallery. While most galleries feature paintings and posters, an increasing number sell sculpture, art glass, or other collectibles. Other lighting tasks include circulating through the gallery, the point of sale, and task areas such as framing.

In general, galleries should be lighted using a track lighting system. The flexibility of track is unparalleled, and it permits the rapid change of lighting to address new artwork. Tracks should be located parallel to all display surfaces, far enough from the surface to permit aiming lights at 30 degrees off vertical to illuminate art hung at eye level. Galleries exhibiting three-dimensional art often have the same lighting needs, although additional tracks or other methods of adding focal lighting would be welcome. Track luminaires should primarily be halogen, largely to minimize risks to the artwork by photodegradation.

Ambient light is an important choice. Many fine art galleries have no ambient light, and the artwork stands out. In other galleries, the ambient lighting system is an important part of the design, setting a mood or stage for the art.

For controls, an automatic time clock system should be used to turn off lights between closing and opening, possibly with a separate clock circuit to turn off alternating lights during stocking and cleaning periods. Dimming may be used to minimize energy use and extend lamp life. Motion sensors can be connected to dimmers to increase light levels as shoppers approach.

The design shown in the following figure shows a typical gallery using mostly track lighting. A limited amount of ambient light is provided via sconces and chandeliers that generate 3–5 fc of illumination, the minimum necessary for circulation and safety and for attracting the eye with sparkle separate from the glow of the artwork.

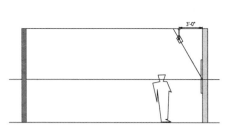

Section

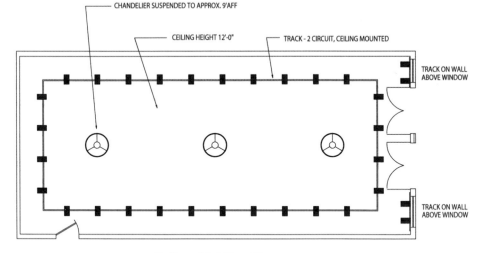

Gallery Lighting Plan

Chapter 15 LIGHTING COMMON SPACES

Almost all buildings have one or more of the spaces that are here defined as *common spaces*. Clearly, halls, corridors, and stairs fall into this category. Public or common-use rest rooms are found in almost every nonresidential building. Large, general-use public spaces, such as malls, airport waiting areas, and atria, also are in this category.

Although common spaces are found in all building types, they present different lighting design requirements and considerations. In residences, corridors and stairs are treated as a part of the personal environment, while in nonresidential buildings they are public domain and often quite anonymous in character. Public rest rooms, while always personal in their use, can vary tremendously from strictly utilitarian to decorative and even luxurious. Creating a personally tolerable environment for large public waiting areas, like those found in airports, is a particularly challenging design problem. Shopping malls, with the constant movement of people and the efforts of individual stores to vie for shoppers' attention, present still another common space design challenge.

The techniques for solving these common space lighting design problems vary as widely as their uses. Their one shared characteristic is that lighting requirements are generally fixed and need not be adjusted to changing conditions; once set in place, the lighting condition usually remains constant. Otherwise, however, every type of luminaire and light source is used in common spaces, from fundamental to complex and from utilitarian to ornamental.

Except for in residential settings, code compliance plays a significant role in the lighting of common spaces because so many of them are, directly or indirectly, part of a building's egress system and must provide safe paths of evacuation in emergencies. Energy consumption code factors are usually not an area of concern because critical visual tasks are normally not performed in these spaces and high levels of illumination are not needed. Nevertheless, minimally adequate vision to find one's way out of a building when power is cut off due to a fire or other crisis situation is clearly essential and required by all building codes. An emergency lighting system, employing accepted industry techniques, must be an integral part of every nonresidential building's overall lighting system. All common spaces that are part of a building's means of egress, including corridors, stairs, lobbies, and malls, must incorporate emergency lighting that is powered by battery and/or emergency generator methods.

Some standard techniques for lighting fire stairs and utilitarian corridors are sensible and acceptable because they are used infrequently. But beyond these purely utilitarian spaces, most common spaces deserve (and sometimes demand) creative lighting design attention. Corridors are rarely thought of as interesting spaces, but they can be saved from their usual pedestrian quality with thoughtful lighting design solutions. This is the case in countless office, apartment, hospital, and hotel buildings. Atria, lobbies, monumental stairs, and other major entrance or gathering spaces typically receive a great deal of design attention, including lighting design attention, and significant budget is applied to make them special. Entrances, in particular, are symbolic spaces, creating the visitor's first impression and setting the tone for what lies beyond. These special spaces typically require extensive collaboration between the architect and/or interior designer creating the space and the lighting designer responsible for a successful lighting design solution.

It should be obvious that the lighting of common spaces runs the gamut from purely functional to dramatic. The case studies in this chapter identify the most frequent of these lighting design problems, expecting that the concepts employed are translatable to a wide range of design conditions.

CASE STUDY **22**

Public Rest Room Lighting

The character and quality of public rest rooms run the gamut from utilitarian and bare-boned to lavish and decorative, depending on the setting and budget. Size and the number of people to be accommodated also ranges from an uncompartmented two-fixture facility to large-scale men's and women's rooms geared to serving large numbers of people, as at airports and sports stadiums. Most people have experienced the vast difference in design intent between rest rooms in fast-food chain restaurants and those in expensive and elaborate restaurants. Obviously, lighting design solutions must be consistent with the design intent and quality of the rest rooms they serve.

The rest rooms shown in the figure at right are in the middle range with respect to both size and elaborateness; they are the kind of facility one might find on a typical floor of a large office building or adjacent to the lobby of a museum. Except for the grooming area provided in the women's room, the lighting requirements of both rooms are identical. (1) Approaching the restrooms there should be just enough light in the small recessed corridor area for users to comfortably see the signage identifying gender. (2) Upon entering each of the rooms comfortable navigational ambient light is needed for finding one's way into the main space. (3) In the urinal area and all of the toilet stalls a general wash of ambient light is needed. (4) A somewhat greater concentration of light is needed at the lavatories, but washing hands and some perfunctory grooming at the mirror above do not require much more than the ambient level of the remainder of the room. (5) The one critical visual task occurs at the vanity counter in the women's room, where high level and properly positioned light is needed. As discussed in chapters 10 (residential) and 12 (hospitality), evenly distributed and relatively shadowless light are best for combing hair and applying make-up. Note should be made that the ADA compliance issues of these restroom facilities do not place special demands on the lighting solution.

The lighting design shown in the figure at right addresses the visual tasks in the following manner:

1. In the recessed corridor area one recessed downlight is adequate for lighting the necessary signage which identifies the signage for "men" and "women." Note that the ceiling height has been raised 4" so a drywall ceiling may be placed in that small area, and the luminaire can be placed without having to conform to the corridor ceiling grid pattern. Under other corridor conditions the drywall ceiling in the recessed area could be lowered by four or more inches.

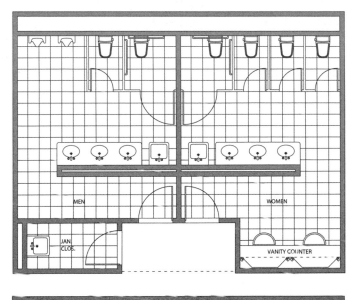

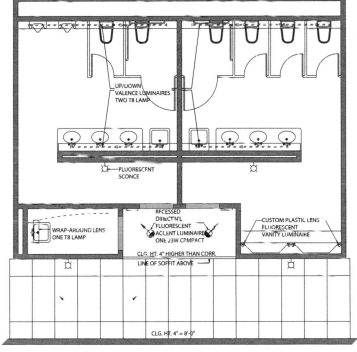

Proposed Toilet Rooms

2. In the entrance area to each restroom, a wall sconce is placed fairly high on the north wall. The luminaire should direct its light equally to the ceiling and the floor, and have a translucent shield or shade to also provide some eye-level glow. The intensity level should be quite modest, in the range of 7 to 12 fc in the general entrance area.

3. In the toilet stall and urinal areas, a continuous, upwardly and downwardly directed valence luminaire is used, shielding three in-tandem fluorescent channels, providing an even wash of indirect light for those areas of both restrooms.

4. In the lavatory areas, a similar vanity luminaire is placed directly above each lavatory; they should be designed and placed to cast nonglare illumination on users' faces, as well as to provide adequate light for hand washing. The overall intensity of light in the room should range from 10 to 15 fc. Unlike the surfaces in most interior spaces, wall and floor surfaces in restrooms tend to be relatively permanent, such as ceramic tile or stone, resulting in equally permanent reflectance values. Because of this, long-term lighting results can be counted on.

5. At the vanity counter two vertically mounted fluorescents with wraparound translucent shield are placed to provide high intensity and shadowless light for each of the two grooming stations. Unlike the grooming light indicated in the residential and hospitality case studies (chapters 10 and 12), where lavatory use also had to be accommodated, the users' functions and positions are fixed and known, and a "perfect" lighting solution can be achieved.

Switching in public situations of this kind is usually controlled at a locally central panel box with the power on during all operating hours and, when needed, time clock operated.

Luminaire and lamp selections should be based on the following considerations:

Downlight: recessed downlight lamped with a 13 watt compact fluorescent

Wall sconces: equal direct-indirect distribution with a translucent shield or shade, and lamped with a 13 watt compact fluorescent

Valence fluorescents: for the north walls, 75% uplight and 25% downlight; for the lavatory surfaces, 75% downlight and 25% uplight. Lamp with 48" units and as directed by manufacturer to achieve desired light levels

Vanity fluorescents: wall mounted, lensed and lamped with 36" units selected for good skin tone color rendition.

Design character and style are primarily determined by the quality and style of the architectural and interior design detailing and materials that are being used in the space. In this case study, and true of most public restrooms, luminaire selection is limited by the impersonal nature of the space and the narrow range of materials, finishes, and toilet stall and plumbing fixture colors and finishes that are normally employed. There are the occasional decorative restrooms, usually in restaurants and other hospitality settings, which permit and call for a much wider range of luminaire selections.

CASE STUDY **23**

Corridors and Stairs

We encounter corridors and stairs just about everywhere. Except in single-story buildings, which do not require stairs, they are a necessary element of every building. They range from utilitarian to decorative and are, on occasion, monumental in character. Critical safety issues are always related to them because they are the means by which we get out of buildings at times of emergency or panic. Stairs present the additional danger of tripping and falling. These safety issues have made corridor and stair design, including their lighting, a major element of all building codes.

Corridors range in width from the typically narrow halls in residences to quite wide corridors in places of heavy pedestrian traffic, such as schools and assembly buildings. They often dominate the design character of a building, particularly in the case of hotels, apartment buildings, and office buildings. Many corridors feel lifeless because the pedestrian traffic is occasional or sporadic. Long corridors present difficult visual problems; their length should be deemphasized.

The design character of stairs range from rarely used fire stairs to grand stairways that are the central feature of an elaborate lobby or entrance. In residences, stairs take on a personal character and fuse with other architectural and interiors elements. On occasion, stairs become a traffic hub, as in an interconnecting open stairwell between the floors of a single tenant in a high-rise office building. In all cases, stairs present an unusual design challenge because of their dynamic volumetric configuration.

The visual tasks in corridors and stairs are primarily navigational and usually not critical. Lighting levels are conventionally low to moderate, similar to those required for casual conversation or other situations where vision is not vital. Occasionally, a corridor or stair is part of a larger space, such as a lobby or exhibit area, where higher levels of illumination are required—for example, at a bulletin board or display panel in a school or hospital corridor. Lighting on stairs must provide a clear view of treads and risers to minimize the inherent dangers of tripping and falling. Generally, the visual tasks in corridors and stairs that are related to safety are critical. More specifically, lighting is critical when providing for safe passage out of a building when a fire or other emergency, or just the fear of such a crisis, creates the need to get out quickly. Because electrical systems often fail at such times, building codes require that auxiliary or emergency lighting be provided in corridors and stairs. While this lighting requirement is minimal in terms of illumination level, emergency lighting must be properly incorporated into every nonresidential building.

This case study is unlike all of the others because it presents generalized lighting solutions for several corridor and stair conditions rather than an in-depth solution for a single example. The purpose of this approach is to provide a needed range of solutions for the many corridor and stair conditions found in buildings.

CORRIDORS

The figure below indicates the typical corridor lighting solution found in nonresidential buildings. Because major mechanical and electrical lines and equipment are often in the corridor plenum, lay-in acoustic tile ceilings are employed to provide easy access. Recessed fluorescent troffers are placed at intervals of about 16', resulting in alternating dark and light areas as one traverses the length of the corridor. And all of the light is downlight, resulting in a particularly flat or unmodulated appearance. The use of a dropped lens, or better still, a surface mounted luminaire with translucent sides, will provide some horizontal light and result in a less flat or better modulated appearance. Instead of the 2' X 2' luminaires shown in this illustration, 1' X 4' or 2' X 4' units can be used, being careful to place the long dimension across the width of the corridor in order to de-emphasize the corridor's length. Luminaires do not have to be placed in the center of the corridor, and ceiling tile patterns can be adjusted to provide an eccentric or asymmetrical arrangement. However, luminaires should not be placed adjacent to the corridor wall, which may cause hot spots on the wall. Lamps must be selected to produce the desired level of illumination directly under each luminaire as well as at the midpoint between two luminaires. Emergency lighting can be provided by supplying emergency power to designated luminaires or by installing wall-mounted battery pack units at the required intervals.

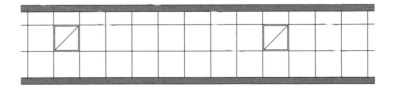

Corridor A

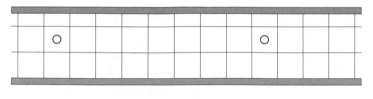

Corridor B

The figure above shows a common solution found in both residential and nonresidential buildings, although the acoustic tile ceiling is rarely used in residences. It presents the same disadvantages of alternating dark and light areas and a flat appearance. Luminaires can be placed off center for an asymmetrical appearance, including placement close enough to one wall to create a scalloped light pattern on it. Lamping can be easily adjusted to produce the desired level of illumination. Emergency lighting can be provided by an emergency generator tied to selected luminaires or by battery pack units at the required intervals.

Corridor C

The figure above demonstrates the use of sconces as the primary approach to lighting corridors. Their advantage in corridors is that they produce both direct and indirect light as well as eye-level glow and a decorative quality, depending on the luminaire(s) selected. Their disadvantage is that they must coordinate with door openings, corridor recesses, and intersecting corridors. To compound this disadvantage, sconces should be placed at fairly regular intervals to avoid creating a visually chaotic vista down the length of a long hallway.

Sconces can be effectively used in apartment buildings, hotels, and other settings where corridor door locations are not subject to change. However, particularly in office buildings, where door locations are subject to frequent change, sconces are impractical.

When they are used in corridors, sconces usually represent a major design element, and their design characteristics should be carefully selected to complement the architectural and interior design characteristics of the corridor. Lamp selection should be based on the levels of illumination desired at the luminaires and at midpoint between luminaires. Emergency lighting can be accomplished with an emergency power system tied to selected luminaires or with battery pack units at the required intervals.

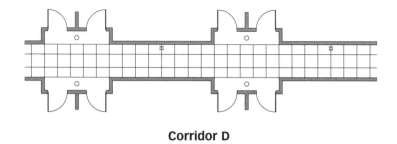

Corridor D

The figure above illustrates a solution often found in hotel corridors, where doors to guest rooms are at quite regular intervals. From a lighting design point of view, this is an opportunity to create a visually interesting result not often found in long, uninterrupted corridors. As a design approach or concept, it is sometimes applicable to other building types in which the recessed doorways occur at irregular intervals. As illustrated here, the recessed doorway areas are lighted with a centrally placed recessed downlight in a slightly raised gypsum wallboard ceiling, so that ceiling tile patterns do not have to be considered. In most hotels, recessed doorway areas occur every 25' to 30' unless there are recessed doorways at the midpoints on the opposite side of the corridor. As shown in the illustration, a ceiling- or wall-mounted luminaire is needed at the midpoint between the recessed doorways.

If a wall-mounted luminaire is used, its design characteristics and style are visually important and must be consistent with the architectural and interior design elements of which it is a part. This lighting solution, in addition to providing a visually interesting alternative to conventional corridor lighting, also supplies the minor task light needed by people looking for where to place their key or reading how to insert a plastic key card. Lamp selection is based on the levels of illumination desired in the recessed doorways and in the areas between the doorways. Emergency lighting can be accomplished with emergency power supplied to selected luminaires or with battery pack units at the required intervals.

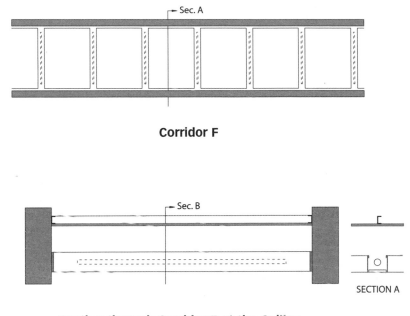

Corridor F

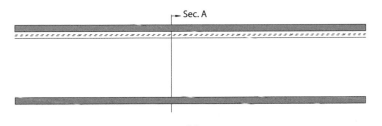

Corridor E

The valence or cove lighting shown in Corridor E has many possible applications. It provides an uninterrupted and relatively shadowless quality of light. The valence or cove can be easily detailed to ride above door heads, but this approach may be impractical in corridors interrupted by recesses or intersecting corridors. Unless the valence or cove is used on both sides of the corridor, one side of the corridor will be appreciably lighter than the other, although it is possible to detail the valence or cove to project its light toward the other side. In particularly wide corridors, especially in hospital or geriatric care settings, the use of cove lighting on both sides of the corridor will provide a desirably even wash of light that will not produce visually disturbing glare on smooth, shiny floor surfaces.

A continuous line of light is needed to produce the desired effect of valence or cove lighting, so lamp selection is limited to readily available straight lengths of fluorescent lamps. In carefully detailed construction of this kind, lamp ends are staggered in order to avoid the minor unevenness of light that occurs between lamp ends. Emergency lighting can be accomplished with emergency power supplied to selected luminaires or with battery pack units at the required intervals.

Section through Corridor F at the Ceiling

Corridor F describes a variation on cove or valence lighting that is particularly applicable to long, uninterrupted corridors and can be installed quite economically. It also has the advantage of visually breaking up a dauntingly long vista of corridor ceiling. The accompanying section drawing, Figure 15.9, indicates how direct view of the lamp is avoided when corridor doors are opened. Also note in the section that enough space is provided between the lamp and the ceiling surface to permit easy relamping by maintenance personnel. Materials for the long central element and the repeated cross-members must meet building code flammability requirements; chemically treated noncombustible wood or formed sheet metal are the obvious choices. An extremely basic industrial channel can be employed for the luminaires. One or two lamp luminaires can be used, depending on the spacing of the luminaires and the level of illumination desired. Emergency lighting can be accomplished with emergency power supplied to selected luminaires or with battery pack units at the required intervals.

Section through Corridor E at the Ceiling

STAIRS

The enclosed stairwell is found in most buildings other than residences. In many buildings, such as high-rise office buildings, hotels, and apartment houses, the stairwells are used only in emergencies. However, in many other buildings, particularly smaller multistory buildings, stairs are the primary means of interfloor circulation. Obviously, regularly used stairs must receive more detailed design attention.

One approach to designing the lighting of enclosed stairwells uses wall-mounted fluorescent luminaires with both direct and indirect light distribution at each landing, providing appropriate and safe lighting. Depending on the luminaire selected, this technique can add to the design character of the space. A ceiling-mounted fluorescent luminaire with both down- and side-light distribution can be equally effective. Avoid luminaires that provide downlight only because they will be less effective, and therefore less safe, in lighting the treads and risers of the adjacent runs of stairs.

For the rarely used fire stair, lighting levels can be at minimal navigational intensity, while for stairs that are regularly used, lamp selection should be geared to the same level as a normally traveled corridor. When windows bring natural light into a stairwell, luminaire placement may have to be adjusted to accommodate the architectural condition as well as the daytime lighting condition. When emergency power is available, all stairwell luminaires are tied to that power system; otherwise, battery pack units are employed.

In the case of an unusually long floor-to-floor run of stairs with a sloped ceiling or soffit following the stair slope, it is often best to use downlights placed directly in or on the sloped ceiling surface. Attention should be given to luminaire selection so people descending the stair need not look directly into the light source. This architectural condition tends to occur more frequently in residences, where luminaire selection may have to be particularly well integrated with surrounding interior design detail.

Several techniques for lighting stairs involve installing the light source close to and directly focused on the treads and risers. While these techniques are ideal for generating safe lighting conditions, they do not provide adequate ambient light for most situations and must be supplemented with ambient light for the overall stairwell. One possible solution is the use of fluorescent lamps incorporated into the stair handrail, which casts light directly on the treads and risers.

Another option is the use of small luminaires recessed into the stairwell's side wall, usually placed every two or three treads and lamped with compact fluorescents. For a dramatic effect, the use of a linear fluorescent lamp placed under each tread nosing is a technique that yields excellent illumination for safe passage. This approach is obviously expensive to construct, install, and maintain, but in special situations where dramatic effect is desired, it may be appropriate.

SWITCHING AND CONTROLS

A commonsense understanding of how people enter and exit rooms and other spaces, including halls and stairs, is a good guide to switching in residential settings. Dimmers should be approached in the same commonsense manner. Three-way switches are particularly useful at the opposite ends of hallways and at the top and bottom of stairs.

Switching for corridors and stairs in nonresidential buildings is typically controlled in centrally located panel boxes that prevent users from arbitrarily turning lights off in critical paths of egress. Timing devices often control switching patterns in which minimal corridor lighting is employed during low-use hours in office buildings and other settings where use patterns are highly predictable.

EMERGENCY LIGHTING

Building codes require that all nonresidential buildings provide emergency lighting when normal power service fails. Simply, occupants must be able to safely see their way out of a building at times of emergency or crisis. Additional requirements for emergency lighting pertain in other specialized building types, such as hospitals and large open work areas. Generally, a minimum lighting level of 1 fc is required, and sources may not be more than 50' apart in corridors and other horizontal exitways. The same 1-fc minimum requirement must be maintained in stairwells.

Power for emergency lighting is accomplished in two very different ways. Remote emergency generators can provide power to designated luminaires. This approach is generally reserved for fairly large buildings where economy of size makes it practical. In smaller buildings, the one-, two-, or three-headed battery pack unit is the preferred approach because the installation of an emergency generator system is economically prohibitive. From an aesthetic standpoint, designers usually prefer to avoid battery pack units because they so often appear to be an uncoordinated afterthought, but construction cost economy typically is the deciding factor.

LUMINAIRES AND LAMPS

Luminaire and lamp selections have generally been addressed in the corridor and stair solutions described above. Almost every luminaire type is employed in corridors and stairs. Lamping is generally dictated by the desired illumina- tion level for each interior condition. Luminaire design character and style should be consistent with the building's architectural and interior design qual- ities. But corridors and stairs, so often thought of as anonymous or uninter- esting spaces, present many opportunities for creative and unusual lighting solutions. They are spaces in motion, and stairs in particular have an inherent- ly dynamic spatial character. When budgets permit, corridors and stairs are good and appropriate places for customizing luminaires and the housing or integration of conventional luminaires. Sometimes, in highly repetitive sit- uations, customization can favorably compete with standard products and solutions.

CASE STUDY **24**

Waiting Room Lighting

Waiting rooms are a common space type in many public buildings, including airports, malls, hospitals, train stations, and government buildings. Many waiting rooms are designed for more than 100 people. Waiting room architecture varies from modest spaces to large structures and volumes.

A common waiting room design problem is shown below. An airport waiting room, also called a hold room, is a space where passengers await planes. The most common visual tasks undertaken there are reading and socializing, although an increasing number of hold rooms also have television screens. Most hold rooms also have large windows, and some modern airports may also have skylights. In this example, almost the entire exterior wall is glazed for daylight and view of aircraft operations.

This plan shows three workable lighting solutions. Each produces an entirely different character and mood to the space.

DESIGN A: RECESSED TROFFERS

Usually, the least expensive solution is 2' X 4' recessed troffer lighting for general illumination in the space. This solution can employ lens troffers, parabolics, or recessed indirect basket luminaires. A regular layout producing 30–50 fc on average supports all of the visual tasks in the space. This design can also be mixed with wallwashers and special lighting for the ticket counter.

DESIGN B: LINEAR PENDANT LIGHTS

Linear fluorescent pendant lights are an excellent solution where the ceiling height is at least 10'. This portion of the plan shows indirect lighting over both the waiting area and the ticket counter. Like Design A, this solution provides 30–50 fc throughout the area. A combination of this design and Design C may be employed to highlight the ticket counter or to wash a wall.

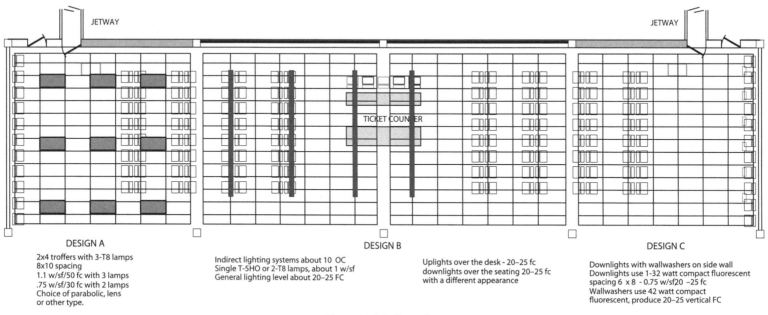

JETWAY

JETWAY

TICKET COUNTER

DESIGN A

2x4 troffers with 3-T8 lamps
8x10 spacing
1.1 w/sf/50 fc with 3 lamps
.75 w/sf/30 fc with 2 lamps
Choice of parabolic, lens
or other type.

DESIGN B

Indirect lighting systems about 10 OC
Single T-5HO or 2-T8 lamps, about 1 w/sf
General lighting level about 20–25 FC

Uplights over the desk - 20-25 fc
downlights over the seating 20–25 fc
with a different appearance

DESIGN C

Downlights with wallwashers on side wall
Downlights use 1-32 watt compact fluorescent
spacing 6 x 8 - 0.75 w/sf20 –25 fc
Wallwashers use 42 watt compact
fluorescent, produce 20–25 vertical FC

Airport Lighting Plan

DESIGN C: DOWNLIGHTS WITH WALLWASHERS

This design illustrates the use of recessed downlights over the seating area combined with wallwashers for the side wall. Many hold rooms feature artwork, graphics, or other displays on this wall, and the indirect light from wallwashers illuminates this portion of the room as well. Downlights are laid out to provide 30 fc of illumination.

DESIGN CONSIDERATIONS: ALL THREE SOLUTIONS

:The style and appearance of a hold room are generally high in priority. Lighting is usually a key element of the overall interior design.

Luminaire and lamp selections should be based on the following considerations:

Downlights: depth of baffle, light distribution spread, compact fluorescent (xx watts)

Troffers: Type (lens, parabolic, recessed indirect), cutoff angle, distribution, style or size, fluorescent lamp type and color (xx watts)

Wallwasher: recessed or semirecessed, light distribution and uniformity, lamp type metal halide or compact fluorescent (xx watts)

Pendant lights: type (indirect, direct-indirect), appearance cutoff angle, distribution, style or size, fluorescent lamp type and color (xx watts)

Note that of the three designs, only the pendant luminaires have significant aesthetic impact on the space. Among the other designs, the aesthetic effects are more subtle; troffers tend to make a space appear more institutional, while downlights tend to make a space feel more tailored and formal. If pendant lights are used, their selection should be closely coordinated with the interior design color, finishes, and furniture.

Lighting controls are sometimes not used in hold rooms because they often are open around the clock. However, most hold rooms should employ the following lighting controls:

- *Automatic daylight sensors* to dim or switch off lights near windows.
- *Time of day controls* to extinguish or dim lights when hold rooms are not scheduled for use, especially in airports and similar places where relatively certain hours of use are known. A manual override permits off-schedule use.
- *Motion sensors* to extinguish or dim lights when hold rooms are unoccupied.

Also consider dimming lights at night even when hold rooms are in use. Lower light levels still permit casual reading and socializing but are more relaxing and better for television viewing and even sleep.

CASE STUDY **25**

Lighting Shopping Malls

The mall spaces within shopping mall complexes are pedestrian thoroughfares or indoor streets designed to provide access to the retail tenant spaces as well as generate an atmosphere that stimulates an interest in shopping. (Stimulating an interest in *buying* is the retailer's job.) For many shoppers, the attraction of the mall is also the opportunity for social experience, albeit a passive one—to get out of the house and see, hear, and even make casual social contact with other people. Successfully creating this kind of complex environment—which is a mix of practical planning, simulation of interesting street vistas, infusing a sense of theater or entertainment (sometimes including a space for impromptu performance), an audio experience of canned music and/or splashing fountains and/or wind chimes, and even subliminal olfactory awareness via food vendor stands and/or piped-in aromas—has a great deal to do with the success or failure of a shopping mall enterprise.

Shopping Mall

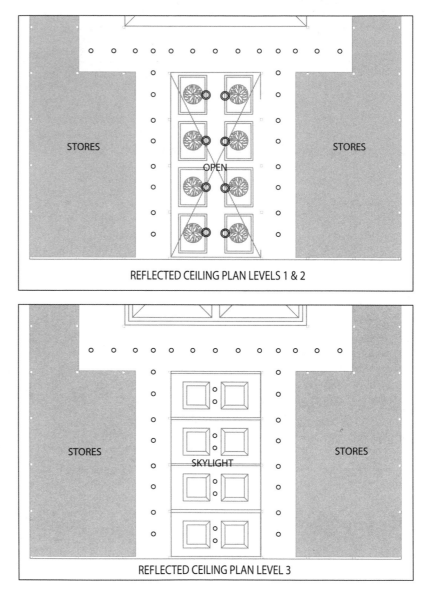

REFLECTED CEILING PLAN LEVELS 1 & 2

REFLECTED CEILING PLAN LEVEL 3

Shopping Mall Atrium

The primary task of the lighting designer is to support the mall's commercial purpose. The important visual focus must be the retail stores. The mall space and its contents should not compete for visual attention. This is rarely a problem, as the mall space itself rarely sports major attractions. Low to modest levels of navigational light are the primary lighting requirement. Even specialty sales carts, often found within the mall space, normally provide their own focal lighting. The exception to this general rule for navigational light is the presence of a central or spectacular visual attraction unrelated to the tenant spaces, such as a large fountain, waterfall, or electronic display, that becomes the complex's identifying feature or sense of place. When these feature attractions are present, their lighting breaks all the rules and requires an individual lighting design focus.

One more generality concerning mall lighting is necessary to note: the use of daylight through major skylights. Most mall spaces are two or three stories high, with the upper level(s) having balconies overlooking the central mall. It is common to find these mall spaces daylighted by large steel and glass skylight roof structures that flood the mall space with natural light during the day. The integration of natural and electric light must be carefully calculated and designed, including the phasing for diminishing natural light as night approaches. Night-time shopping is of major importance to mall complexes, and the effects of the full electric lighting system are critical, even when large skylights are incorporated into the overall building design.

Chapter 16 THE PROFESSIONAL PROCESS OF LIGHTING

Lighting design is a relatively new part of the process of building construction. Many of the principles and standards needed for lighting come from architecture and engineering, and for good reason—architects and engineers are the licensed professionals who design buildings. However, because of the rapid changes in lighting technology and design technique, unique lighting issues must be addressed by the lighting designer.

DESIGN DOCUMENTATION

General Information

During the process of design, it is important to record project criteria, decisions, and other information so the information can be reviewed and checked as the project advances. For each space being designed, it is a good idea to record:

- Area and dimensions of the space
- If available, room elevations and sections
- Finishes on all surfaces
- Furniture
- Visual tasks and locations, including focal tasks
- Architectural or interior design concept
- Light level(s) selected, including task, ambient, and focal
- Light color temperature and CRI
- Control requirements
- Cost budget
- Power or energy budget
- Code requirements
- Additional requirements specific to the project

Recording this information serves the project in a number of ways. First, it ensures that you are reasonably thorough in collecting the information needed to properly execute your work. Second, it challenges you to identify the design problems and how you might solve them. Finally, it provides a paper trail for liability protection. For this reason alone, many designers keep every sketch or marked-up plan they produce during the design phase.

Calculations

Some type of calculation is required on almost every commercial project. Even when the lighting design is intuitive and artful, as for the design of a restaurant or hotel lobby, many cities now require point-by-point lighting calculations for emergency and path-of-egress lighting.

As a practical matter, most architects and interior designers (and many electrical engineers and lighting designers, too) have calculations performed for them by manufacturers or agents. While there is nothing wrong with this, you should be familiar with the input data as well as the output reports so you can make sure the right luminaire, lamp, and room finishes have been used. The results of all calculations actually used in the design should be retained and labeled for future retrieval.

Conflicts and Issues

Lighting can be a touchy subject, with many opinions about a particular design. It is not uncommon for a preferred lighting design to be altered or rejected for many reasons, including personal preference, cost, energy use, and interference with pipes or ducts. Often these changes compromise the integrity of the lighting design.

While lighting is generally more forgiving than, say, structures, the failure of a lighting design to be correctly implemented can have major implications, such as:

- Insufficient light levels for the tasks to be performed
- Unattractive luminaires or layouts
- Systems that use too much energy
- Systems that are expensive to maintain
- Potentially unsafe conditions for people or vehicles

Good lighting is often considered frivolous and dispensable, particularly when building costs are over budget. It is common to change the design,

reduce the number of lights, or change the type of light without performing new calculations or considering the impact. The most common reason is so-called value engineering, whereby the contractor proposes cost-cutting measures to the building owner. The lighting design may be changed without the designer's knowledge. Having good records of your design and decisions is important in protecting yourself from liability in case the changes don't work.

Potential liabilities in design make recording and resolving design criteria especially important. For instance, the rising costs of energy and new energy codes tend to decrease lighting levels. But the growing population of aged persons requires more light and more energy to see. This is a classic conflict, of which many more involving light will emerge. By properly documenting your decisions, you can appeal to authorities and perhaps resolve problems more quickly. Again, you will be protected from liability.

Products of Design

A lighting design is documented by the following:

Documents for Review and Reference

Lighting Plans	Lighting designs shown in plan form using base floor plans and/or reflected ceiling plans (see chapter 7). The lighting plan is not a contract document until it is used by a licensed professional or contractor (see below). It is common to draw a lighting plan because it is important in showing the complete lighting design. But the lighting plan is often only an intermediate step in developing a suitable electrical drawing.
Cut Sheets	A collection of the product cut or tear sheets corresponding to the lighting schedule. The cut sheets sometimes can be used in place of a lighting schedule if the project is easily understood. Cut sheets permit detailed examination of the intended lighting equipment, often for the benefit or approval of the client or other team members.
Narrative	A written document describing the lighting design and how it will work.
Design Sketches	Drawings, often hand-drawn, that illustrate lighting design concepts or details in the context of the project.
Calculations	Hand calculations and computer printouts containing the input data and results of calculations used in the design.

Documents for Bidding or Construction

Contract Document Drawings	Electrical lighting plans that are drawn by the architect, engineer, or other licensed professional or contractor to establish the scope of the contract work with respect to lighting. While these plans are often based on the lighting plan (see above), they include additional information such as branch circuit design.
Lighting Schedule	The schedule or list of luminaires listed by tag. The schedule should include all information about each luminaire, including tag, description, operating voltage, connected power (watts), number and type of lamps, number and type of ballasts, mounting, finish(es), and approved manufacturer and model number (see chapter 7).
Details	Drawings indicating specific details of luminaire attachment. These are especially vital to coordination of cove lights and similar applications.
Lamp Schedule (optional)	The schedule or list of lamps by type. This is especially useful on very large projects or projects with an unusual number or type of lamps.
Written Specifications (optional)	The specifications for lighting, which are generally Section 16500 of the electrical specifications. Written specifications are required for major projects. Describes lighting and lighting control equipment and requirements for procurement, installation, adjustment, and programming the operation of all lighting systems.
Isocandle Plots (when required)	For some types of lighting, authorities require isocandle plots on floor plans or site plans. Exporting a calculation plot file to the appropriate plan drawing generally does this.
Control Riser Diagram (when required)	Indicates the components and suggests the operation of a lighting control or dimming system.

Seldom are lighting documents used without review and approval by an electrical engineer. As a minimum, an engineer must design branch circuits to power the lights. Both the lights and the circuits must appear on the engineer's electrical drawings for the project. If the engineer is also the lighting designer, the point is moot, but if the lighting designer is independent of the electrical engineer, conflict or coordination issues may need to be solved.

PHASES OF DESIGN

A lighting design is part of the building design. Historically, the engineer added lighting during later design phases. However, due to increasing demand for energy efficiency and daylighting as well as to better integrate lighting in the overall design, lighting design should begin early in the project.

Following the standard phases of the American Institute of Architects (AIA), here are the lighting design activities that should occur as the project progresses.

Project Phases of Lighting Design

AIA Design Phase	Activity	Products
Programming	Determine what role lighting and daylighting are expected to play in the project. Establish appropriate budgets.	Narrative and budget line items
Schematic Design	Assist in developing a daylighting strategy. Assist in conceiving spaces, especially those requiring specific lighting performance or aesthetics. Establish an energy budget and strategy, if needed. Develop lighting concepts using preliminary plans, sketches, or other illustrations. Perform preliminary calculations. Identify products for possible use. Test the concepts for budget compliance.	Narrative with cut sheets, sketches, and preliminary plans. Budget line items. Results of preliminary calculations of critical lighting systems. Renderings, if developed.
Design Development	Assist in developing plans, sections, and details, especially reflected ceiling plans. Complete lighting concepts and begin lighting plans and details. Begin lighting schedule. Identify lighting controls equipment and devices. Perform final calculations and layout lighting on plans. Confirm budget and energy compliance. Begin lighting specifications.	The following should be at least partially complete: lighting plans and details, lighting schedule with cut sheets, specifications, code compliance documents. Also provide controls narrative.
Working Drawings	Design and engineer lighting controls and add circuits to the drawings. Complete all documents. Make final adjustments as required. Confirm budget and energy compliance.	All of the following should be complete: lighting plans and details (turn over to engineer for branch circuit design), lighting schedule, lighting and controls specifications.

The role of the lighting design continues into construction to the extent needed. As a minimum, the lighting designer should check lighting submittals and aid the contractor in making minor changes to suit field conditions. In addition, if value engineering occurs, the lighting designer should be given an opportunity to review the proposals and to advise whether or not the proposed changes will work.

Once construction is complete, the lighting designer should help commission the building by doing the following:

1. Walk through the building and make sure that the lighting is installed correctly and without defects. A list of defects, called a *punchlist*, is turned over to the contractor for repairs.
2. Adjust or direct the adjustment of lighting systems that are aimed, such as track lighting and accent lights. Add filters, lenses, and other accessories.
3. Check the operation of controls systems and set dimming systems.
4. Instruct the owner's personnel in using the lighting systems.

These steps are especially important if the lighting design is sophisticated, creative, or unusual in any way. It is impossible to specify and expect a contractor to complete the artistic vision of a highly creative lighting design. On a more mundane level, many lighting controls systems, especially motion sensing, daylighting, and preset dimming systems, are not set up and calibrated properly. This results in energy waste and, worse, the disconnection of the system by frustrated occupants.

Post-Occupancy Evaluation

After your design is built, make every effort to evaluate your work. Give the client an opportunity to criticize and comment on the lighting systems and how they work. Be open and self-critical, and listen carefully. The best designers are those who learn from prior success and failure.

DESIGN INTEGRITY AND COST MANAGEMENT

Every lighting design relies heavily on the appearance and performance of the lighting equipment. When the designer specifies lighting equipment, the specified equipment usually will meet the project needs. If more than one product will do the job, the lighting schedule should list as many options as possible.

The electrical sales industry, however, does not always fully respect the specification. Electrical distributors compete for projects. Distributors in turn receive pricing from manufacturers' representatives (or *reps*). The trend in the industry is for each rep to offer a package in which he or she represents one major manufacturer that makes a wide range of common luminaires (see chapter 3) and a number of specialty manufacturers. Thus every project will face competing packages, and often the specified product is only part of one package.

Substitutions are products the rep feels are the same as the specified product. This is often true, and designers should review substitution requests and accept them if possible. This is especially the case with standards of the industry. Most designers today require substitution requests to be made early in the project. It is a good idea for the lighting designer to review and approve substitutions rather than find them installed without his or her knowledge.

The evolution of the package and standards of the industry began with government work. Government agencies generally build ordinary buildings and want to ensure they receive competitive pricing on all materials. The standard requirement became to list three manufacturers for every product. This requirement persists today for both government and private work, although designers are permitted to specify particular products (and one manufacturer) if the design requires specific performance and the product is unique in the market.

Uniqueness in the lighting industry is rare. As in the furniture industry, some members of the lighting industry have little respect for the ownership of intellectual property, including designs and patents. Most reps have one or more copy companies in their package, enabling them to furnish every luminaire on the project by substituting the unique products with knockoffs—blatant copies of otherwise unique products. Most knockoffs violate patents or design style protection, but the cost of litigation generally prevents action being taken against the copy company.

Recently, a few companies have fought back, but the situation is impossible to police, and manufacturers have turned to professional designers to help prevent the copying of lighting equipment. Professionals, in turn, can do a great deal to protect intellectual property through specifications and subsequent actions, including:

1. Write specifications and lighting schedules with packaging in mind. As often as possible, list three manufacturers of acceptable, if not equivalent, products. Avoid the phrase "or equal" in specification writing; if the specification must be general in nature, use the phrase "or as approved."
2. Isolate unique products in the specifications and schedule. Make it clear that these products are not part of bidded packages and that the products will be individually priced and purchased.

3. Require contractors to submit a unit price schedule so you can check for unusual pricing or gouging.
4. Require contractors to submit substitution requests and receive approval prior to bid. Remember, the drawings, schedules, and specifications form the contract, and the contractor is legally required to provide the specified products *unless* a substitution is permitted.

Unfortunately, reps having the unique product in their package often use this to their advantage by not selling the unique product to other reps at a fair price. This practice is common despite being a violation of federal antitrust laws. One way to control pricing is to actively work with reps, distributors, and the contractor to manage pricing. Another approach is to work closely with the owner to purchase (or threaten to purchase) unique lighting products separately.

Value engineering is often seen as a chance to substitute lighting systems willy-nilly. Contractors and reps work together to reduce the scope and quality of the design, but seldom does the owner receive the full financial benefit of this activity. The normal result is that the owner pays a little less for the lighting and gets a lot less.

Protecting the design is critical to the success of the project, and designers must play an active role in cost management if they want their projects to come out well. Protection of the intellectual property of others is important because most innovations come from the smaller and more creative companies. If the industry does not respect their property, they won't stay in the business. For more information, contact the International Association of Lighting Designers and read the Specification Integrity document.

AVOID TYPICAL LIGHTING DESIGN PROBLEMS

Lighting designers encounter many problematic conditions and situations when attempting to create high-quality lighting design solutions. Be sure to examine your preliminary solutions for these common problems:

Excessive energy consumption: Use energy-efficient lamps and don't overlight. In nonresidential situations, energy code limitations place a not-to-exceed control on wattage use, but the spirit of energy consumption and staying within dollar budget constraints should be added incentives for being economical with energy use.

Direct glare: Use luminaires that shield the eye from direct visual contact with lamps or built-in reflectors. This is sometimes accomplished as much through luminaire placement as by luminaire selection. When eye-level glow is desired, make sure the selected luminaire does not create offensive glare.

Veiling reflections: Place luminaires in nonoffending positions in situations where visual task and user positions are relatively fixed. The classic example is the freestanding desk, but many other work situations are prone to conditions involving veiling reflections.

Light source reflections in computer screens: This common problem, particularly found in large offices and other workplaces, is typically resolved with the use of an indirect lighting system or deep cell parabolic lenses on recessed fluorescent luminaires. The employment of a combined task/ambient system significantly reduces the severity of the problem. Even in small work settings, attention should be given to avoiding this situation, which creates human discomfort and negatively affects work production.

Problematic lamp color selections: These have an adverse visual effect on materials and colors used in a particular room or space. Typically, this is a complex and interactive process. Lamp selections often are made before material and color selections are known, in which case the materials and colors must be selected with the light source in mind. However, it is not uncommon for basic architectural materials and colors to be chosen prior to lamp selection, in which case the lamp color should accommodate them. In general, being aware of the lamp spectrum relationship to finishes and colors helps avoid a multitude of potential color problems in the finished interior.

Chapter 17 COLLABORATING WITH LIGHTING DESIGNERS

Architects and interior designers typically are responsible for lighting design within their building and interior projects, and, in all likelihood, continue to provide those services for the many basic spaces they design. Quite often, the assistance of lighting manufacturers' sales representatives, lighting showroom personnel, and electrical engineers and contractors is sought to help complete a lighting design solution. Because lighting design technology has expanded and become more complex, and because many building owners and managers have become knowledgeable about the growing capabilities of lighting effects, a new kind of professional, the *lighting designer*, has emerged over the past few decades specifically to solve the lighting design problems in special or atypical spaces. Lighting design is integrally involved with architecture, interior design, and electrical engineering; this integration has yielded the ability to achieve significant and often dramatic improvements in performance and aesthetics over the basic lighting of a space.

Typically, the lighting designer works as an independent consultant on a contractual basis with and for the architect and/or interior designer. The services of a lighting designer are most often sought when projects require specialized lighting where aesthetics, drama, and mood are critically important, as in the case of restaurants, hotel lobbies and function rooms, casinos, art galleries and museums, and high-end retail stores. As the importance of lighting has become more explicitly understood, particularly in terms of its effects on day-to-day activities, lighting designers are more frequently retained for the lighting design in office, health care, educational, and other institutional settings. It should be obvious that special lighting design consultation is essential in the design of uncommon or one-of-a-kind building types such as zoos, performance spaces, and exposition and convention centers.

While this book instructs in lighting design for basic interior spaces that architects and interior designers may often perform without the assistance of a lighting designer, it is becoming more routine to retain a lighting designer for the overall lighting of large projects that, in addition to many basic interior spaces, contain visually demanding spaces such as lobbies, atria, performance spaces, and malls that require the attention of a specialist. In these cases, a lighting designer may also be called upon for knowledgeable judgment related to code compliance and budget constraints.

When special effects are appropriate, the lighting designer can be of particular help. Special effects can be for a wide variety of purposes, such as the display of artifacts in a lobby or living room, the lighting of exotic plants, or creating an evening view of exterior sculpture or flora. Situations of this kind are usually found in projects for high-end clients, as in the case of an executive's penthouse office, an extremely elegant boutique, or an extravagant house. When budgets permit, the lighting designer can create strikingly unusual and dramatic results.

Collaborating with a lighting designer confers a wide range of benefits. The most obvious of these is their depth of experience in lighting from both aesthetic and technical perspectives; it is the rare architectural or interior design practitioner who has had the time to focus in an in-depth manner into lighting, considering the broad range of their responsibilities. The lighting field is constantly and rapidly undergoing technological change and has become the province of the specialist, not the average design practitioner. The introduction of new lighting product lines is equally difficult to stay in touch with; again, most architects and interior designers have neither the time nor the inclination to develop adequate knowledge about that complex marketplace.

One of the most valuable aspects of service provided by the lighting designer is coordination with the project's electrical engineer who designs the electrical power system; that coordination is essential for a professionally managed project and saves countless hours of on-site problem-solving. Code compliance, if dealt with intelligently, is a complex issue requiring the detailed attention of a specialist; again, the lighting designer brings that expertise to a project, providing techniques for getting the greatest lighting value from the fewest watts. Budget issues can be among the most demanding design problems; as with code compliance, getting the greatest lighting value from limited budget dollars is an art. In addition, lighting designer can bring a fresh, other-directed, and valuable point of view to many aspects of architecture and interior design that are just indirectly related to lighting design.

Because lighting designers are relative newcomers to environmental design teams, it is not uncommon to work with clients who are unfamiliar with the special value they bring to a project and may subsequently be reluctant to incur the additional cost of still another specialist consultant. In these situations, it is entirely appropriate for the architect or interior designer to persuade the client that the lighting designer's value to their project is of major importance. It is becoming a more widespread practice for architects and interior designers to routinely include the cost of a lighting designer's services in establishing an overall compensation package for a proposed project.

The process of selecting a lighting designer is like selecting any of the other consultants normally engaged to work with an architect or interior designer, such as mechanical and electrical engineers and foodservice consultants. Some design firms routinely work with the same group of consultants on all of their projects, preferring to work with a familiar personality or professional firm. Other design firms vary the consultant group based on the nature of the project at hand and the specific project backgrounds of the consultants. More specifically, the design firm may wish to use a lighting designer with extensive experience in shopping mall design for a project of that kind. Regardless of these issues of familiarity or specialization, the generally accepted methods for selecting a professional consultant include:

- *Referral:* Seek the recommendation of other architects or interior designers whose opinion is respected.
- *Evaluate previous project results:* Travel to, observe, and talk to users of those facilities. Note that simply looking at photographic results provides limited and sometimes misleading information regarding the success of a lighting design project.
- *Credentials/experience:* Investigate educational background, previous employment experience, and membership and activity in professional organizations; this is a conventional and sometimes useful aspect of the selection process. Special note is made at the end of this chapter concerning the professional organizations related to the lighting field and a relatively new certification process for the lighting industry.
- *Working methods and philosophic compatibility:* Assess the many important issues in this aspect of consultant relationships:

  –At what stage of the project does the lighting designer enter the process?
  –What tasks will be performed, and at what stage of project development?
  –What does the lighting designer expect from the architect and interior designer?
  –Is there basic philosophic compatibility about major professional and design concepts?

- *Contractual relationship:* Discuss in depth the details of the work process, compensation, professional liability insurance, involvement in the bidding and negotiation processes, and involvement in contract administration, including on-site presence.

These thoughts on selecting a lighting designer purposely have been kept quite basic. Working with consultants generally entails complexities that are not discussed here because they go far beyond the intent of this book, including core issues of trust and working rapport that apply to all consultant relationships.

THE COLLABORATION PROCESS

Programming Phase

Ideally, the lighting designer enters the design process early in the project's development. Shortly after the design programming is complete and the first physical plan arrangements can be seen is a good time to start the working relationship. In preparing for the first working discussion with the lighting designer, the architect or interior designer should review all of the expected spaces in the project and record his or her preliminary thoughts and expectations concerning lighting results for each space, including issues related to practical functions, intensity of light, color effects, special effects, code concerns, budget, emergency lighting needs, aesthetics, and unusual architectural features. After carefully thinking through all of these factors, the architect or interior designer should record those thoughts in a concise and communicative manner so the lighting designer does not have to rely on memory or meeting notes. One good technique for concisely recording these lighting design thoughts is to develop a simple matrix format in which the initial thoughts about lighting for each of the project's rooms or spaces is briefly identified, including thoughts on the visual tasks involved, level(s) of illumination required, color factors, and anything else that will impinge on the lighting design solution.

Schematic Design Phase

During the first working discussion, the lighting designer probably will have many questions, the answers to which will amplify the thoughts on lighting recorded in the programming phase. In addition, the initial project discussion often opens several new avenues of thought. Following this first exchange, the lighting designer prepares a preliminary lighting design solution. When the lighting designer presents this first preliminary solution, the stage is set for dialog, the purpose of which is not to question the lighting designer's

expertise but rather to discuss the interpretation of the programming matrix; in other words, to be sure the architect's or interior designer's thoughts and intentions concerning lighting are appropriately understood and preliminarily resolved.

Design Development Phase

As with any design process, it is likely that the review and discussion of the preliminary lighting design schemes by the project designer and the lighting designer will result in a need for revisions, and an interactive process involving the two professionals is set in motion. In the case of large and complex projects, this review process can involve many of the professionals working on the project's design. After basic lighting design issues are resolved, the review process will move on to the details of luminaire and controls selections and placements, until the lighting design process is completed.

During the latter phase of design development, the lighting design process usually reaches completion. In this period, the lighting designer works with the architect, interior designer, and other project consultants, such as the electrical and mechanical engineers and landscape architect, to assure that the lighting design works within the context of the balance of construction. Critical activities include checking ceiling plenum depths, coordinating duct sizes and locations, developing and checking lighting mounting details, confirming ceiling and soffit heights, and coordinating with fire protection.

Often the lighting designer's work is mostly completed by the end of design development. Because the lighting designer's drawings often do not serve as contract documents, the architect, interior designer, and electrical engineer must use them to produce actual working drawings.

Contract Documents Phase

Once the major lighting design decisions are agreed upon, the lighting designer is ready to prepare his or her portion of the project's contract documents, including drawings and specifications, or serve as consultants for incorporation in the contract documents preparation. Many details of coordination are required in this process, such as working with the electrical engineer on issues related to providing power, checking with the mechanical engineer on the availability of plenum space, and working with the architect or interior designer on ceiling and other construction details and the compatibility of finishes. In many cases, the lighting designer's involvement with contract documents is fully coordinated with the electrical engineer, and the lighting designer's solutions are incorporated with the final electrical working drawings and specifications.

Bidding and Negotiation Phase

When contract documents are complete, some form of construction cost bidding or negotiation typically takes place. Quite frequently, the bidding or negotiation process reveals significant cost overruns, requiring design revisions to reduce overall project cost. Except where overruns are so great that overall project size must be reduced, the details of finishes and installed products, including luminaire and lighting controls, are targeted for cost reductions. Frequently, the lighting designer is one of the players called in to adjust the contract documents and/or negotiate cost reductions with the construction manager or electrical contractor. Unfortunately, it is not uncommon for lighting design quality to be significantly compromised in this cost-cutting process. The experienced lighting designer can be of invaluable benefit here through his or her ability to preserve lighting design quality while making significant contributions to saving costs.

Contract Administration Phase

During the construction phase of a project, the lighting designer is often called in to advise on a variety of details, from the precise focusing of accent lighting to the fine tuning of complex control systems. Unexpected problems inevitably require expert troubleshooting, such as plenum space conflicts with ductwork or sprinkler runs or last-minute luminaire substitutions created by the late shipment of specified items.

Post-Occupancy Evaluation

For projects in which post-occupancy evaluation services are provided, the contributions of the lighting designer can be extremely valuable. Often, small adjustments made to luminaires and lamps can have major positive results. Of equal importance is the mutual learning process involved in discovering what works well and what doesn't—not only so mistakes in design judgment are not repeated but also to gain new insights and innovative ideas for future projects.

PROFESSIONAL DESIGN ORGANIZATIONS

Special note should be made of the professional organizations in the lighting design field. Similar to the qualifying examination process for both architects and interior designers, the lighting industry, through the National Council for Qualifying Lighting Professionals (NCQLP), has an examination-based certification process. Certified individuals—those who pass the NCQLP exam—have demonstrated that they possess minimum qualifications in the field of lighting technology and are called Lighting Certified (LC). The NCQLP lighting certification program encompasses a broad range of people working in the lighting industry, including those connected with manufacturing, sales, and other business and professional relationships to the field of lighting. The International Association of Lighting Designers (IALD), active in North America and much of the world, focuses much more specifically on people involved in lighting design and requires its professional members to pass a review of their design portfolios and to then practice according to strict ethical standards.

Chapter 18 COMPUTERS AND LIGHTING DESIGN

Since the early days of personal computing, lighting computer programs have enabled relatively accurate predictions of light levels for both interior and exterior lighting. Today, these programs determine light levels at specific locations in a space. They can also predict the brightness of room surfaces and give the patterns of light on the ceiling, walls, and floor. Some programs can generate perspective renderings as well, generating a lifelike representation of lighting in the space. However, lighting software cannot choose an appropriate lighting system based on the designer's requirements. The designer must develop a design first, then analyze it with the computer.

TYPES OF PROGRAMS

Most current programs designed for everyday use in lighting design employ *radiosity*, a type of calculation that is relatively fast, especially on a modern personal computer. A simple calculation and rendering for an empty room can be generated in less than a minute, making this type of program highly effective as a design support tool. Radiosity's primary drawback is that the calculation assumes that all room surfaces have a matte finish, and renderings lack a lifelike quality.

To create more realistic images, a few programs use a far more precise form of calculation called *ray-tracing*. By tracing each ray of light from each source, surfaces of any texture and finish can be accurately depicted. These programs, however, require considerable computer resources, and the analysis for a simple room could take hours on a personal computer. Sophisticated analysts using graphics workstations can use this type of program effectively, but it is not an everyday tool for the designer.

At least one program uses a combination of radiosity and ray-tracing to provide more realistic images while operating at reasonable speed on an ordinary personal computer. The results of this type of calculation can be improved by permitting longer computer execution times. As long as an experienced operator uses the program, this is a powerful presentation tool that is practical to own and use.

INPUT DATA

To use a computer lighting program, you must first enter the data needed to perform the lighting analysis. All programs, even the most basic radiosity programs, require the following input data:

- Room dimensions, work plane height, and luminaire mounting height (for pendant mounted luminaires)
- Room surface reflectance, including inserts—portions of room surfaces that may reflect differently
- Detailed luminaire photometric data in IESNA format. Photometric data files for interior and exterior luminaires are supplied by manufacturers in IESNA format via diskette, CD-ROM, or website.
- Precise location and orientation of luminaires using *x, y, z* coordinates or an interface with computer-assisted drawing (CAD) programs
- Light loss factors and any other multiplying factors to adjust the lamp and ballast output from the assumptions used in the luminaire photometry

For a basic radiosity program, data entry can be rapid. Using CAD-like commands, a simple room can be described in a few minutes, ready for analysis.

Some radiosity programs also permit the use of objects in space, which include tables, partitions, chairs, ductwork, and other items present within the room's volume. Objects in space help improve the realism of the analysis and rendering but can considerably increase analysis time as well. For instance, the single minute needed to calculate and render a simple room might increase to five minutes if two chairs and a table are added.

A few programs also calculate the effect of daylight. To analyze daylighting effects, it is necessary to enter information about windows and skylights, including coordinates and characteristics, and to choose the time of day, date, and weather conditions. This increases the calculation time of a radiosity program.

Input data for ray-tracing programs can be significant. Most programs accept three-dimensional CAD data, including objects in space. However, the operator must describe the finish and texture of every surface of all room finishes, including the furniture, and must enter the three-dimensional data file for each piece of furniture or furnishing. Daylighting data may also be added; the most photorealistic images require that site and landscaping information be added as well.

INTERIOR LIGHTING CALCULATIONS

Lighting calculation programs calculate the lighting effects caused by specific luminaires in specific rooms at specific points. Output includes:

- Illuminance (lux or foot-candles) on a horizontal work plane at selected points in the room; summary statistics such as average, maximum, minimum, and standard deviation of illuminance values
- Room surface luminance (candelas per unit surface area) or exitance (lumens per unit surface area). These results are based on the assumption that room surfaces have a matte, not shiny, finish.
- Lighting power density (watts/m² or watts/ft²)
- Visibility and visual comfort metrics. UGR (uniform glare rating), ESI (equivalent sphere illumination), RVP (relative visual performance), and VCP (visual comfort probability) are the principal metrics computed by these programs. They are calculated for a specific location in the room and for a specific viewing direction.

Output from these programs is usually a chart of calculated values, an isolux (isofoot-candle) plot, or a shaded plan with gray scales representing a range of light levels. All programs print results, and most display the results directly on the screen.

Some programs offer three-dimensional black and white or color-shaded perspective views of the room showing light patterns produced on the room surfaces by the lighting system. Ray-tracing programs produce exceptionally realistic renderings.

EXTERIOR LIGHTING CALCULATIONS

Exterior lighting programs are used for parking lots, roadways, pedestrian paths, and special situations such as airport aprons, car sales lots, and sports fields. Exterior lighting calculations are similar to interior calculations except that they are simpler, as no light reflectance from room surfaces is calculated. Input data typically include the following:

- Plan dimensions of the site to be studied, usually entered in x, y coordinates or through a CAD interface
- Points on the site where illuminance is to be calculated. Some programs permit blocking out the printing of light levels on areas of the site where light levels are not critical, or where buildings or trees would block the light.
- Luminaire photometric file in IESNA format
- Mounting heights, site locations, orientations, and tilt of luminaires
- Lumen output of the specified lamp
- Light loss factors due to lamp aging, ballast factor, and luminaire dirt accumulation

Chapter 19 DEVELOPING SKILLS BEYOND THE BASICS

If this book has served its intended purpose, it has provided a methodology and techniques for creating high-quality lighting design solutions for many, if not most, of the rooms and spaces for which architects and interior designers are responsible. More specifically, creating a high-quality lighting design solution for a private office, a living room, or a nursing station should be a comfortable challenge. When working with a lighting designer on a large or complex project, such as a major conference center, urban medical clinic, or gambling casino, one should be able to easily communicate overall lighting design intentions and establish a comfortable working relationship with the consultant, the result being a successful lighting installation.

But this book has not provided, nor has it intended to provide, in-depth information on the vast amount of technical detail related to lighting, such as the wide range of lamps and luminaires the marketplace offers, the many possibilities that control systems offer, and finding the best balance of lamps to meet a stringent energy code requirement. For the great majority of architectural and interior design practitioners, an appropriate foundation has been laid for their day-to-day practice needs as they relate to lighting. The challenges of designing lighting for basic spaces or working with an experienced lighting designer now should be met with comfort.

For some architects and interior designers, involvement in lighting design to the point developed in this book simply whets the appetite for deeper involvement in the lighting process—not necessarily to function as a lighting designer but rather to gain more specific control of the subtleties of lighting spaces, such as the color of light employed, creating gradations of light, developing techniques for lighting exhibits, or enhancing a sculpturally shaped room.

Several approaches achieve this more accomplished level of lighting design skill. These approaches are generally informal, meaning that they are without a planned curriculum of courses or a structured internship with a lighting designer. They include:

- Working with the manufacturers' representatives of lamp and luminaire producers; many reps are quite knowledgeable, and they have an economic incentive for designers to understand and appreciate their product line.
- Working with to-the-trade showroom salespeople in hands-on demonstrations; again, many of them are quite knowledgeable and have the same economic incentive.
- Attending short-term courses, such as those sponsored by IESNA or lamp and luminaire manufacturers. In addition, professional organizations such as AIA, ASID, and IIDA offer continuing education unit (CEU) courses. Distance learning courses may be accessed without the need for travel and at one's own convenience.
- Attending intensive programs or courses at lighting lab facilities, such as those maintained by General Electric (NELA Park in Cleveland, Ohio) and Phillips (Edison, New Jersey), can be especially valuable because of their specialized demonstration rooms and equipment. Some of the seminars and presentations offered at national and regional conferences and trade shows can also add to one's knowledge base.
- Regularly reviewing professional periodicals for focused articles is still another source of information and ideas. These publications are particularly helpful in keeping in touch with current trends and products.
- Working with lighting designers on a prearranged project-by-project basis in what is essentially a mentor relationship. This kind of working relationship is hard to come by, but if the parties have worked together in the past and the personal chemistry is good, this can be an ideal learning mode for architectural and interior design practitioners.

Ultimately, the process of deepening one's involvement in lighting design must be put into action in actual projects. Over time, by working with manufacturers' reps and lighting designers in the development of relatively standardized specifications, many projects can be completed with minimal expert consultation. Standardized specifications must be updated periodically because of the rapidly developing technologies in lamps and luminaires. Architects and interior designers can feel confident that, with a concerted effort to learn, they can have significant control of the quality of lighting in their finished projects.

While only a small number of architects and interior designers decide to redirect their careers into lighting design, this direction is reasonable and real-istic if the interest in lighting design is compelling. Clearly, lighting design has become an independent specialty within the architectural and interior design fields. If working informally with the many aspects of lighting design is satisfying and creates a feeling of wanting to know more and to spend more time with it every day, a career redirection might be considered.

The routes to a career in lighting design are numerous. Because it is a relatively new design specialty, lighting designers have come to the field from a variety of backgrounds, including architecture and interior design but also theater and stage set design, electrical engineering, industrial/product design, and lamp and luminaire manufacturing and sales.

The educational or training paths to lighting design are equally varied. Many lighting designers have found their way into the field through a mentorship or internship by working for established lighting designers, learning by doing, and being of value in the process by offering the knowledge and skills from their original professional discipline. Because there are still relatively few formally trained lighting designers, the route of mentorship/internship has been and continues to be a well-worn path. To gain perspective on this approach, note that the majority of architects were not formally schooled in architecture until the 1920s, and the majority of interior designers were not formally trained in interior design until the 1960s and 1970s. The mentorship method remains a viable entry port for aspiring lighting designers.

Over the past 25 to 30 years, formal educational programs have been established in colleges and universities at both undergraduate and graduate levels. The focus of these programs varies widely, with some primarily directed to aesthetic and design issues and others with the technical and engineering aspects of the field. (A list of certificate and degree programs is provided in Appendix B.) Clearly, a well-organized curriculum in lighting design that covers information in a thorough and sequential manner has many advantages, particularly if coupled with an integrated cooperative education program in which students concurrently work in a professional office setting. Specific curricular structure is highly individualized to the degree that generalizations cannot be made; each program's curriculum must be scrutinized for applicability to the individual's career interests. Over time, more and more professionals in the field will have had some form of formal lighting design training; eventually it may become a requirement for practice.

Many professionals now have established careers in lighting design, but this specialty is no more nor less competitive than architecture or interior design. The lighting design field has grown over the past decade or two because many architects and interior designers and their clients have come to understand the critical need for specialists in lighting. In addition, the worldwide need for conserving energy resources has led to both general awareness and specific code requirements that demand the attention of a knowledgeable lighting professional.

As with all design professions, lighting design as a career pursuit is sensitive to the economy. When the economy is good, many opportunities occur in both the construction of new buildings and the renovation of existing facilities; when the economy is poor, the potential for work in any of the construction-related fields is diminished. This certainly is not news to anyone aware of the realities of the construction industries. As always, creative professionals, by necessity, find methods for coping with the current economic environment.

Some lighting designers have developed specialized careers within the field. Much of that specialization focuses on entertainment-oriented environ-ments such as theater and concert facilities, film and television performance and production, and theme park complexes. As the worlds of entertainment and retail continue to fuse, additional opportunities in this area are likely to emerge.

From a broad perspective, it is clear that the world of lighting design will continue to grow and produce an expanding array of specialties. For many people, this is a world full of personal appeal and opportunity in terms of both creative fulfillment and financial reward. It is impossible to predict the future of the lighting design field, but all indications are that the factors that have driven its tremendous recent growth will continue to accelerate its potential. As is true in all creative fields, a strong element of passion for one's work is the best ingredient for a satisfying career.

EDUCATIONAL PROGRAMS IN LIGHTING

The following colleges and universities offer undergraduate and/or graduate programs in lighting design and applications:

- *Rensselaer Polytechnic Institute*, Troy, New York. A graduate program associated with the Lighting Research Center and offering a master of science degree.
- *Parsons School of Design*, New York, New York. A graduate program offering a master of science degree.
- *Pennsylvania State University*, State College, Pennsylvania. An undergraduate and graduate program offering bachelor of science, master of science, and doctoral degrees in architectural engineering with a lighting specialty.
- *University of Colorado*, Boulder, Colorado. An undergraduate and graduate program offering bachelor of science, master of science, and doctoral degrees in architectural engineering with a lighting specialty.
- *University of Nebraska*, Lincoln, Nebraska. An undergraduate and graduate program offering bachelor of science, master of science, and doctoral degrees in architectural engineering with a lighting specialty.
- *University of Kansas*, Lawrence, Kansas. An undergraduate program offering a bachelor of science degree in architectural engineering with a lighting specialty.
- *Kansas State University*, Manhattan, Kansas. An undergraduate program offering a bachelor of science degree in architectural engineering with a lighting specialty.

Programs are also offered in Europe, Asia, Australia, and New Zealand.

A number of colleges and universities offer excellent lighting classes within architectural, interior design, and engineering colleges.

Appendix B   ENERGY CODES

Some of the following information is contained in the *Advanced Lighting Guidelines* (2001 draft).

Energy codes establish a minimum level of energy efficiency or product performance for lighting systems installed in buildings. The wide variety of energy codes and standards ranges from national model energy codes, which must be adopted by a state or local jurisdiction to have the force of law, to locally developed and adopted standards.

The U.S. Energy Policy Act of 1992 requires mandatory lighting efficiency standards in all states. These energy codes must be at least as stringent as the ASHRAE/IESNA Standard 90.1–1989. Over time, energy codes will be gradually tightened and made more stringent. The latest national model code is ASHRAE/IESNA 90.1–1999, and some states have already adopted its more stringent requirements. The new International Energy Conservation Code (IECC) adopts the ASHRAE/IESNA 90.1 code by reference. Remember, however, that these are just model codes. In order for them to be legally required, they must be adopted into law by a city or state. In adopting model codes, cities and states sometimes add local amendments or changes, so it is important to read the local energy code carefully.

Some states have developed their own lighting efficiency codes. Because of the state's large population and construction volumes, California's Title 24 Building Energy Efficiency Standards have produced substantial energy savings over the years and have led to relatively energy-efficient lighting design norms compared to many other regions of the country. Other states, including Washington, Oregon, Minnesota, and New York, have also developed their own energy codes, in some cases from scratch and in others creating local variations of energy codes developed elsewhere. Oregon, for instance, created a simplified lighting code that matches Universal Building Code (UBC) classifications but also permits ASHRAE/IESNA 90.1 to be used instead.

The current energy code of every state can be found at http://www.bcap-energy.org.

In addition to state energy codes, a number of other energy codes may apply to any given lighting project. For instance, on federal projects, the Federal Energy Standards, which are similar to ASHRAE/IESNA 90.1, must be used instead of a local code. Likewise, countries other than the United States have energy codes that apply to projects located in them. However, whenever you use ASHRAE/IESNA 90.1–1999 or a similar standard, your design will probably be considered sufficiently efficient.

You can order the lighting portion of the ASHRAE/IESNA Standard from the Illuminating Engineering Society of North America (IESNA) as LEM-1, or you can obtain the entire standard from ASHRAE.

ENERGY CODE STRUCTURE

Energy code requirements for lighting may be grouped into several broad categories.

Lighting Power Limits

Lighting power limits establish a maximum allowable installed lighting power level, typically expressed in watts per square foot (W/ft^2); the value is multiplied by the area of the space to determine the overall limit. This may be given for a whole building, with a single W/ft^2 number specifying a limit applied to all the spaces in it. Limits may also be established by space category, with higher values allowed for spaces with more demanding visual tasks and lower values for spaces where visual demand is less.

For buildings with special lighting needs, neither the whole building nor the space category method may produce a fair lighting power limit—that is, the limit may be too low to adequately serve the needs of the building. In these cases, energy codes may provide special lighting power allowances for special purposes. An example is the tailored method under California's Title 24 energy standards. Some energy codes also provide extra lighting power allowances for special applications on a use-it-or-lose-it basis. These allowances may be applied only to the specific lighting equipment used to illuminate the special application; they may not be used as general allowances to boost the whole building lighting power limit.

Most energy codes also provide a whole building performance-based method for setting an overall building energy budget. Such a method may allow users to obtain higher lighting power allowances by trading off energy with other building components. For example, installing a high-efficiency air conditioning or heating system could yield an energy credit that allows for a less efficient lighting system (more lighting power).

Outdoor Lighting Power Limits

A few energy codes extend requirements for lighting efficiency to the building's outdoor lighting, such as façade lighting, overhead canopy lighting, walkway lighting, and even parking lighting. These requirements seldom extend to roadway lighting or other types of outdoor lighting that are not powered from the building's electrical system.

Calculation of Installed Lighting Power

All energy codes that specify limits on installed lighting power also include rules for how the installed lighting watts are calculated. These rules require that the types and quantities of lamps, ballasts, and fixtures be called out and that the wattage of lamp-ballast combinations be identified. The rules may also provide default lamp-ballast wattages, which typically are conservative for a given type of equipment but which may be used when the make and model of the equipment are unknown. These rules encourage lighting designers to select more efficient lamp-ballast-fixture combinations because they yield lower installed wattages, but they also require the designers to document the better performance of the equipment. Energy codes may also provide rules for calculating the installed wattages for tricky situations, such as track lighting or screw-in compact fluorescent lamps, which might be easily replaced with higher-wattage alternatives after the compliance-checking process is completed.

Mandatory Switching Requirements

Most energy codes include mandatory requirements for lighting controls; these requirements typically are independent of the lighting power limits. Mandatory control requirements may include requirements for independent light switches in every room, bilevel switching or daylit area switching, and time clocks or photocell controls on outdoor lighting. Many of the more recently updated energy codes, such as the 90.1–1999 code, include a requirement for automatic sweep controls that shut off building lighting during typically unoccupied hours, such as nighttime and weekends.

Mandatory Control Specifications

Energy codes also typically set minimum performance requirements for automatic lighting controls, to assure that they are likely to function as intended and not cause user dissatisfaction. These requirements include such things as time delays for occupancy sensors, or sensitivity adjustments for photocell controls.

Optional Lighting Control Credits

Some energy codes also provide credits for automatic lighting controls that are installed as options. These credits allow the designer to calculate a reduced, adjusted lighting power level for the design. If the adjusted lighting power meets the allowable maximum set by the code, then the design is in compliance. In effect, the designer is trading off the energy savings expected from the automatic control for the extra energy usage from the increased lighting power. Optional lighting control credits have been dropped from some energy codes—the 90.1–1989 code had them, but they are not part of the 90.1–1999 edition—because they can be complicated, confusing, and open to abuse. Nevertheless, controls credits can provide designers flexibility in meeting lighting power limits, and they encourage the use of automatic controls. If the controls operate as intended, a net savings in lighting energy should accrue over time because the control credits usually are set to be conservative about their energy savings expectations. Lighting control credits have been offered for such devices as occupancy sensors, daylighting photocontrols, tuning controls, and lumen maintenance controls.

Compliance Documentation

Most of the advanced energy codes provide standard forms for designers to use in demonstrating that their lighting designs comply with code requirements. The intent of these forms is to make it easier for both designers and code enforcement officials to verify that a given lighting design falls within the lighting power limits, includes the mandatory controls, and correctly accounts for control credits. Because these forms can become rather long and cumbersome for large buildings, some jurisdictions provide lighting code compliance software tools so the documentation may be prepared electronically and with a minimized chance of calculation errors. The compliance forms are then printed out and submitted along with the electrical plans. The codes may also have requirements for the level of specificity of lighting system elements and controls that must be shown on the plans. All of these requirements can make for more successful enforcement of code requirements, leading to a higher level of achieved energy savings.

IMPORTANT POINTS TO REMEMBER ABOUT ENERGY CODES

- Codes vary from state to state and, sometimes, from city to city. Always check with local authorities. The BCAP website given above is generally current and useful; it often lists the URL (Web address) of the state code office. Some states publish their energy codes on the Web.
- Some states require that calculations be submitted with plans for permit approval. Other states require little or no documentation.
- Many states do not require compliance except for state or local government projects.
- The federal standards usually apply to federal projects or those undertaken on federal land, including military bases in other countries.
- Energy codes tend to regulate nonresidential lighting only. The exception is California, where residential lighting is also regulated, but only to the extent of requiring high-efficacy light sources for general illumination in kitchens and baths.

RESOURCES

Each year, the Illuminating Engineering Society of North America (IESNA) publishes a lighting software survey in *Lighting Design and Application*. Products are surveyed in many areas, including hardware requirements, analysis features, applications, types of output, user features, and price. The following are some of the more readily available and recognized software programs available at the time of the IESNA survey's development.

Lighting Software Programs

Category	Program	Manufacturer	Description
General-Purpose Programs and AutoCAD Extensions	CALCU-LITE 5	The ScreenMaker Williamstown, NJ	Basic lighting program
	AGI	Lighting Analysts, Inc. Littleton, CO	Advanced radiosity lighting program with rendering
	Luminaire Global Illumination Tools	Jissai Graphics	Radiosity add-in to 3D Viz with rendering
	LUMEN-MICRO 2000	Lighting Technologies, Inc. Boulder, CO	Advanced radiosity lighting program with rendering; also, Simply Lighting basic lighting programs
	LITE-PRO	Columbia Prescolite Spokane, WA	Radiosity lighting program with rendering
	LUXICON	Cooper Lighting Peachtree City, GA	Radiosity lighting program
	VISUAL	Lithonia Lighting Group Conyers, GA	Advanced radiosity lighting program
Radiosity and Ray-Tracing Program	LIGHTSCAPE 3.2	Autodesk San Rafael, CA	Combines radiosity with ray tracing for rendering accuracy
Ray-Tracing Program	RADIANCE (Unix) and Desktop RADIANCE (Windows—AutoCAD 14)	Lawrence Berkeley National Laboratories University of California, Berkeley, CA	Ray-tracing program that is computationally intensive but produces the most realistic renderings

Note: These listings are not exhaustive and do not imply applicability or endorsement. Additional programs are available. Refer to the annual lighting software survey in *Lighting Design and Application* magazine and http://www.lightsearch.com for additional sources of software and comparative analyses. *Source:* Advanced Lighting Guidelines 2001.

INDEX